D1478687

PRODUCTION OF LANDSCAPE PLANTS

by

Carl E. Whitcomb, Ph.D.

Library of Congress Catalog

Title: Production of Landscape Plants

Author: Whitcomb, Carl E.

Major Areas: 1. Plant production
              2. Plants in the field
              3. Methods of planting and harvesting

Includes bibliographies and index

Library of Congress Catalog Card Number: 87-50631

ISBN 0-9613109-3-6

Printed in the United States of America

Lacebark Inc.,
Publications and Research
P.O. Box 2383
Stillwater, Oklahoma 74076

This book is dedicated to the production of trees. Trees shade, protect, enhance, cool, beautify, screen, complement, soften, enframe, color, and provide a vast array of visual and physical benefits to man. Yet trees are poorly understood by the general public as well as many horticulture professionals. The better the root system, the healthier the tree or shrub and the healthier the plant, the more resistance it has to diseases, insects, and other stress factors. If these books aid the production, health, or preservation of a few trees, then it will have been worth the tremendous number of hours.

A special thanks to Cara Beer, Dr. Frank Carpenter, Susan Kenna, Ruth Ann Stuart, Andy Whitcomb, Benjamin Whitcomb, and LaJean Whitcomb, for reviewing and editing the manuscript and offering suggestions. A book of this nature requires a great effort on the part of the author's family. Without their assistance, it would have been far more difficult.

TABLE OF CONTENTS

About These Books

College professors are generally held just below politicians at being able to "waltz around the question without ever giving an answer". While an undergraduate at Kansas State University, I came across a comedy record by 'Brother' Dave Gardner. At one point in a dialog with himself he made the statement, "Don't give me your doubts, I have enough doubts of my own. Tell me what you believe in!" Since I had encountered several professors, even at that early age, who would talk of various theories but would not tell what they believed, the statement stuck--permanently. In the ensuing years, it became more and more clear that when people ask a specific question they expect an answer that is reasonably specific, even from university professors.

These books are "what I believe in"! I have attempted to include some of the research, experiences or observations on which that belief is based.

No area remains unchanged over time. By the time this book is printed, some points may be subject to modification. However, be cautious and make sure the new information is well founded and not a fluke or the result of poorly designed and conducted research or simply misinformation.

In 1986 I first wrote *Landscape Plant Production, Establishment and Maintenance*. My view was to show the relationship between how a plant was produced, harvested, transplanted, established and grew. After one printing of the book and exposure to the nursery and landscape industries, it quickly became clear that there were two distinct interests: 1) production of landscape plants and 2) establishment and maintenance of landscape plants. As a result of those two distinct interest groups and the fact that there was additional material I wanted to add to the book anyway, two books now exist instead of one.

Production of Landscape Plants is an attempt to describe the various field techniques used in the production process and offer suggestions for improvement. Field production is a viable and practical technique for the production of trees and large shrubs. Field soil provides a great buffer against the extremes and stimulates natural root growth. Stem diameter and overall quality of the crown of a tree grown in the field is superior to plants grown in containers. Clearly the better the root system, the

i

healthier the plants. Likewise, the healthier the plant, the fewer the problems in transplanting and establishment.

Establishment and Maintenance of Landscape Plants is an attempt to share all of the findings and feelings derived from a vast array of transplanting studies done over a period of more than 20 years. Some of the current "horticultural" practices are wrong. In this book the correct way, as I currently know it to be, is presented along with the why! The more successful the performance of all landscapes, the greater the vitality of the nursery/landscape industry and the greater the beauty of our great country.

Carl E. Whitcomb
November, 1989

About the Author

Carl E. Whitcomb was Professor of Horticulture at Oklahoma State University 1972 to 1986. An innovative researcher, he has received patents on a successful solar-heated greenhouse, a unique micronutrient fertilizer (Micromax), unique container designs for improving the root systems of container nursery stock and other inventions. He has written over 400 technical and semi-technical publications on plant propagation from cuttings and seeds; plant nutrition and production, both in containers and field; and factors affecting the transplanting, establishment and performance of landscape plants. He is author of three other books, *Know It & Grow It II: A Guide to the Identification and Use of Landscape Plants* and *Plant Production in Containers*, and *Establishment and Maintenance of Landscape Plants*. He has traveled extensively throughout the U.S.A. where he is a frequent speaker at nursery meetings as well as Canada, Europe, Australia and New Zealand.

A native Kansan, he received a bachelor of science degree from Kansas State University and master of science and Ph.D. degrees from Iowa State University. He taught and conducted research for five years at the University of Florida and 13 1/2 years at Oklahoma State University. He was the 1977 recipient of the Porter Henegar Award given annually by the Southern Nurserymen's Association for excellence in research; the 1983 recipient of the L.C. Chadwick Award, presented by the American Association of Nurserymen, "to an exceptional educator for superior teaching, guidance and motivation of students in the nursery and landscape arts and sciences"; in 1985 he was named Outstanding Oklahoma Nurseryman; in 1986 he was made Honorary Life Member of the Oklahoma Horticulture Society and received the Slater Wight Memorial Award for 1986 presented by the Southern Nurserymen's Association for outstanding contributions to the nursery industry. In 1987 the Florida Nurserymen and Growers Association named him "outstanding industry person".

Currently, Dr. Whitcomb is a private research horticulturist/consultant/author/lecturer for Lacebark Inc., Publications and Research, P.O. Box 2383, Stillwater, Oklahoma 74076.

Introduction

The production of landscape plants has changed in many ways in the past 30 years and yet some aspects have changed very little. Certainly the production of plants in containers is a big change with both promise and problems. The fabric containers hold a great deal of promise in reducing transplant stress by building a better root system and storing energy in the root system to enhance root growth on the new site. The New Generation RootBag solves the problems of the old style bags.

On the other hand, little has changed in the production of bare root and balled-in-burlap (B & B) plants. Nutrition of field soils has improved as well as weed control and storage conditions, but these are minor refinements in an old system.

This book is an attempt to bring together various aspects of field production of nursery stock. The stock may begin as bare root seedlings planted in the field to be dug B & B. They may be unrooted hardwood cuttings placed in the field to root and grow, to be harvested and marketed bare root or in packages. In recent years more and more trees and shrubs are begun as rooted cuttings in one-gallon containers, then planted into the field at the end of the growing season for growing on to a larger size.

There is no best or ideal way to produce nursery stock. There are a mass of variables from soils, water, length of growing season, length of the day, market objectives, geographic location, attitudes of customers, fads or trends and many other factors that affect a nurseryman's decision to grow and sell plants in a certain way. There are, however, studies and experiences that can suggest various advantageous production techniques that make a more marketable product at an economical price.

Whenever possible, not only what to do or what not to do is presented, but why or why not as well. The numerous brief summaries of experiments are included to show the basis for many suggestions.

The 1990s may well be the decade of the "greenhouse effect" as a major watchword or emphasis. Trees have a great impact in modifying/moderating the urban concrete desert into more habitable places. The Global Releaf program may help stimulate the planting of millions of additional trees during the next decade and more. If the new emphasis on tree planting is truly to have an influence on our global environment, the trees must be healthy, rapidly growing, well adapted species. Thus the quality of the root system and other nursery practices can and will influence the long-term outcome of such a program. If the trees provided by the nursery industry grow and function well, the program should expand further. However, if many people have the experience I have heard lamented many times, "Well, I planted a tree and it died", the program will be only a brief flurry.

I believe it is critical for every one in the nursery industry to strive to ensure that every plant they sell is the best they can produce---so it will perform well for the customer. I still believe the best advice I can offer anyone in the nursery business is, "If in doubt, throw it out!" In other words, do not sell marginal quality plants. When questionable plants are sold, someone is taking the short-term profit in lieu of a long-term satisfied customer.

One of the greatest frustrations and hidden economic costs of tree production is the large number of culls that are present in any nursery field. I now believe many of those trees are runts or culls because they have a poor root system. Techniques now exist that substantially improve the percentage of good trees from a block. Let us sell the good trees, learn something from the poor ones, and make further improvements in the products of the nursery business.

A Summary of Field Production

1) Begin with the best quality transplants possible. "If in doubt, throw it out"...Whitcomb!

2) The better the soil on the nursery site, the healthier the plants and simpler the process.

3) Prepare the soil. Add fertilizer(s), lime, or sulfur as needed. Modest levels of nitrogen are important but excessive levels are not. Do not raise soil pH above 5.5.

4) Subsoil for aeration or drain the field if necessary.

5) Plant at the most desirable time relative to the method of handling the liners: plant bare root in spring only, plant container-grown in fall in most areas or perhaps spring in hardiness zones 5 and northward.

6) Water plants immediately following planting. The first thorough watering is critical to settle the soil and re-establish capillary contact between the soil loosened for planting and the surrounding soil. For this initial watering, hand- or flood-type watering around the plant is preferred over overhead or drip irrigation.

7) Apply pre-emergent herbicides. Do not procrastinate. Weeds germinate faster than you think. Once germination occurs---you lose.

8) Fertilize as needed. Nitrogen is the primary element of concern if other materials have been properly adjusted under Point 3. Remember, the key factor that controls how much and how often nitrogen should be applied is the porosity of the soil.

9) Prune/direct new growth. Stake only if necessary. With properly grown liners, staking should not be necessary and is a practice to avoid if possible. Light "guidance pruning" is preferred over less frequent but more severe pruning. Remember, the plant can not grow without energy and the only source of energy is the leaves.

10) Spot spray escape weeds with contact herbicide. In some situations, it works well to mix a pre-emergent herbicide with a post-emergent "contact" herbicide. This prevents other weeds from germinating once the current weeds are killed.

11) Drip irrigate or otherwise apply water as needed during periods of drought.

12) Keep a keen eye out for disease or insects. With cautious monitoring, most problems can be stopped early, and with less pesticide as spot sprays.

13) Do final pruning/lower limb removal one season before sale. This allows callus growth to cover pruning wounds.

14) Harvest when the terminal buds are fully developed. These buds are the growth/control centers of the plant. If they are immature, poorly developed or damaged, recovery following transplanting will be slowed and the plant will encounter more stress.

15) Keep storage times to a minimum. Storage means deterioration in health and vigor.

16) Have the root ball in soil or soil mix when spring bud swell begins. Take advantage of the harvest/transplant recovery process by providing a favorable environment for new root development with spring bud swell. The first bud swell following harvest provides the strongest recovery signal for new root growth. If you miss it, stress level builds rapidly.

17) Drainage and water management in addition to timing (Point 16) are the key factors to recovery and re-establishment.

18) The first flush of growth after harvest reflects conditons in the nursery and the plant tissue. The second flush reflects the conditions/recovery/reaction to the new site.

CHAPTER 1

METHODS OF PLANT PRODUCTION

METHODS OF PLANT PRODUCTION

Landscape plants have been grown in field soils then dug bare root or wrapped and tied in some way since man began caring about his immediate surroundings. The classical bare root or balled-in-burlap (B & B) technique for transplanting plants grown in the field has remained unchanged for many years. As labor costs increase and the size and quality of nursery stock grown in containers improved, the demand for bare root and balled-in-burlap plants has decreased. In addition, the general performance of bare root or balled-in-burlap trees following transplanting is only fair on marginally suitable landscape planting sites and/or when digging and transplanting is not done timely and with care. As the nursery and landscape industries have grown in size and sophistication, so have the general expectations of consumers. Plants that require a growing season or more to establish and lend the full desired effect to the landscape are no longer acceptable.

Work by Watson and Himelick (5) showed that up to 98% of the roots of field-grown trees are lost when dug conventionally (balled-in-burlap or with a tree spade). This is probably the single most important factor in understanding the marginal performance of plants grown conventionally in the field and dug and transplanted bare root or balled-in-burlap.

Bare Root. The greatest limiting factor in the trans-planting of nursery stock bare root, is the short time in late winter/early spring when it can be done. Sizable plants of some species may be dug and transplanted bare root with acceptable success if it is done timely and carefully.

The advantages of handling trees and shrubs bare root are:
a) The investment per plant is low.
b) Cost of plants to the consumer is low.
c) Plants are lightweight, making shipping economical.
On the other hand, the disadvantages are:
a) The time appropriate for digging and transplanting is short.
b) Only those deciduous species easy to transplant are tolerant of the technique.
c) Since all fine roots are killed during digging, handling and storage, no root activity occurs until bud swell in the spring. Consequently, planting in

1

fall or winter is generally not suitable due to bud and twig dehydration. In many geographic areas, the lowest humidity of the year occurs during the winter.

d) Small plants can be handled bare root with acceptable survival rates, but larger plants generally have more problems.

e) Only those plants very stress-tolerant and capable of rapid recovery following transplanting can be handled successfully.

Most plants dug bare root are grown in sandy loam field soils so that the soil can be easily removed from the roots. This is normally done by mechanical diggers using a U-shaped blade with a lifting unit or fingers that lift and agitate the soil (Figure 1.1). In some cases a modified potato harvester is drawn behind the U-shaped blade to further lift and shake the plants and soil to hasten separation (Figure 1.2). The plants are either loaded onto trailers and taken to a storage area where they are later graded and sorted as to size and quality or in some cases, they are rough sorted and tied into bundles in the field (Figure 1.2). With either procedure, sufficient dehydration occurs to kill all fine roots leaving the larger roots roughly 1/8-inch or larger to re-establish the plant on the new site. Fortunately, the energy level inside the plant is generally good, which further aids re-establishment on the new site. Handling plants bare root can work well if the storage time is brief or nonexistent. The greatest problem with bare root nursery stock is the storage rather than the digging process.

Figure 1.1. A U-shaped blade is used to cut the roots on three sides of the plant (above). Most units have some type of lift or finger apparatus attached to the back of the U-blade to further shake or move the soil to aid separation. A crawler tractor was modified to give more belly clearance for stradling the rows and equipped with a U-blade (below).

3

Figure 1.2. A modified potato harvester is drawn behind the U-blade to further aid in soil separation (above). The potato harvester shakes the plants and soil vigorously and in many soil/soil moisture situations, leaves the roots relatively clean. The plants may be taken directly to a storage area or rough-graded and tied in the field (below).

4

Balled-in-Burlap. Balled-in-burlap (B & B) is the time-honored method of transplanting most field-grown nursery stock, primarily during the dormant period. The plant is carefully dug with a block of soil surrounding the base of the plant. The soil is generally wrapped in burlap, secured with pinning nails and/or wrapped with twine (Figure 1.3). If the process is completed correctly, the soil ball is held securely and is not broken or allowed to shift during shipping, handling and planting into the landscape. Because only a very few active root tips are present in the soil ball they must sustain the plant until it is planted into the landscape and new roots develop from the cut ends of the larger roots (Figure 1.4). breakage or disruption of these few small roots may mean the plant dies.

Advantages of the B & B method are:
   a) Digging and transplanting season is extended compared to bare root.
   b) Plants with poor survival percentages handled bare root can be transplanted with moderate satisfaction, particularly are the broadleaf evergreens and conifers: pines, spruce, fir, etc.
   c) A soil ball placed in the landscape creates minimal textural and water movement differences compared to container-grown plants in soilless mixes where the texture of the mix and the soil at the planting site are vastly different and create water stress problems.
   d) Plants may be dug ahead of time and held for moderate periods of time above ground if handled properly, thus extending the transplanting time.

Note: Transplanting with tree spades and other mechanical digging devices would have the same advantages and disadvantages as the B & B method.

Figure 1.3. Once the ball of soil is shaped (above), burlap is used to hold the soil ball in place around the roots during digging, handling and planting (below). Pinning nails are used to secure the ends of the burlap. Twine may or may not be needed to further secure the burlap and soil mass.

6

Figure 1.4. Plants dug bare root, B & B, or with tree spades must be sustained by the very limited absorption of water by the sections of large roots and the few fine roots. New roots develop just behind the cut surface of the root in most cases. These roots are slow to develop following planting, thus considerable care and maintenance is required. The plant on the left was grown in a fabric container that stimulates root branching. The plant on the right has an excellent root system for a plant dug B & B but note there are very few fine roots present.

Disadvantages are:
a) 98% or more of the roots of the plant are lost at digging (5).
b) Digging is limited to the dormant season for all but a few of the very tolerant species.
c) Some species still cannot be transplanted with satisfactory survival percentages using this technique. Examples: Kentucky coffee tree (*Gymnocladus dioica*), blackgum (*Nyssa sylvatica*), sassafras (*Sassafras albidum*), and gums or eucalyptus (*Eucalyptus* spp.).

d) considerable labor is required, and the labor must be skilled at this technique (it is not as easy as it looks or sounds and balls are different sizes (Figure 1.5).

e) Soil moisture conditions can limit digging. Very dry or very wet soils are unsatisfactory.

f) The root balls are heavy and awkward to transport, yet if broken or allowed to shift, chances of plant survival decrease.

g) Root balls must be kept moist but not overly wet during handling and shipping (Figure 1.5) Soil balls with excess water may end up shaped like pancakes after being hauled considerable distance.

h) Heavier soils work best since the soil ball is less likely to break and damage the few small roots that must sustain the plants until replanting. Some species, such as pines and other conifers in particular, grow best on well-drained, sandy loam soils. However, since they are evergreens and must be dug B & B, they must be grown on soils sufficiently heavy for satisfactory digging.

i) Planting should be completed in the spring before natural bud break for the species (elongation of the buds at the ends of the many twigs and branches). The growth regulating chemicals sent downward by the expanding buds are responsible for the development of new roots from the cut ends of the larger roots. This early root development plays a major role in reducing the stress experienced by the plant during the critical first growing season.

Many plants are dug B & B and "heeled-in" (placed above-ground and surrounded with mulch such as sawdust, bark or straw) to protect the roots in the ball of soil (Figure 1.6). These plants are often held for planting after the normal spring flush of new growth for the species. Under these conditions, the major development of new roots occurs into the mulch material. When plants are removed from these conditions, many of the new roots outside the original soil ball are damaged or killed, either by exposure to air or physical breakage (Figure 1.6). When the initial spring bud break is past, there is less chemical signal to stimulate a new burst of roots to rapidly establish the plant in the new site. Consequently, the plant has new foliage, with a high rate of water loss, with an extremely limited root system and no major chemical signal to develop new roots until the following spring. Conditions are further complicated by the fact that the energy level in the plant drops substantially with the extension of the new top growth. Also, because of the very limited root system, the supply of water and nutrients to the leaves will be minimal throughout the growing season which prevents the normal replenishing of energy in the plant following the initial spring flush. Energy levels in the plant decrease sharply during spring growth then slowly build to a peak in fall just before leaf drop, with only a slight decline during winter until the spring flush again (1, 3, 4).

Energy (carbohydrate) and growth regulator levels of root tissue are probably the limiting factors in new root growth when trees are transplanted during or after the spring shoot growth period (2, 6).

All these factors strongly emphasize the importance of: a) planting B & B plants **before** the spring flush of growth, or b) holding these plants in some type of container to minimize the disruption of the new roots produced prior to time of planting. As one nurseryman put it, "Balled-in-burlap is a lot of work just to keep the roots moist."

Figure 1.5. Trees dug balled-in-burlap ready for sale or shipping. Frequently the root balls are of different size, shape, and weight, making handling and shipping awkward (above). Watering must be done carefully. Because the root ball is small in comparison to the top and the burlap further promotes evaporation, the root balls can dry out very quickly (below).

10

Figure 1.6. Trees heavily mulched to protect the roots from heat and cold and to help stabilize soil moisture (above). Unfortunately, if the trees remain in this position very long, the burlap deteriorates and roots grow into the mulch or into the soil below, making further movement of the ball difficult and increasing plant stress (below).

11

When first considered, placing plants dug B & B into containers for holding seems like a very desirable alternative (Figure 1.7). The roots are comfined to the volume of the container and subsequent movement can be done without root disturbance. However, several factors must be considered to avoid complications. Every container has a perched water table caused by the bottom restricting the normal downward movement of water (see the chapter on landscape containers in *Establishment and Maintenance of Landscape Plants* for a detailed definition). This is why very porous soilless mixes are used almost exclusively for producing plants in containers. When the ball of field soil is placed in the container, the potential for a very high perched water table and rapid suffocation of roots exists (Figure 1.8). If the ball of field soil is surrounded by a suitable soilless growth medium such as would be used if the plant had been grown in the container, drainage of excess water proceeds normally and the plants can be held for considerable time under these conditions. On the other hand, if the soil ball is placed in a container and surrounded by additional field soil, water management must be precise. In most cases, plant losses, particularly of sensitive species, are great. Given two trees dug B & B and placed in containers the same diameter and depth, one surrounded by soil while the other is surrounded by a suitable mix for the depth of the container, the one with the soil may lose part or all of its root system to suffocation. Taxus, pines, and other conifers, as well as dogwoods, redbuds and certain other hardwood species are especially sensitive (8). The soilless mix used around the B & B soil ball should contain reasonable levels of all nutrients required for plant growth. For a discussion of soilless mixes and nutrition of these soil substitutes, see *Plant Production in Containers* by Carl Whitcomb (7). Proper nutrition of B & B trees held in containers greatly reduces the stress experienced by the plants before, during and after transplanting.

12

Figure 1.7. These upright junipers were dug in the field and placed into paper mache pots for holding or shipping. This can be an acceptable practice if water is managed carefully but often it ends in plant death due to root suffocation.

Both bare root and balled-in-burlap plants are most effectively dug and planted in early spring before growth begins. This greatly limits the length of time nursery plants can be offered for sale. Therefore, various techniques such as cold storage, shade and heeling-in with sawdust, bark, straw or similar materials are used to extend the digging and selling season. These techniques are successful to varying degrees. However, the consuming public does not understand the limitations of these techniques and sufficient plant losses occur to discourage many gardeners.

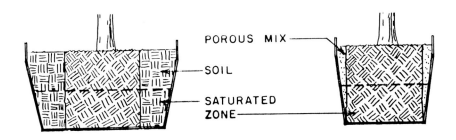

POROUS MIX

SOIL

SATURATED ZONE

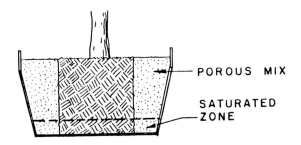

POROUS MIX

SATURATED ZONE

Figure 1.8. If the root ball is surrounded by soil, the saturated zone in the container will be deep (above, left). Likewise, if the sides of the root ball are large enough to touch the sides of the container, the saturated zone will be deep and many roots are likely to suffocate (above, right). However, if the root ball is surrounded by a porous mix, the saturated zone will be shallow and plant performance will be good (below).

Tree Spades. Many trees are dug with a mechanical tree spade, then placed in wire baskets lined with burlap to better secure the root ball for shipping and handling (Figure 1.9). This technique adds considerable harvest expense, but does help in keeping the soil around the roots from shifting.

Recently the effect of the wire basket on future root growth and plant health has been questioned. In order to observe this closely, several trees were dug that had been placed in wire baskets for transplanting. The wire baskets were in very good condition even though they had been in the soil for six years and were made of painted, not galvanized, wire. Root restrictions and injury as a result of the wire could be observed at several locations (Figure 1.10).

14

Figure 1.9. A field-grown tree is dug with a tree spade (above). The root ball is placed in a wire basket lined with burlap and tied securely. By making crimps or twists in the wire the burlap can be drawn securely around the root ball to reduce the likelihood of shifting or breaking during shipping and handling (below).

15

*Figure 1.10. Root growth of a sycamore tree in relation to a wire
basket. Several roots have been partially restricted by the wire
(above). Looking at the overall root system (see white arrows,
below) several roots have been partially restricted but they
represent only a small portion of the supporting root system on
this six-inch caliper tree. The painted wire basket had been in
the ground six years, yet little deterioration had occurred except
near the soil surface.*

16

The effect of the wire on the future health of the trees remains to be seen. However, the many roots partially restricted, and the limited deterioration of the wire, suggest that the wire baskets do somewhat jeopardize plant health. Whether the benefits of the wire baskets in moving larger plants and keeping the soil ball from breaking or shifting, justifies the restriction of a portion of the lateral root growth remains to be determined. Many nurserymen and landscape contractors are either for or against wire baskets based on their own feelings and observations. Until a good study is made of the long-term effects of wire baskets on tree growth and health, the jury is still out.

One of the most costly practices for both B & B and tree spade harvest field nurseries is the hunt-and-harvest practice. If all of the trees are of a consistent size and quality so that they can all be harvested at one time, mechanical digging with tree spades works fairly well. However, if only an occassional tree is salable, so that either the machine operator or B & B digging crew must hunt for an acceptable tree, the cost of harvest goes up dramatically (Figure 1.11).

Figure 1.11. If all of the trees are of marketable size and quality such that all can be dug at one time, labor/ machinery efficiency is good (above). However, if only an occasional tree is of marketable quality, the cost per unit to harvest is much greater and space use efficiency in the field is decreased (below).

18

Container Production. After World War II a new nursery industry began developing in southern California where techniques common to greenhouse production of pot plants were used. Because temperatures were mild and moisture fell only when the irrigation system was on, container production procedures which worked in the southern California sun lead to disaster when employed elsewhere. Southern California is unique in that it provides an outdoor environment similar to the climate in greenhouses in other parts of the world.

Despite numerous setbacks and frustration for growers outside southern California, the production of a assortment of plants in containers continued to increase. The consuming public eagerly purchased them for several reasons:

a) Plants were in full leaf and sometimes flowering when offered for sale, thus the stigma of buying a "dead" (dormant) plant was removed.

b) The container provided a neat package, easily displayed, handled, and transported in the trunk or back seat of an automobile.

c) In general, container-grown plants could be planted anytime during the growing season, instead of just during a limited period in the spring.

d) For the less informed public, the container-grown plant provided a greater chance of success.

By the early '60s, container production of nursery stock had spread throughout the southern United States and in other parts of the world. However, many problems existed because the unique environment of the container was not understood. Productive field soils failed to support good plant growth in containers. Peat and sand were frequently added to field soils to try to improve drainage but with little benefit. During this period, growth of plants in containers was slow because of poor nutrition and losses were high due to root rot organisms such as *Phytophthora* and *Pythium* which flourished in these overly wet and poorly aerated conditions. With each improvement in container plant production techniques, the weeds grew better than the crop plant, and because the roots of the crop plant were confined to a limited volume, the growth restrictions due to weeds were tremendous. (For detailed information regarding containers, see *Plant Production in Containers*, 1988, Lacebark Inc., P.O. Box 2383, Stillwater, OK 74076).

The Unique Container. Growing plants in containers does not alter the basic physiological principles involved in the production of any crop. Neither are the genetics of the plant altered (Figure 1.12). On the other hand, the conditions in the container are unique compared to any other plant production system. Consider that no plants have evolved in containers as compared to the immense diversity of climatic conditions and soils that exist in nature. Plants are grown in containers for the convenience of man, **and** only when conditions in the container have been highly refined and carefully maintained, do the plants grow well.

Figure 1.12. These small trees were field-grown then dug when dormant in the fall and placed in storage. Before spring growth began, they were placed in containers with a good growth medium. These field-grown plants are now 'container-grown' (once a good root system has developed). The growth characteristics of the plant are not altered, but the environment of the root system has been radically altered. If the container growth medium is correct, plant top and root growth will be excellent. However, unless the container conditions are understood and managed correctly, disaster can occur.

The length of time a plant can be grown or held in a container without repotting, is limited. The air spaces in the container growth media (soil mix), so essential to active root growth, are rapidly filled by roots as the plant grows. In a sense, the plant restricts itself as the demand for aeration due to growth of the root system increases and the availability of air decreases due to filling of the air spaces with roots and settling and decomposition of the media. When the aeration level in the mix declines beyond a certain point, root activity declines, and, unless shifted to a larger container with new mix, the plant will stop growing, regardless of additional fertilizer or water. This is especially true for woody plants. A further complication is the fact that with conventional containers, 90% or more of the roots of most plants are in the outer sheath of growth medium next to the inner container wall. The vast proportion of the medium provides little towards plant health and vigor other than serving as a water reservoir and ballast to hold the plant upright. **Because of this container-root-media-aeration relationship, the time a plant can remain in a specific container is limited. Thus the point is reached where container-grown nursery stock must be sold, shifted into a larger container, or thrown away.**

The Fabric Container. In 1982, a new system became available for producing trees and shrubs. It essentially combined the advantages of growing a plant in a container with the buffer, safety and simplicity of producing plants in the field. The system consists of a porous fabric container that allows plant roots to penetrate the fabric as they extend outward. However, as the roots grow in diameter, they are restricted by the physical strength and resistance to expansion of the unique fabric. Because absorption of water and nutrients is almost exclusively at the root tips, the more fibrous the root system, the more plant growth and health is enhanced. Likewise, since the   translocation of water and nutrients from the root tips to the leaves is through the xylem (the central core of the root and stem) the fabric provides little restriction. However, the physical restriction of the fabric causes the root system to branch inside the fabric container and restricts the downward flow of energy (carbohydrates or soluble sugars) from the leaves at the inner surface of the fabric container, since the downward flow of energy is in the phloem (the outer sheath of the root and stem) (Figure 1.13).

21

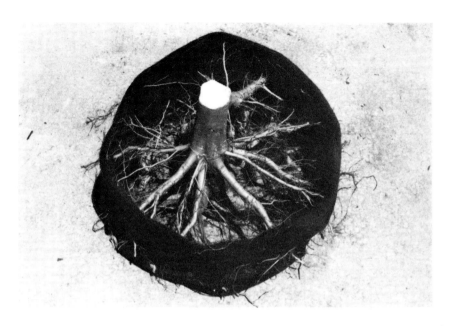

Figure 1.13.   Root development inside a fabric container.   In this case the tree was dug, the bottom removed, and the soil washed away while leaving the fabric/root complex undisturbed.   Trees grown conventionally and dug balled-in-burlap have a far inferior root system.

With this unique system, plants can be dug and transplanted over a much longer time during the year than can bare root plants or those dug balled-in-burlap.   The root ball is generally smaller than with B & B, making handling and shipping easier.   Some roots are lost at time of harvest, but these nurse roots mostly have been deprived of energy from the leaves since they are outside the fabric wall and are of minor consequence.   The plants re-establish very quickly because of the tremendous root systems and energy storage within the roots.   These "containers" cannot blow over like conventional above-ground containers, and because of the tremendous insulating effect of the soil, the plants' roots are in their natural environment, protected from the extremes of heat and cold that are so devastating to plants in conventional above-ground containers.   The complete system is described in a later chapter.

It is very important to note that not just any fabric works; the physical requirements are quite specific. If the roots cannot grow through the fabric, the plant is stunted and if the roots are not restricted by the fabric, few, if any, benefits occur. In addition, this is a patented invention and with further improvement patents pending, the patent protection will last for many years.

There is no one "best" system. Each plant production system has advantages and disadvantages. Market demands and labor costs will, no doubt, cause further evolution of production techniques used in the nursery business.

Literature Cited

1. Kramer, P.J. and T.T. Kozlowski. 1960. *Physiology of Trees*. McGraw-Hill Book Co., New York.

2. Reich, P.B., R.O. Jeskey, P.S. Johnson, T.M. Hinckley. 1980. Periodic root and shoot growth in oak. Forest Sci. 26:590-598.

3. Siminovitch, D., C.M. Wilson and D.R. Briggs. 1953. Studies of the living bark of the black locust in relation to its frost hardiness. IV Seasonal transformations and variations in the carbohydrate: starch-sucrose interconver-sions. Plant Physiology 28:383-400.

4. Wargo, Philip. 1979. Starch storage and radial growth in woody roots of sugar maple. Can. Jour. Forest Res. 9:49-56.

5. Watson, Gary W. and E.B. Himelick. 1982. Root distribution of nursery trees and its relationship to transplanting success. Jour. of Arboriculture 8:225-229.

6. Watson, Gary W. and E.B. Himelick. 1982. Seasonal variation in root regeneration of transplanted trees. Jour. of Arboriculture 8:305-310.

7. Whitcomb, Carl E. 1988. *Plant Production in Containers*. Lacebark Inc., Stillwater, Ok.

8. Whitcomb, Carl E. 1985. *Know It & Grow It: A Guide to the Identification and Use of Landscape Plants*. Lacebark Inc., Stillwater, Ok.

CHAPTER 2

ROOT DEVELOPMENT AND PLANT HEALTH

ROOT DEVELOPMENT & PLANT HEALTH

A direct relationship exists between root branching and plant growth, particularly with the woody plants. In 1968 Stoner and Whitcomb (7) were studying the root development of tree seedlings in containers. While working with Jerusalem thorn (*Parkinsonia aculeata*), a legume with a strong primary root, they observed that when young seedlings six to eight inches tall were removed from a deep flat and the primary root was cut at different distances below the root-stem interface, some trees grew rapidly following transplanting while others did not. When the seedlings were examined after several months, the seedlings that had grown well had well developed lateral roots, whereas, those that had grown poorly had re-established a primary or taproot. Subsequent studies with other species showed a similar response (Figure 2.1).

Figure 2.1. When a taproot is manually pruned, it may quickly redevelop and suppress lateral root branching (left) or it may lose its apical dominance thus allowing many lateral roots to develop (right). This is a typical response of a tree seedling with a strong taproot (in this case, Kentucky coffee tree, **Gymnocladus dioica**)*, thus the need for a technique to prevent the taproot from redeveloping.*

25

Thus began the search for a technique that would prune the primary root of every seedling without the labor of removing and cutting. The further complication of re-development of the primary root by some seedlings could also be eliminated. Deep flats with wire bottoms quickly provided the good news and bad news. The good news was that the wire bottom, covered only by a layer or two of newspaper to retain the medium, worked well for pruning the primary root and stimulating secondary root branching and accelerating growth of seedlings. The bad news was that with many seedlings in a flat and the development of many secondary roots, the root system became an unmanageable mass that could not be separated without severe damage to most seedlings.

Air Root Pruning. In 1969, bottomless milk cartons were used as individual containers for seedlings (7). Quart-size milk cartons 2.75 x 2.75 x 11 inches deep were used. Species with strong primary roots such as Jerusalem thorn, (*Parkinsonia aculeata*) and eastern red bud (*Cercis canadensis*) worked well, however, there was little benefit to several species of pines. Inspection of the root systems showed that pine roots never reached the bottoms of the containers in a three-month growth period. On the other hand, the species with strong primary roots had developed a mass of secondary roots at both the bottom and top of the containers with only the primary root extending through the center. Studies by Davis and Whitcomb (2) confirmed that there is an optimum depth and diameter of container for growing tree seedlings. Containers 2.5 inches square were superior to smaller sizes and depths greater than nine inches provided no benefit (Figure 2.2). Since the size of the container is important and the length of time a tree seedling is grown in a container influences root quality, studies were conducted with larger containers. Gibson and Whitcomb (3) and Whitcomb, Kazokas and Gray (9) studied the growth of tree seedlings planted in half-gallon or one-gallon milk cartons. Larger tree seedlings were produced by extending the time seedlings were left in the container, but root system quality and overall plant size and quality were not increased proportionately to the space, labor, and other expenses required for the larger containers. Growth of pines and other conifers was especially sluggish in the larger containers. As will be shown later in this section, this was probably due to the limited root branching at the root/stem interface. In these larger containers,

26

the roots that developed laterally from the taproot following air-root-pruning grew out, contacted the side wall, and were directed downward. When they were air-pruned at the bottom, secondary roots formed only a few inches back, thus the key root formation at the base of the stem was not affected.

Figure 2.2. The depth of the air-root-pruning container is important in that secondary root branching will occur only a limited distance behind the pruned primary root. In this case, the container was about six inches deep and secondary roots developed about 4.5 inches back from the pruned primary root tip. If the container had been shallower, the lateral roots would have formed over the entire primary root.

Further work by Wall and Whitcomb (8) with 2.5-inch square milk cartons for tree seedlings showed that containers 5.5 inches tall stimulated more root branches than deeper containers. Hathaway and Whitcomb (4) observed:

a) Proper nutrition was very important to growth and development of Japanese black pine and river birch seedlings.

b) Root-to-shoot ratio **was not** related to survival and growth when planted in the field.

c) Seedlings grown in containers with the proper depth, diameter and nutrition were larger after three months than two-year-old bed-grown plants and continued to out-grow the bed-grown seedlings after one full year following transplanting (Figure 2.3)

Figure 2.3. A three-year-old Japanese black pine seedling grown in a ground bed for two years before being transplanted into the container (left) and a one-year-old seedling that was grown in an air-pruned container for three months to stimulate root branching before being transplanted into the larger container (right).

28

For maximum growth and plant health, time of transplanting tree seedlings from the containers either into larger containers or the field is very important. Plant growth is also related to the size of the seedling container in which the seedling is grown. Appleton and Whitcomb (1) found that the milk carton approximately 2.5 inches square, 5 inches deep was superior to other containers of similar or less volume. The benefit of the best container size was still evident two years after the seedlings were transplanted into larger containers or the field (Figure 2.4). They also noted that **rapid-growing species should be transplanted out of the propagation containers earlier than slow-growing species.** At the time these studies were done, the optimum time of transplant was thought to be related to volume/nutritional aspects of the container growth medium. However, in light of further investigations, the benefits may have been due to the time required for the container size/growth rate aspect of the species to develop maximum root branching.

*Figure 2.4   Scotch pine (**Pinus sylvestris**) seedlings 18 months from seed planting date (left) in milk cartons 2.5 by 2.5 by 5 inches deep and (right) in Nu-pots 2.25 by 2.25 by 3.0 inches. Both seedlings were transplanted into the larger containers on the same date.*

29

Propagation Container Design. The shape, depth and volume of containers can have a striking effect on the growth of tree seedlings. Wall and Whitcomb (8) observed not only a vast difference in the growth of tree seedlings relative to container design, but a difference in root quality as well (Figure 2.5). Klingaman and King (6) carried the study further and observed that containers more than four to six inches deep for growing tree seedlings are not compatible with nursery practices. Most roots developed from the air-pruned bottoms of the containers, therefore, when the trees were harvested, most of the new roots developed below the depth of the soil ball at harvest time. They concluded that tree seedling containers should be no more than four to six inches deep to insure that new roots will be sufficiently near the surface to be retained in the soil ball when harvested B & B.

*Figure 2.5. Root development on lacebark elm (**Ulmus parvifolia**) seedlings as a result of different propagation containers. Notice the constriction of the roots at the bottom (left). The round-bottomed container with the center drain hole (right) caused much root spiraling. The shallow bottomless container (center) developed the best root system of these three.*

Examination of trees grown in tube-shaped ('plug') containers with only a large drain/air-root-pruning hole at the bottom, typically shows a terrible root system. For example, when live oaks that were originally grown in 'plug' containers, then transplanted into two-gallon conventional containers, were examined for root growth, a mass of distorted roots were found. The original 'plug' had been 1.5 inches x 5 inches deep. The roots in this area were spiraled, twisted, and contorted so that several roots had begun girdling or strangling the main stem near the soil surface (Figure 2.6). Because of the 'plug' container design, most of the active root tips at time of transplanting were aimed down (Figure 2.6). This is in response to the air-root-pruning at the bottom drain/pruning hole. The longer a seedling stays in such a container, the more distorted and undesirable the root system. Unfortunately, the root systems are least undesirable if transplanting occurs six to eight weeks after the seed has germinated. This is rarely done since the top is still small and it is perceived that the plants are not yet ready to be transplanted. Once the permanent roots of a woody plant are deformed, there is no practical method to correct the problem. A tree such as the one in Figure 2.6 is doomed to slow growth and a short life.

Further information on this subject is included at the end of this chapter. *Plant Production in Containers* by Carl E. Whitcomb, 1988, covers this and related aspects of propagation of seedlings in detail.

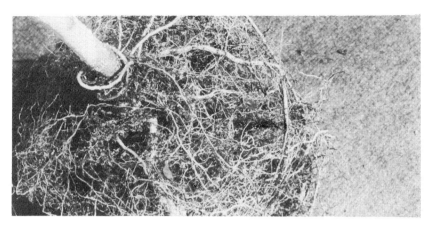

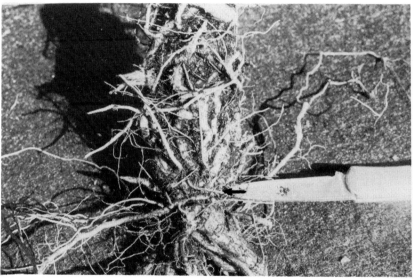

Figure 2.6. *This live oak tree was grown for several months in a 'plug' container before being transplanted into a larger container. Note the dimensions of the original 'plug' container are still readily visible two years later (above). Several circling or strangling roots are present near the top as well as at the bottom. Note that most of the roots developed from the bottom of the 'plug' container, providing little lateral support for the young tree. This tree had grown poorly in the nursery and was doomed to poor growth and an early death because of the root system.*

Root Development/Root-bound. The question frequently arises, "When does root development in a container reach the point of being 'root-bound'?" The answer is not simple. Root-bound begins at that point where the growth rate of the plant begins to decline due to a decrease in available space in the container for further root development. It continues to the point where plant growth cannot be stimulated to proceed at even modest rates, regardless of fertilizer, water, light, or temperature conditions. The greater the decline in plant growth and vigor, due to decreased root activity, the more difficult establishment of the plant will be in a larger container and especially in the landscape. At some point, the plant becomes so stunted that the only value remaining is as organic matter in a landfill or compost heap. Being root-bound is, therefore, not a specific point or condition but rather a progressively undesirable condition from the ideal state of root development to the very undesirable point where the plant should be thrown away. The point where the plant should be discarded varies with species and, to some degree, how the plant was propagated, but in general, if no white root tips are visible when the container is removed, establishment and subsequent growth in the field or landscape will be poor at best and losses are likely to be substantial.

Plants that are propagated from cuttings develop secondary roots more readily than those grown from seed. The roots that form on the base of a cutting are the secondary or adventitious roots. The fact that these form rather easily and quickly also means that as roots restrict roots, secondary roots are formed, thus slowing somewhat the rate at which a plant reaches the severe root-bound condition, where no white root tips are visible when the container is removed. Plants grown from seed generally do not develop secondary roots readily, therefore, as the initial root growth progresses to the point where space becomes limiting to plant root growth, the decline in numbers of white root tips is rapid. A tree grown from seed in a container with no white root tips is unlikely to grow following transplanting into the field or landscape. A higher percent of these undesirable trees will survive if shifted into a larger container if they are managed very carefully, essentially as a large cutting. However, their growth will be slow, problems many, and their value minimal.

A key point to remember is that once the plants normal growth is restricted, for any reason, the plant will never catch up with

33

plants that have not been restricted---assuming all other factors are equal. This can be readily observed in the photos in this chapter dealing with the time of transplant of tree seedlings. The ideal point of transplant to avoid any root-bound stress is as soon as the root development has progressed so that it will hold the soil mix together, no more. This is **much** sooner than would normally be anticipated from observing the root system.

The emphasis on white root tips, visible when the container is removed, cannot be over-emphasized. The white root tips play a key role in establishing the plant in the field or landscape. Unfortunately, not all of the white root tips visible when the container is removed grow out into the surrounding soil. In studies with several species only 38% to 61% of the white root tips continued to grow following transplanting. In these studies care was taken to assure that the root tips did not dry out while the counts were being made or during the transplanting process. The reason for an apparently active and white root tip to cease to extend following transplanting is not understood. See the chapter on spring vs. fall transplanting and establish-ment of container-grown nursery stock in *Establishment and Maintenance of Landscape Plants* for further information on this topic.

Figures 2.7, 2.8, 2.9, 2.10, 2.11, 2.12, 2.13 show plants with root development from near ideal to severely root-bound. **Perhaps the best advice is simply, "If in doubt, throw it out".** To put it another way, it is far better and more economical to throw it out than to go to the expense of planting only to have it die and have to be replaced. Plants that perform poorly or die after installation in the landscape are "black eyes" to the nursery and landscape industry and related businesses. The "man on the street" generally attributes a dead or dying plant to some-thing, the lack of rain, too much rain or irrigation, "that particular species won't grow here", poor planting procedures by the contractor or nursery, and on and on. On the other hand, plants are supposed to be green and healthy so little notice is given to good plant performance. One dead or dying plant in a landscape probably does more harm to the image of the industry than the favorable appearance of several hundred healthy ones. Once container-grown nursery stock gets root-bound beyond a certain difficult-to-define point, it becomes a liability, not an asset. **When a plant reaches the point of optimum root growth** it should be sold or shifted into a larger container. If not, at some point shortly thereafter a point is reached where its value and performance decreases very rapidly. That is the price for the convenience of plant production in containers.

Figure 2.7. Nearly ideal root development in a container prior to transplanting. Note the white root tips on the sides and bottom of the root ball which will extend and support the plant physically as well as with water and nutrients.

Figure 2.8. The pyracantha (above) has visible white root tips, but they are mostly at the base of the root ball and the root mass around the sides is very tangled. This plant will likely survive in the landscape and because it is from a species that develops secondary roots with relative ease, will probably function for a reasonable time, although its life will be shortened by the root-bound condition. The roots of the juniper (below) will mean poor establishment and landscape performance if it survives at all.

36

Figure 2.9. This ligustrum is very root-bound and will be slow to establish in the landscape. Like the pyracantha in the previous figure, if it survives the transplant stress and does eventually get a few roots out into the surrounding soil, it will probably function for a moderate period of time. Keep in mind that a ligustrum or pyracantha are much more tolerant to the undesirable root-bound condition than many other species.

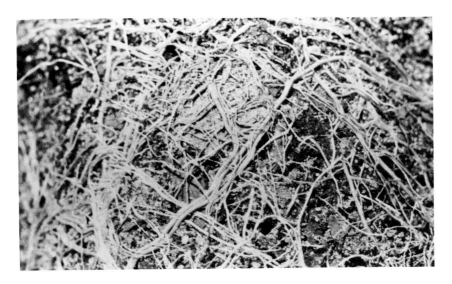

Figure 2.10. The oak tree (above) is severely root-bound and will never make a good tree with adequate anchorage even if it does survive transplanting. Throw it away, is good advice. The roots of this elm tree (below) are so intermingled that it would be permanently stunted to some degree even if it survived transplanting. There were no white root tips visible on the outer surface of the root ball, thus intensive, extended care would be required in order to get this tree to survive in the landscape. If it survived, it would be poorly anchored and stunted, thus subject to disease and insect problems and blow-over.

38

Figure 2.11. With the spring flush of growth, many root-bound plants will develop some new actively growing root tips. On the outer surface of the root ball, only a few white root tips can be observed (above). These are the key to survival of the plant. Unfortunately, for every active white root tip, there are masses of roots showing no activity (below). The bottom photo is a close-up of the center of the bottom of the above plant.

Figure 2.12. In many cases, if a root-bound container-grown plant is planted either in a field nursery to grow on or a landscape, its performance is poor and its life is short. The oak (above) was grown in a three-gallon container for one year, then planted in the field. When it was dug two years later, the only roots that grew out from the container root mass were from the bottom and on one side (with one exception, see left, center). Once the tree reaches any appreciable height and a strong wind blows from left to right.... (there were no roots growing downward either). This has nothing to do with a taproot, but rather with container design.

*Figure 2.13. These two elm trees are the same age and the
difference in container volume is only about 20% (5-gallon poly
bag, left, and 4-gallon rigid plastic container, right), however,
note the many white root tips on the tree grown with the poly bag
which stops root circling and stimulates root branching as opposed
to the poor root system with most roots at the very bottom of the
container. Container design can have a great influence on root
development and plants becoming root-bound*

     *In the case of container-grown plants, it is mostly a matter
of "what you see is what you get" in terms of root growth into the
surrounding soil at time of transplanting. If few white root tips
are visible when the container is removed, establishment of the
plant will be slow. By contrast, if many white root tips are
visible, establishment will be rapid and problems few. White root
tips continue to grow in the same direction following planting,
they do not "remember" the container.*

Root Development and Larger Plants. Many containers and other
root modification techniques have been tested and reported.
However, a major clue as to the importance of the number of
roots at the root/stem interface resulted from an unplanned
experiment. A study had been planned with considerable care since

41

differences in plant response to treatments was expected to be relatively small. Four species were selected and 180 trees of each species were planted in the field. In order to have very uniform plants in the beginning, about 300 trees of each species had been grown in two-gallon polyethylene bag containers. The 180 most uniform trees were selected for the study. Two years later and three unsuccessful attempts to establish various treatments among the trees ended in a great deal of difference in tree size and quality but without any treatments. Since the trees were very uniform when planted, the vast difference in tree growth was a surprise and mystery.

At the end of the second growing season, all of the trees were dug using a 24-inch backhoe, and the soil removed in order to see if a relationship existed between root development following planting and top growth. All large trees had many small to medium-sized roots, whereas, some small or medium-sized trees had a few large roots. Counts of large roots (over 3/4-inch or more in diameter at the root/crown interface) were not correlated with stem diameters or tree heights. Likewise, counts of various sizes of roots alone or in combination at a point approximately 12 inches out from the stem revealed only poor correlations with stem diameters and tree height. However, when counts of roots, approximately 3/16 inches (5 cm.) or larger arising from the root/stem interface were taken, a striking correlation resulted (Figures 2.14 and 2.15)

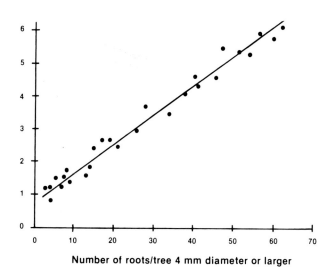

Number of roots/tree 4 mm diameter or larger

*Figure 2.14. Relationship of number of roots arising from the root/stem interface and stem diameter of lacebark elm (**Ulmus parvifolia**) trees. It is striking how well the relationship between number of roots and the stem diameter exists since all values are very close to the line.*

*Figure 2.15. Uniform trees of lacebark elm (**Ulmus parvifolia**) were planted in the field from two-gallon containers then dug two years later. The vast difference in tree size as affected by the number of roots arising from the root/stem interface shows the importance of proper root development on plant growth in the nursery and landscape.*

43

This suggests that the number of roots arising from the root/stem interface is more important to tree growth than the number of roots developed on the ends of a few larger roots as a result of root pruning or other techniques. Looking back, this was suggested by earlier experiments but the relationship was missed in evaluating the results of those studies (1, 2, 7).

The fact that the trees were uniform in age and size when the study began points up a pronounced weakness in evaluating container-grown plants using only the visual quality of the top. With the luxury of water, root zone aeration and nutrition in a well managed container production system, a plant of good size and visual quality can be produced with a poorly formed root system (Figure 2.16). Following transplanting into a less favorable environment, the quality of the root system greatly influences root proliferation and soil contact on the new site and gradually plants with superior root systems grow faster because of the additional water and nutrient absorption.

Figure 2.16. Root development of two English oaks as a result of root-modifying seedling containers. However, due to the abundance of nutrients, water and aeration in the larger containers, the tops of the two trees grew similarly while having vastly different root systems. When these trees were planted into the field, their performance was very different.

The striking relationship between the number of relatively small roots arising from the root/stem junction and plant growth in the landscape suggests several management practices:

a) Root pruning of bed-grown seedlings should be done earlier and shallower than is currently practiced.

b) Tree seedling containers should be relatively shallow in order to stimulate root branching at or near the root/stem junction (as opposed to the deep containers sometimes used). Transplanting should be prompt and much earlier than is normally practiced.

c) Trees that can be propagated from cuttings with a substantial numbers of roots stimulated on the base of the cutting should have superior growth compared to the same species grown from seed. Hickman and Whitcomb (5) observed far better growth with several cultivars of lacebark elm propagated from cuttings compared to the best seedlings. They concluded that the difference was due to the genetic superiority of the cultivar propagated from cuttings as opposed to the seedlings. In retrospect, the difference may have been equally or more related to the number of roots developed at the root/stem interface. Similar growth differences have been obtained using red maple (*Acer rubrum*), osage orange (*Maclura pomifera*), and London planetree (*Platanus acerifolia*) (unpublished data).

The Future. As a result of these data and observations, a new container design was developed for propagating woody plants. It features a bottom for easy filling and handling, yet the bottom is designed such that the taproot of a seedling is air-pruned, only without having the messy open bottom and wire benches. The secondary roots that develop from the taproot are air-pruned on the **sides** of the container to further increase root branching. The result is a seedling or cutting that has many lateral roots from the root/stem interface. In addition, the roots are positioned so that they will grow out in all directions following transplanting, thus securely anchoring the plant while providing maximum root surface area for rapid absorption of water and nutrients. Named the RootMaker, this propagation container is the first to stimulate root branching while directing the new roots as well (Figure 2.17). Eventually a one- and two-gallon size will also be available.

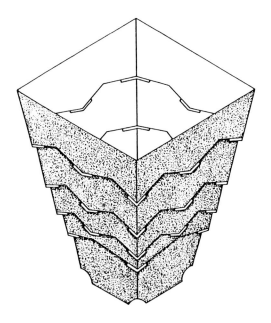

Figure 2.17. Original drawing of the new propagation container featuring air pruning on the sides in conjunction with offset and sloping sections that direct the roots into the opening (see the following chapter for details). This design will eventually be made in larger sizes as well.

The data supporting root branching is dramatic. At this print negative effects of "excess" root branching have not been observed. How many roots are enough? It is not known, but clearly the better the supply of water and nutrients from the roots to the tops, the healthier the plant. It may well turn out that plants with very fibrous and perhaps more compact root systems are better suited to the many landscape settings where root space is very limited. Trees grown conventionally can not or will not develop secondary roots at the base of the stem. This branching process must be done when the seedling is in its infancy. See the next chapter for further information on roots and containers and the RootMaker propagation container specifically.

Literature Cited

1. Appleton, Bonnie L. and Carl E. Whitcomb. 1983. Effects of container size and transplanting date on the growth of tree seedlings. Jour. Environmental Hort. 1:89-93.

2. Davis, Randy E. and Carl E. Whitcomb. 1975. Effects of propagation container size on development of high quality seedlings. Proc. Int. Plant Prop. Soc. 25:448-453.

3. Gibson, John D. and Carl E. Whitcomb. 1980. Producing tree seedlings in square bottomless containers. Ornamentals South 5:11-15.

4. Hathaway, Robert D. and Carl E. Whitcomb. 1984. Nutrition and performance of container-grown Japanese black pine seedlings. Jour. Environmental. Hort. 2:9-12.

5. Hickman, Gary, Bonnie Appleton and Carl E. Whitcomb. 1982. Vegetative propagation and evaluation of five *Ulmus parvifolia* selections. Okla. Agri. Exp. Sta. Res. Rept. P-829:16-18.

6. Klingaman, G.L. and John King. 1981. Influence of container design on harvestability of field-grown oaks. New Horizons (A pub. of Hort. Res. Inst.) pg. 21-22.

7. Stoner, David and Carl E. Whitcomb. 1969. Root development of Parkinsonia seedlings. Nursery Field Day memo. Univ. of Florida. 22 pages.

8. Wall, Steve and Carl E. Whitcomb. 1980. A comparison of commercial containers for growing tree seedlings. Okla. Agri. Exp. Sta. Res. Rept. P-803:72-75.

9. Whitcomb, Carl E., William Kazokas and Charlie Gray. 1983. Growing super tree seedlings. Okla. Agri. Exp. Sta. Res. Rept. P-829:38-39.

CHAPTER 3

CONTAINER DESIGN AND TRANSPLANT SUCCESS

CONTAINER DESIGN AND TRANSPLANT SUCCESS

The design of a container can influence transplant success whether going into the field or the landscape. This chapter is included to give insights into some of the background work and how container design can influence the rate of root development into the surrounding soil. Since many plants begin life in containers, then are transplanted into a field to grow larger, many practical aspects exist. Rapid growth of roots from the container mix out into the surrounding soil is important to field production of nursery stock, since this is the only practical way to overcome the complicated water relationship problem that always exists when a plant grown in a soilless growth medium in a container is planted into soil. The textural difference of the two materials (the mix and the soil) is always such that the finer textured soil quickly draws the moisture away from the more coarse-textured container mix, leaving the plant high and dry. However, as soon as the plant gets roots into the surrounding soil, the moisture content of the container mix becomes of minor importance. Here lies the basis for these many studies.

In 1970, a soldering iron was used to create rectangular holes in the sides of conventional round plastic containers in an attempt to study the effects of aeration and drainage on plant growth (9) (Figure 3.1). The holes in the sides of the containers were not tapered or offset relative to the side curvature of the container, therefore, the roots grew past the openings with no effect. Because there was no effect, a number of years went by before the factor of container design was reconsidered.

Figure 3.1. Plastic containers with many rectangular holes in the sides. Roots were unaffected by the holes. Likewise, the holes had no effect on water management and aeration in the growth medium. Carissa grandiflora was used as a test plant because at that time it was in great demand, but difficult to grow in containers. As growth media became lighter and better aerated, the problem attributed to many "diseases" subsided. The difference in these two plants is no micronutrient fertilizer (left) and four pounds of Perk micronutrients per cubic yard (right).

The next change in container design came with ribs or baffles in the containers in an attempt to stop roots--especially roots of trees and other woody species grown from seed--from wrapping or circling in the container. With each advancement in nutrition, growth media, watering and weed control, growth of the top of the plant increased. Likewise, the root system grew larger and became more twisted, distorted and undesirable (5, 6, 7). Plants of many species quickly became "pot-bound" and were slow to establish in the field or landscape and were generally poorly anchored. As a result, life was short (Figures 3.2, 3.3, 3.4).

*Figure 3.2. A northern red oak (**Quercus rubra**) (above) planted in the field after one year in a round, standard, one-gallon container. In this instance, erosion removed part of the soil exposing the greatly deformed roots. Note the extent of root girdling likely to occur if the tree ever reaches a stem diameter of only two to three inches. The live oak (below) has a large root that encircles the stem. Roots such as this may eventually branch and extend out into the soil, but provide little anchoring of the tree.*

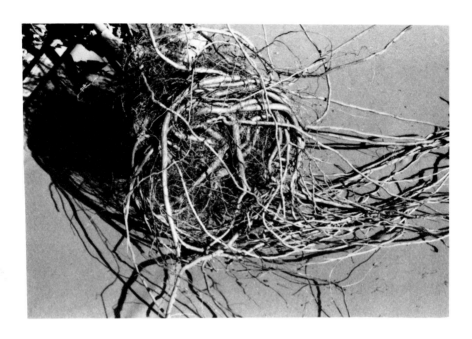

Figure 3.3. *Root system of a shumard oak* (**Quercus shumardi**) *that was grown in a three-gallon container for one growing season prior to planting in the field. After one year in the field, the tree was dug, all soil was washed away and the photo taken. Notice that the roots continued to grow in whatever direction they were oriented when planted in the field. The roots did not continue circling as has been proposed. However, the circled and tangled roots that developed in the container will remain in this undesirable position throughout the life of the tree. Roots of trees intertwine in nature to some degree, but never to this extent. The downward flow of growth regulating chemicals and energy from the leaves is in the outer sheath of the stem and roots. Therefore any restriction on the outside of a root will reduce the flow of materials back to the many smaller roots, thus slowly but surely placing additional stress on the tree. In most cases, the death of a tree is not directly due to the poor root system, but to some other cause. Nonetheless, the stress predisposes the tree to problems and hastens its demise.*

*Figure 3.4. Roots of pecan (**Carya illinoensis**) are probably the most aggressive in developing heavy circling roots when placed in conventional containers. Note that the heavy root on the left makes one full revolution. These deformed roots anchor the tree poorly and restrict normal water and nutrient absorption.*

Birchell and Whitcomb (1) glued vertical ribs inside one-quart containers with or without bottoms in an attempt to improve root branching and quality. River birch (*Betula nigra*) and bald cypress (*Taxodium distichum*) were used as test species. The vertical ribs stopped the river birch roots from wrapping and directed many of the roots downward (Figure 3.5). As some of the roots contacted the rib, they were restricted and developed secondary root branches. In order to evaluate the quality and distribution of the root system, the young trees were transplanted into one-gallon containers and allowed to grow for 10 days. At that time the one-gallon container was removed and many roots had already reached the sides and bottom of the larger container (Figure 3.6). When the new growth medium was removed, the distribution of the new roots growing out from the original container root mass could be observed (Figure 3.7). Root growth from along the ribs could be seen resulting in more root branching (Figure 3.7). These roots would aid in the lateral stability of the plant following transplanting. Unfortunately, the ribs were not strong enough to restrict the roots of the bald cypress and the roots continued to circle.

Figure 3.5. Root development of a river birch seedling affected by a vertical rib attached to the inside of a container. Note the downward orientation of most roots with some secondary root branches along the rib.

Figure 3.6. After only 10 days, the transplanted river birch seedlings grew roots from the surface of the one-quart containers to the side and bottom of full one-gallon containers.

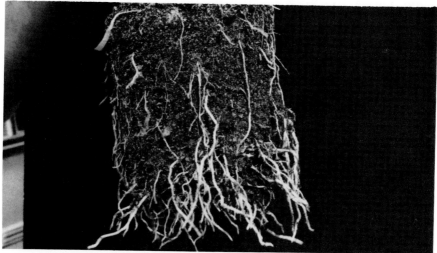

Figure 3.7. When the growth medium was removed after 10 days to expose the original root ball, the improved lateral root development as a result of the rib is visible.

Dickinson and Whitcomb (6) carried the rib concept one step further by using ribs across the bottoms of the container but only partially up the sides to allow the container to partially stack for shipping and handling. Most roots of Japanese black pine (*Pinus thunbergiana*) were stopped by the vertical ribs that extended upward about one-third the height of the container and root quality was improved (Figure 3.8). Plant height and stem caliper was also stimulated by the vertical ribs. Unfortunately, the ribs across the bottoms of the container had little, if any, beneficial effect.

It is also important to note the reaction of the roots to the various ribs or barriers placed in the containers. When the roots contacted the ribs, it was almost always at some angle greater or less than 90', thus the root was guided or deflected. However, when a root contacted a rib or barrier at 90 degrees it was nearly always stopped, then secondary branch roots would form. The latter situation is rare because of the curvature of the container and the general downward growth of the roots. Consequently, the overall root quality was improved very little by the ribs or barriers, so the search went on.

Hathaway and Whitcomb (8) grew bur oak (*Quercus macrocarpa*) seedlings in containers of identical volume and depth with and without bottoms to study root growth and quality. Bur oak in the bottomless container on a raised wire bench had a very fibrous root system and a larger top compared to the tree seedlings grown in conventional round containers (Figure 3.9).

56

Figure 3.8. Root development of Japanese black pine with and without vertical ribs added to the inside of a conventional plastic container (above). Note the root development as a result of the vertical rib (below). Plant height and stem caliper were also stimulated by the vertical ribs.

Figure 3.9. Root quality and branching of bur oak seedlings as a result of a bottomless container (right) and a conventional round plastic container with a bottom (left).

Polyethylene Bags. British and Australian nurserymen have been using polyethylene bags made of four- or six-mil black polyethylene sheets for years. Some feel the bags offer several advantages. The bags are more economical than rigid plastic or metal containers, easy to use and generally acceptable to customers once they get accustomed to them. They also use up several times less petroleum in manufacture than do rigid plastic containers.

Polyethylene bags are flexible and store easily. They come folded flat in boxes. A box about six inches by 12 inches by 22 inches can hold about 250 five-gallon bags. The same number of rigid plastic containers of the same volume would require about 40 times as much storage space (Figure 3.10).

Figure 3.10. Polyethylene bags require much less storage space than containers of the same size. The bags and containers above each hold five gallons. There are 10 bags laying on the plant on the left and 10 rigid containers on the right.

Some nurserymen still use metal food containers with straight sides for nursery stock. These cans must be cut with a special tool before they are planted. The rough surfaces often cut fingers during handling and planting. Disposing of used cans is also a problem. Plastic containers, although not a hazard, can create disposal problems if they are not re-used.

In contrast, polyethylene bags can be easily removed from the root ball. They may be slipped off and re-used or cut off and thrown away (10).

Polyethylene bags do have drawbacks. Filling the bags takes longer than with rigid containers, but other handling operations appear similar. Bags of two-gallon size or larger are filled and handled most easily. Six-mil bags are filled more easily and withstand handling better than four-mil bags. The thinner bags tend to collapse while filling.

Transplanting liners into one-gallon bags is difficult without some device to hold the bags in the filled position. However, transplanting liners or seedlings into larger bags is accomplished easily.

At the end of one growing season, plants in the bags are generally 5% to 15% larger than those in rigid container (12) (Figure 3.11). The reason for the greater growth was highly visible when the root systems were observed. Plants produced in the polyethylene bags had more fibrous root systems than plants grown in the rigid containers. They had six times more white root tips visible on the root ball surfaces (Figure 3.12).

Figure 3.11. A comparison of plants grown in rigid container (right) and a polyethylene bag (left). Plants produced in polyethylene bags are generally 5% to 15% larger than those grown in rigid containers of the same color.

*Figure 3.12. A comparison of the root system development of two elm, (**Ulmus parvifolia**) in a polyethylene bag (left) and a rigid plastic container (right). The cultural practices were identical for the two plants, but the one grown in the polyethylene bag has a more fibrous root system. Also, it did not develop circling roots as did the one in the rigid container. Note the greater number of white root tips on the left poised to grow into the surrounding soil following transplanting.*

Root Reactions to Containers. As a root grows in a rigid container, it contacts the side wall and is directed around the inner wall and/or downward. When it reaches the bottom, it follows the curvature of the container. Root development proceeds similarly in a polyethylene bag, except that when the root reaches the bottom, it is trapped in one of the four folds (Figure 3.13). Because the root tip is unable to elongate further, it ceases to grow. When the root tip ceases to grow, the apical dominance (control by the root tip over what happens to the tissues further back) is lost and lateral secondary roots quickly form.

Figure 3.13. **Elaeagnus macrophylla** *grown in a two-gallon poly-ethylene bag, with the bag removed to show how roots become trapped in one of the folds (see white arrow). This helps produce a better root system.*

This process continues as additional root tips reach the folds and are trapped. It is similar to the lateral branch development that occurs on a tree or shrub when the terminal branches are removed.

The increased number of roots helps plants become established in the landscape more quickly. Roots that continue to develop while plants are being held in retail outlets are forced to branch. This increases the holding time of container nursery stock somewhat, but little, if any, loss in plant vigor occurs as long as good cultural practices are continued.

White on black polyethylene bags failed to pass durability tests, even though they reduced soil temperatures by 10 to 15 degrees F and accelerated plant growth (Figure 3.14). Until further refinements are made, only black polyethylene bags are recommended.

Figure 3.14.   High temperatures in containers restrict root growth and functions during much of the summer.   The difference in these two rows of trees is due to the lower temperature of the roots from the white containers.   This is a white (outside) black (inside) laminated poly bag that reduces root temperature without light penetration to support algae growth.   It is of interest that plants in the white containers are larger even after the containers are mostly shaded by the foliage.   This is probably due to an advantage gained by the plants in the white containers before the tops provided any appreciable shade, yet the advantage continues.   Careful plant spacing is the only practical temperature control available at the present time.

Clearly, polyethylene bags are not for everyone in the nursery business. However, small nurseries and retailers who grow part of their own stock should consider using them. Observations indicate that retail customers are more interested in plant quality than container types.

Trees and other plants grown from seed develop better roots in polyethylene bags over those produced in rigid container, where root circling is a major problem. Consumers know very little about how plants grow, but even they know that tree roots should not look like bedsprings.

These various container design studies showed that the root system of a plant grown in a container could be improved as in the case of:
a) vertical ribs,
b) the bottomless containers on raised wire benches, and
c) in polyethylene bags which trap most of the roots at the bottom before they can circle. Unfortunately, each of these ideas have serious flaws that limit practical use: the vertical ribs prevent stacking of the containers, producing container nursery stock on raised wire benches is impractical, and polyethylene bags are awkward to fill and somewhat more cumbersome to handle. Nonetheless, progress was being made.

The Pyramid or Stair-Step Container. A container was needed that would stimulate root branching without openings in the side wall and would be easy to handle. By trapping roots on the sides of the container, perhaps an effect similar to the plastic bag could be obtained. In order to study such a container, Whitcomb and Williams (13) constructed containers from six-inch polyvinyl-chloride thin-wall drain pipe, six inches long. The internal surface of the container was:
a) left smooth,
b) fitted with 4 vertical ribs approximately 3/8-inch wide and 3/16-inch thick,
c) fitted with 4 stair-step sections about 1/8-inch thick, or
d) fitted with 4 stair-step sections about 3/16-inch thick (Figure 3.15).
The four sections added to the interior container surface were equally spaced around the container. Bottoms of all containers were notched to provide drain holes and glued onto flat Plexiglas sections for bottoms.

All containers were filled with a growth medium of three parts ground pine bark, one part peat and one part sand amended with nutrients for good plant growth. Test plants were crapemyrtle (*Lagerstroemia indica*), Virginia pine (*Pinus virginiana*), and Mojave pyracantha (*Pyracantha* X 'Mojave').

Figure 3.15. Cross section of container made with the vertical rib (left) which had showed promise in earlier studies but was judged impractical and the stair-step rib with the recessed edge (right). In practice the stair-step rib would have many more steps than is shown here. The sides of the vertical and horizontal portions of the stair-steps are recessed to trap the root tips, thus stimulating root branching much like the folds in the bottom of the polyethylene bags.

After four months, counts of white root tips of Virginia pine increased most where the thick stair-step rib was present (Table 3.1). Number of white root tips was increased both on the sides and bottoms of the containers (Figure 3.16). The conventional style container with no ribs had the fewest roots at the bottom of the container.

65

Table 3.1. Effects of container design on number of white root tips of Virginia pine on the sides or bottoms of six-inch plastic containers.

Root tip count	Round Container no ribs	4 vertical ribs	4 shallow stair-step ribs	4 thick stair-step ribs
Bottom	75	144	108	253
Sides	69	77	121	187
TOTAL	144	221	229	440

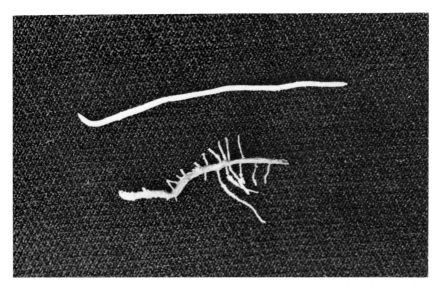

Figure 3.16.   Root development in containers with the stair-step form which traps the root tip and stimulates branching (below) and in a smooth conventional container (above).

The Virginia pines were transplanted into two-gallon containers and allowed to grow for 22 days. At that time the number of root tips reaching the side or bottom of the container were determined. The number of roots reaching the bottom was greatest with the standard container, whereas, the container with

66

thick rib had 26% less at the bottom. On the other hand, the container with the stair-step rib had 213% more roots on the sides compared to the standard container (Table 3.2). Response of the crapemyrtle and pyracantha was similar. This container design was briefly manufactured by Imperial Plastics, Evansville, Indiana under license by Oklahoma State University (Figure 3.17).

Table 3.2. Effects of container design on number of white root tips of Virginia pine in six-inch containers reaching the sides or bottoms of two-gallon containers 22 days after transplanting.

Root tip count	Round container no ribs	4 vertical ribs	4 shallow stair-step ribs	4 thick stair-step ribs
Bottom	48	42	38	36
Sides	66	99	123	141
TOTAL	114	141	161	177

Figure 3.17. The one-gallon container made by Imperial Plastics with 120 root-trapping points compared to 24 used in the studies..

67

The design of a container can increase root branching. The greater the number of white root tips on the sides and bottom of a container root ball, the more rapid establishment of the plant following transplanting. The first commercial containers made using this technique successfully trapped root tips, prevented root spiraling and increased root branching (Figure 3.18). As of this date, the container is no longer being made.

*Figure 3.18. Roots of Virginia pine (**Pinus virginiana**) grown in the pyramid container (left) vs. a conventional round container (right). Note the trapping of the root tips by the pyramid container and the aimless circling of the roots in the conventional container.*

The Air-Root Pruning Container. During February 1981 the idea of air root-pruning the root system on the sides of the container instead of the bottom was born (11). In order to study this container modification, the sides of conventional polyethylene containers were cut and re-positioned to create vertical slits and offset side walls (Figure 3.19). The vertical slits created were about 1/8-inch wide. Some slits opened clockwise and others counterclockwise. It is important that slits extend to the bottom of the container and they must be offset. If they are not, roots do not grow out and are not air-pruned as was observed in Figure 3.1. *Pyracantha* X 'Mojave' cuttings were planted in the new containers and in conventional containers of the same size and color. The growth medium and nutrition for both containers were identical. Both containers were located in full sun and watered as needed from overhead sprinklers.

Figure 3.19. The container design with vertical slits to air root-prune root tips as they circle the container. By alternating the opening of the slit, the root tips will be pruned whether they circle left or right.

With nursery stock grown in conventional containers, only a few root tips exist on the sides of the container at time of transplant, whereas, many are present with the vertical slits (Figures 3.20 and 3.21). At time of planting in the landscape, the root tips extend into the surrounding soil (3). With the vertical air root-pruning container, a great increase in number of root tips extending into the surrounding soil at planting time occurs (Figure 3.21 and Table 3.3). Thus, establishment of the plant in the landscape is accelerated. Other advantages of the container are:

    a. It can be filled by existing commercial pot fillers, without modification.

    b. This container will "nest" or stack so that freight costs for shipping containers from manufacturers to nurserymen will not be increased.

Figure 3.20. *Above, root development of a pyracantha shrub in a container with vertical slits (left) and in a conventional round container of the same size and composition (right). Note that some roots in the conventional container circle halfway or more around the container even though these plants are only three months old. Below, a close-up of the root branching as a result of the vertical slit.*

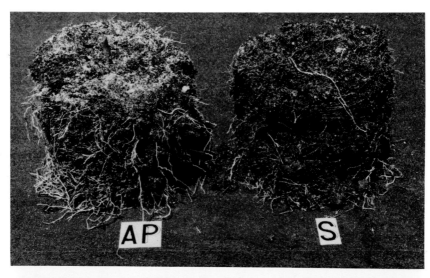

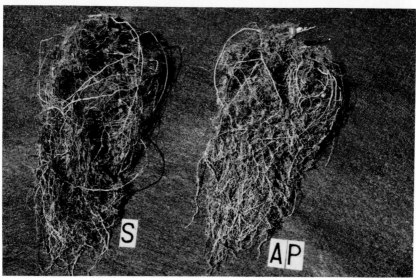

Figure 3.21. *Root development of pyracantha grown in two-gallon containers then transplanted into five-gallon containers and allowed to grow for 10 days before the containers were removed for inspection (above). Note the greater number of white roots on the vertical air root-pruned container (AP) as opposed to the standard pot(s). The production of new roots is even more dramatic when the new soil mix was removed (below).*

71

Table 3.3. Effects of vertical air root-pruning on growth of Pyracantha X 'Mojave'

	Standard Pot	Air-pruned Pot	Percent increase
Branches/plant	12.5	32.2	158
Number of roots 2 inches long 10 days after transplant	44	126	187
Top weight (grams)	93.3	152	63
Root weight (grams)	109	192	38

Manufacture of this container design has not worked out. The offsets in the side create mold design complications and in order to have adequate openings in the sides, the container must have an extreme taper which would mean poor stability.

By air root-pruning the roots on the sides of the container, root circling was eliminated (Figure 3.20) and objections of previous techniques were overcome:

a. Containers have a conventional bottom for ease of filling, handling and shipping.

b. Roots are more evenly distributed throughout the container medium, not mostly along the sides and in the bottom (Figures 3.21).

c. Vertical air root-pruning stimulates branch root development. The increase in root surface area results in increased absorption of water and nutrients, which in turn results in increased top growth (Table 3.3).

Container design can have a dramatic effect not only on the quality of the root system but on the growth of the top of the plant as well. Once containers that stimulate root branching become available, they will be quickly accepted because:

a) less pruning of the top will be required,

b) stem caliper of both trees and shrubs will be increased, reducing or eliminating the need for staking,

c) nutrition programs will need to be adjusted to allow for the more rapid growth and

72

d) establishment of these plants in the landscape will be very rapid.

The RootMaker Container. U.S. patent #4753037 is the result of data presented in Chapter 2 regarding the importance of stimulating secondary roots near the base of the tree (see Figures 2.14, 2.15, specifically). In order to force secondary roots to form at the base of the stem, the container can be no more than four inches deep. Note the development of secondary roots on the tree seedlings in Figure 2.2. The propagation container was too deep, thus secondary (side) roots were formed behind the point where the taproot was air-pruned, but they did not extend to the base of the stem. If the point of air-pruning had been moved up the taproot (a shallower container) the secondary roots would also have moved up. Another factor that influences tree seedling growth and development is adequate space for the top to grow. If seedlings are crowded they will be tall and spindly and require staking at transplanting. By contrast, if they are adequately spaced, they will be shorter and with stronger stems and generally staking is not required. The RootMaker container is 2.6" X 2.6" X 4" deep and contains about 18 cubic inches of mix (Figure 3.22). The containers are made in clusters of four for stability and ease of handling. An overlap strip on the edge helps create a surface without cracks between pots (Figure 3.23). The one-half inch strip between containers helps ensure sufficient top space for good stem development. Note the shape of the bottom of the containers. The RootMaker has a bottom for ease of filling and handling, yet the "hip and valley roof" design of the bottom consistently directs the tip of the tap root into one of the four openings for air pruning. This design also increases the volume of mix in the bottom of the container where the first root branches develop and prevents the crowding at the bottom so common in pots with a single bottom hole for air pruning.

Figure 3.22. The RootMaker container. As roots develop on a seedling or cutting and reach the bottom of the container, they are air-root-pruned. By limiting the depth of the container, secondary root branching occurs back to the base of the stem. As secondary roots reach the sides, they too are air-root-pruned. Root system quality, transplantability and stress tolerance are all improved by this unique container.

Figure 3.23. The clusters of four containers are very stable and can be placed on a wire bench, creating a uniform surface. The overlap edge interlocks the containers, creating a uniform surface for watering or broadcasting fertilizer. Wire 14-gauge and one-inch and two-inch openings makes a good wire bench surface.

Once the taproot has reached the bottom and has been air-pruned, the secondary roots form back up the taproot to the base of the stem. As these secondary roots grow outward they strike the container side wall and are directed into air-pruning openings. The tertiary roots are also directed into openings on the sides and so on. The result is a seedling or cutting with a very fibrous root system without the root circling or spiraling that occurs with conventional containers (Figure 3.24). When seedlings or rooted cuttings are transplanted from the RootMaker, root extension occurs in all directions vs. mostly downward for conventional bottomless pots Figure 3.25)

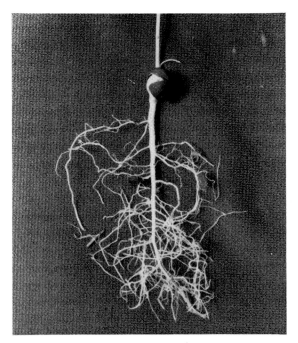

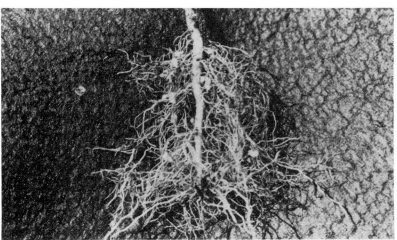

Figure 3-24. The western soapberry seedling (above) has been in the RootMaker for about five weeks. Note the near-horizontal secondary roots. The green ash seedling (below) has been in the RootMaker for about 10 weeks. Note the third and fourth set of root branches yet there is no root circling.

76

Figure 3.25. These two green ash seedlings were grown for 10 weeks in the bottomless "milk carton" type sleeve vs. the RootMaker. They were transplanted into three-gallon containers, allowed to grow for three weeks then removed to observe root growth. Note that there are no horizontal "stabilizer" roots and the root growth is down with the bottomless plastic sleeve. By contrast, the seedling grown in the RootMaker has root growth in all directions.

Even with the design of the RootMaker, it is crucial for the nurseryman to realize that a plant can only spend a limited time in such a small volume container. The purpose of this container is to stimulate secondary roots near the base of the stem of the plant. Once this is accomplished and sufficient roots have developed to hold the root ball together, it is time for transplanting into a larger container or the field.

Unfortunately as of this writing, there is not a good one-, two-, or three-gallon container to shift seedlings into from the RootMaker. Until those containers are available, the practical advice is to transplant or shift tree seedlings before they begin root wrapping. Unfortunately that is sooner than is generally realized in conventional smooth-walled containers. The poly bag does prevent major root wrapping and is an economical alternative.

The RootBuilder Container. Containers with taper are very subject to blowing over, especially when trees are grown (Figure 3.26). Taper in round conventional containers is to allow stacking or nesting for shipping. Taper in wooden boxed trees is to prevent the root ball from falling out when the tree is lifted and the bottom has rotted out. In addition, the spaces between the tapered container allows cold air readily to dissipate heat and damage roots if the temperature is sufficiently low. A square container with no taper would need to have either a non-deteriorating bottom or some mechanism to hold the root ball in place if a woody bottom that might decay were used. In addition, trees that are grown or placed in conventional containers with smooth inner walls have wrapped, twisted and entangled roots.

Figure 3.26.   These trees in boxes have been placed on individual concrete pads so they may be tied down to prevent blow-over.   It also served to prevent roots from growing into the soil below.

First came the concept of a box with no taper and a locking apparatus at the corner (Figure 3.27). Next came the idea of a root-trapping design built into the side walls to prevent root wrapping and to further stimulate root branching (Figure 3.27). The side walls would consist of injection molded panels with diamond shapes and a sloping section from top to bottom that creates a triangular root-trapping point (Figure 3.27). This would provide physical strength for the side wall while using a minimum of plastic. This container is not economical to produce at the present time.

After an assortment of attempts to make a less expensive version of the root-pruning box, a workable modification resulted. The RootBuilder Expandable or modular container (U.S. patent #4716680) consists of individual modules or panels, each 19 inches long and 14 inches tall with a self-contained lock to form a container. The length of the panel is simply six inches by 3.1416 (pi) so that the container increases six inches in diameter with each unit added. Thus two panels make a 12-inch diameter container, three equals 18 inches, four equals 24 inches and so on (Figure 3.28). Each panel consists of 200 hexagonal funnels in the side wall, open at the tip. These funnels direct roots to the open tip where they are air-pruned. The funnel design prevents root circling and the air-pruning stimulates root branching. The 200 openings in the funnels on a panel amount to only three percent of the side wall surface area, thus watering is virtually the same as with a conventional container of comparable size.

79

Figure 3.27. First came a box with no taper and easy locking corners (above). This would allow the box to be removed by pulling opposite pins. This removal procedure allowed for a container side wall that otherwise would not work. The diamond shapes have a sloping section from top to bottom that creates a triangular root-trapping point.

Figure 3-28. The RootBuilder panels locked together to form an 18-inch, 15-gallon container. In this case they are setting on roofing paper and are watered by "spray stakes" from a central line.

The bottom of the RootBuilder can be any material impervious to roots (Figure 3.29). Plastic or roofing paper works well. If the trees are to be shipped some distance, simply place weed barrier fabric over the plastic or roofing paper before placing the RootBuilder and filling with a good container mix. The roots will grow into the weed barrier fabric and knit the unit together. When trees are established in these containers, the weed barrier fabric and the panels can be moved as a unit. At planting, remove the fabric from the bottom, unlock the panels for re-use and plant. Because the root ball is wider than normal and has a flat bottom, only very tall trees need staking.

The size of the container can be adjusted to fit any size tree. Two panels equals 12-inch diameter, 7-gallon container; three equals 18-inch, 15-gallon; four equals 24-inch, 25-gallon;

five equals 30-inch, 40-gallon; six equals 36-inch, 60-gallon; seven equals 42-inch, 85-gallon (Figure 3.29); eight equals 48-inch, 110-gallon and so on.

Since all panels are the same size, they can all be in use whether the need is for 15-gallon or 85-gallon container. They are shipped flat, 100 per carton, and require a minimum of storage space. Since there is no taper to the side wall, they are much less subject to blow-over than conventional containers and have more earth contact to provide a temperature buffer during the winter.

It should be noted that when six or more units are locked together, the top and bottom of each unit should be secured by a strip-lock tie such as is used to secure a bundle of wires. The self-contained lock works well on level surfaces but on uneven surfaces and with six or more units, extra pressure on a connection can allow the RootBuilder to release.

When the first experimental RootBuilder containers were opened to inspect the roots, it was surprising. Containers with metal liners inside to create a smooth interior side wall (for comparison) were opened first. As expected, many roots were visible at the outer surface of the mix and some were pencil size or larger. When the RootBuilder was opened, only upon close inspection were a few white root tips visible, nothing more (Figure 3.30). However, when approximately one-half inch of mix was brushed away, masses of fine roots were visible. Even more striking was the fact that healthy roots were present on the southwest side of containers exposed to full sun. Apparently the design of the side wall with the network of hexagonal funnels reflects and shades enough of the side wall surface to limit heat stress.

When RootBuilder containers were filled with field soil and watered, the drainage was poor and the weight was excessive. However, when a good container soil mix was used around the root ball of a tree dug in a fabric container (then fabric removed) or B & B, drainage was good, water management was simplified and the weight of the overall root ball was reduced (Figure 3-31).

82

Figure 3-29. Once the roots have been air-pruned at the side wall and have reached the bottom, the container can be moved without a bottom (above). However, a weed barrier fabric bottom is inexpensive and helps protect the roots during shipping and handling (below). In this case the fabric was cut around the perimeter of the container.

Figure 3-30. Root development was compared between RootBuilder and smooth-walled conventional containers (above). Note the many wrapping roots against the inside surface of the conventional container (center) whereas with the RootBuilder, only a few root tips were visible at the surface (bottom). Only after some of the mix was removed were the roots visible.

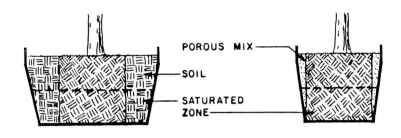

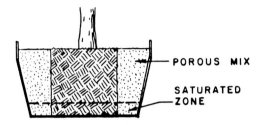

Figure 3.31. *When placing a root ball of soil in a container, be sure there is at least one inch of space between the side of the soil ball and the side of the container. If space is present and if a porous mix is used to fill in the space, the porous mix controls drainage and the plant will remain helathy. However, if the space is filled with soil or the soil ball contacts the sides of the container (above), the saturated zone will be much deeper and many roots will likely be suffocated.*

One of the uses of this container is to prevent shrinkage in nursery stock. The shrinkage referred to is the loss of material while they are being held for landscape installation or sale. When 100 trees are purchased by a retailer, rarely are 100 trees sold. If bare root, B & B or bag-grown trees were installed in the appropriate size container, they would be recovering from the harvest shock, establishing in the container and increase in value while they were being held (Figure 3.32). The alternative is the present system of harvest, hold, stress, root-out-into-surrounding-mulch, movement, more stress due to loss of roots, and eventual recovery or death (Figure 3.32).

The RootBuilder container builds a root system superior to any conventional container. Since the root branching occurs back in the mix, roots are less subject to stress of heat and cold. Likewise, when a tree is planted, the roots are poised to grow horizontally and anchor and establish the tree quickly. This is a very new product, but results from the first first year of use suggest it solves a number of problems in the nursery business.

As of this writing, no one has had any experience with shipping trees grown in this unique container. Can they be placed horizontally? Must they remain upright? Overwintering techniques also remain to be determined. Wrapping an insulating material such as heavy microfoam around the outside of the RootBuilder will help a great deal. How thick does the insulation need to be for a given geographic area? As answers to these and other questions are worked out they will be made available.

What Lies Ahead. Further improvements in container design are bound to occur. The question is, "Will the nursery business recognize the benefits of these containers and the need to improve the nursery product and utilize this technology?"

A one-, two-, or three-gallon version of the RootMaker container will be built as soon as economic conditions allow. The reason the small version was made first was due to the cost of the mold and thus the containers. It was a way to solve a problem and expose the concept with a minimum of expense.

Certainly the better the root system, the healthier the plant. Plants grown in a good field soil are generally fuller, thicker, and of better visual quality than those in containers. Yet clearly, the mobility and attractiveness of containers are major sales factors when combined with the "plant anytime" message.

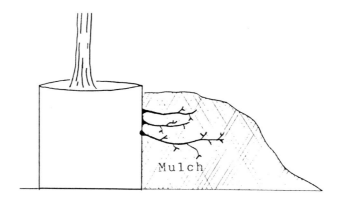

Figure 3.32. When trees are dug B & B and mulched-in, roots grow out into the mulch and are lost or damaged when the tree is moved (above). With the RootBuilder container, roots grow out, contact the side wall and are air-pruned. The trees are growing in size, value and quality of the root system while they are being held (below).

87

One of the sequences that may find use in nurseries of the future is to grow trees or large shrubs in relatively small fabric RootBag containers in the ground. Once the tree has reached near marketable size, it would be harvested, fabric removed and placed in a container such as shown in Figure 3-32. In most of North America, this would/could be done during the winter months when demands on labor are few. If sufficient space for the container mix is allowed around the root ball, it becomes the "mulch" for cold protection, and **no mulch is placed round the container.** This leaves the area neat and attractive. When the trees root out following the spring flush of growth, in six to 10 weeks they assume the mobility of container-grown trees while retaining the visual quality of a field-grown specimen. While the trees are establishing they are also growing in size and increasing in value. This technique provides the best of both worlds, so to speak, as long as it is carefully planned for and incorporated into the overall nursery scheme. This keeps the up-front cost limited and the greatest costs, (the container, mix, and care for the container) short-term while creating a very mobile/flexible product.

Summer sales of large trees in containers will likely increase regardless of the container techniques used. There is the desire by the customer to see the tree in full leaf go into the landscape and clearly, if the root system is not disturbed, late summer and fall is when maximum root growth occurs. Not only does this establish the tree quickly, but by the following growing season the tree is truly established and no longer requires the maintenance otherwise required.

Another item for the future is the further realization by the nursery industry that root-branching complements branch branching. It does little or no good to start all seedlings in RootMaker containers if they are shifted into conventional one-gallons and allowed to remain until they are root-bound. On the other hand, if a tree seedling or cutting is propagated in such a way as to create a very fibrous root system, then planted into a 14-inch fabric RootBag in the field, the initial root branching complements the next sequence of root-branching, then if the tree is harvested in a fabric RootBag and placed in a series of RootBuilder panels with a good container mix around the outside, another multiplication of the root branching occurs. Any plant grown with such a sequence is likely to live to a ripe old age.

All indications are that plants grown with this sequence will not only grow faster and be of better quality, but a much higher percentage of those planted will be harvested. Losses and culls very subtly erode what on paper looks like a profitable business.

Literature Cited

1. Birchell, Robert S. and Carl E. Whitcomb. 1977. Effects of container design on root development and regeneration. Okla. Agri. Exp. Sta. Res. Rept. P-760:39-45

2. Davis, Randy E. and Carl E. Whitcomb. 1975. Effects of propagation container size on development of high quality tree seedlings. Proc. Int. Plant Prop. Soc. 25:448-453.

3. Dickinson, Sancho M. and Carl E. Whitcomb. 1977. The effects of spring versus fall planting on establishment of landscape plants. Nurs. Res. Jour. 4(1):9-19.

4. Dickinson, Sancho M. and Carl E. Whitcomb. 1978. Effects of container design on root quality. Okla. Agri. Exp. Sta. Res. Rept. P-777:35-36.

5. Harris, R.W. 1967. Factors influencing root development of container-grown trees. Proc. Int. Shade Tree Conf. 43:304-314.

6. Harris, R.W., Dewight Long and W.B. Davis. 1967. Root problems in nursery liner production. Univ. of Calif. Agri. Ext. Serv. Bulletin AXT 244:1-4.

7. Harris, R.W., Dewight Long and W.B. Davis. 1967. Root pruning improves nursery tree quality. Jour. Amer. Soc. Hort. Sci. 96(1):105-108.

8. Hathaway, Robert D. and Carl E. Whitcomb. 1976. Growth of tree seedlings in containers. Okla. Agri. Exp. Sta. Res. Rept. P-741:33-38.

9. Whitcomb, Carl E. 1972. Growth of *Carissa grandiflora* 'Boxwood Beauty' in varying media, containers, micronutrient levels. The Florida Nurseryman 17(4):12-13, 43.

10. Whitcomb, Carl E. 1980. The effects of containers and production bed color on root temperatures. The Amer. Nurseryman 136(11):11, 65-67.

11. Whitcomb, Carl E. 1981. A vertical air root-pruning container. Proc. Int. Plant Prop. Soc. 31:591-596.

12. Whitcomb, Carl E. 1983. Containers vs. poly bags--which are better? The Amer. Nurseryman 157:101-103.

13. Whitcomb, Carl E. and Jerry D. Williams. 1985. A stair-step container for improved root growth. HortSci. 20:66-67.

CHAPTER 4

THE FABRIC CONTAINER

91

THE FABRIC CONTAINER

In 1965 the idea occurred that there should be some way to restrict root growth of trees and shrubs grown in the field, thereby making them easier to dig, with less stress and with better survival during most of the year. The occasion was one of the first demonstrations of the Vermeer tree digger in Iowa. The tree diggers would aid in harvesting trees grown conventionally, but why not grow the trees in a different way so that such an expensive machine would not be necessary? In the spring of 1967, while evaluating a study on how trees influence the growth of grass and vice versa, a way to restrict tree root growth was discovered (8). The study had been set up with a tree in a large container with four roots from that tree extending through the side wall. The ends of the roots were inserted into holes drilled in the sides of conventional, rigid, one-gallon containers (9). If the tree root was snug in the hole either in the side of the large or small container, a nodule or swelling occurred and the production of new roots from the root end was restricted. It was clear that if there was a way to restrict the roots of a tree while it was being grown, benefits would occur in terms of transplantability. The nodulated root was reproduced by using a fine mesh welded wire or drilling holes in rigid plastic pots and inserting a small root, but neither of these techniques were practical. In order for the concept to be functional, a container needed to be made from some economical material that had the strength to restrict root expansion and that could be handled and installed in the field. During the following years, many alternative techniques were tried, and all failed to produce the desired results. Steel rings with plastic in the bottom or with various chemicals restricted tree growth both above and below ground (Figure 4.1). Fabric that did not allow roots to penetrate created horizontal trees (Figure 4.1). However, the basic concept of root restriction still seemed sound. The idea remained semi-dormant until 1980 when a new stronger fabric was found. It was far tougher and more durable than any previously tested.

The fabric was sewn into about 3000 containers of approximately 16 inches and 22 inches diameter and 12 and 14 inches deep for testing. Holes 24 inches in diameter were made by an auger in a sandy loam soil, a single disc of six-mil polyethylene of 24-inch diameter was placed at the bottom of the hole, then the fabric containers were placed in the hole and filled with the loose soil removed by the auger. The disc of polyethylene had been very successful in stopping downward root growth and aiding harvesting in previous studies. Tree seedlings that had been air-root-pruned in bottomless containers for about three months, then grown in two-gallon polyethylene bags for the remainder of the growing season were planted in the containers.

All trees grew as well with the fabric as without. After 21 months, loblolly pine (*Pinus taeda*), river birch (*Betula nigra*), and green ash (*Fraxinus pennsylvanica*) had reached nine to ten feet tall with 2 1/2-inch stem calipers (Figure 4.2). The question had been growing, "What is happening to the root system, and how will these trees react when transplanted?" In order to evaluate tree performance, a time of harvest least favorable to the trees was chosen. On August 30, 1982, three trees of two species and one of another were dug by inserting a sharp square-pointed flat-blade shovel around the fabric container to the depth of the polyethylene sheet and the trees were lifted from the soil (Figure 4.3). The trees were transported approximately 38 miles and planted into a sandy loam soil the following day. The temperature was 100 degrees F on the days the trees were dug and planted, yet no wilting occurred. Other trees were dug and sacrificed to determine the relationship of roots with the fabric.

As roots grew outward and downward from the two-gallon container, they had penetrated the fabric. But as the roots that penetrated the fabric grew in diameter, the fabric restricted the root expansion and caused a swelling both inside, and to a lesser extent, outside the fabric. This restriction stimulated secondary root branching inside the container similar to the branching accomplished by air-root-pruning. Because the root system became very fibrous, the soil ball was less sensitive to handling than normal balled-in-burlap (B & B) trees (Figure 4.4) and all of the root balls for a given container size were the same size. Likewise, following removal of the fabric and planting, many more root tips were present to grow very rapidly into the surrounding soil and anchor and establish the tree.

93

Figure 4.1. Above, bald cypress (**Taxodium distichum**) trees grown conventionally (left) and with a metal ring and an herbicide in the bottom of the hole to restrict root growth (right). Below, a horizontal tree resulting from no horizontal roots through the fabric. In this case the fabric on the bottom was different from the fabric on the sides. The system failed if either roots could not penetrate the fabric or roots penetrated the fabric but were not restricted.

94

Figure 4.2. Loblolly pine (left) and river birch (right) after two growing seasons in the original fabric containers in Oklahoma.

Figure 4.3.   One of the original river birch dug in a 22-inch fabric container (above).   One of the original loblolly pine in a 16-inch container (below).   A total of seven trees were planted the following day to evaluate root development following transplanting in late summer.

96

*Figure 4.4.   Trees dug B & B being held for sales or shipment.
Because of the relatively few roots, workers must be careful not
to disturb the soil ball.   Notice the variation in size and shape
of these B & B root balls.*

*Figure 4.5. This fabric container was placed too deep and the
large root on the right escaped over the top.   If the large root
had grown through the fabric, it would have been similar in size
to the many smaller roots around the bottom portion of the root
ball.*

A few of the fabric containers were planted too deep, or the soil was not packed sufficiently and with settling, the top of the fabric was below the soil surface. Roots of several species "escaped" over the top. There was a tremendous difference in size of the roots above the fabric as opposed to those that were forced to grow through the fabric (Figure 4.5).

The trees dug in full leaf in mid August and transplanted did not wilt, and only one river birch dropped a few leaves using this system. This was due to the much higher proportion of the roots retained in the ball as a result of the additional root branching in the soil ball, and the carbohydrate accumulation effect of the fabric on the roots.

Seven weeks following transplant, a green ash tree was dug with a ball about six inches larger in diameter than the original ball and evaluated for root growth. Counts of roots that had grown one inch or more from the surface of the transplanted root ball revealed over 5000 roots (Figure 4.6). This compared with about 150 roots for the best treatments from previous transplant studies with the same species transplanted B & B. Partial excavation of the river birch revealed some roots 20 inches long (Figure 4.6) and pine roots seven inches long. After only seven weeks, these trees were sufficiently established to require little, if any, further watering or maintenance. This was confirmed even more dramatically with the following spring flush of growth. The loblolly pines all grew 24 to 30 inches in the spring which was growth similar to the previous spring **before** they were dug and transplanted. With pines dug B & B the spring following transplanting, the length of the new growth was very limited and the new needles were short compared to trees that are not transplanted.

These studies showed that early fall harvest and transplanting of trees was practical using this technique. However, questions remained. How late can trees be dug in the spring? What will the permanent root system be like? Do the new roots develop in a similar manner to trees dug B & B? What about starting out with bare root whips instead of container-grown trees? Only further studies would provide the answers.

Spring Digging. In order to determine if new root growth would occur on trees grown in the fabric containers when dug and transplanted after spring growth is well under way and if new root

98

growth occurs only at the swollen ends of controlled (restricted) roots, a 2 1/2-inch caliper sycamore was dug well after the spring flush had begun. The tree had been growing for two years in an 18-inch fabric container in a sandy loam soil with drip irrigation and good fertility. When dug, the new shoots were one to two inches long and the largest leaves were only 1/4 to 1/3 full size. The major spring chemical signal from buds to roots that occurs at bud swell should have been partially or completely past. After digging, about 1/2 of the soil was removed from the perimeter of the root ball to expose the root ends. Twelve root ends of similar size were tagged and four each were cut back zero, one, or two inches behind (nearer the tree) the girdled area where the root grew through the fabric (Figure 4.7). The idea was to compare the rate of root growth on these cut root ends compared to the undisturbed swollen root end created by the root restriction by the fabric.

Following cutting and tagging the roots, the tree was placed in a 28-inch diameter container and surrounded with a bark-peat-sand mix used in container production. The container was watered as needed, but the top of the tree was not sprinkled or syringed. The young leaves and shoots on the tree drooped for about four days then regained their normal position. Within 7 to 10 days further elongation of the shoots could be observed. After 30 days the spring flush of growth was 4 to 7 inches long and most of the first leaves were approaching full size. The tree was removed from the large container in order to evaluate root development.

Some of the roots had grown ten inches in the 30 days from digging to observation, and the root ball of the tree had hundreds of new white roots visible when the soil mix was washed away (Figure 4.8). This was surprising in light of the season and extent of new growth when the tree was dug. Root growth from the root ends varied considerably. In general, the undisturbed root ends had more roots than those cut back one or two inches, but all root ends had produced many new roots.

This and subsequent studies show that trees grown with this technique may be successfully dug and transplanted later in the spring than is normally recommended for those dug B & B. However, the mild spring temperatures and relatively high humidity probably aided in reducing stress experienced by the young shoots and leaves. Under hotter, drier conditions the rapid recovery of the top and rate of new root development would probably be less.

99

Figure 4.6. Above, the roots of a green ash 7 weeks after transplanting in late summer. Note the many fibrous roots, even though many were lost during the washing process to remove the soil. Below, root growth from a river birch seven weeks following transplanting. The distance from the trunk to the side of the original root ball was about 12 inches. The new root marked by the two white stakes was about 20 inches long and had grown in seven weeks.

Figure 4.7. Above, exposed root ends of similar size that were cut back none, one or two inches inside the fabric restriction. The fabric restriction and size of the root inside and outside the fabric can be seen on the root on the left. Below, the remaining root ball of the sycamore was transplanted then dug again after one month (see Figure 4.8)

101

Figure 4.8.   Above, one month after digging, removing the fabric and cutting back part of the roots where they penetrated the fabric, a tremendous mass of new roots had developed.   Compare this photo with the original root ball in Figure 4.7 to gain a better perspective of the new root growth.   Below, some of the roots were over 10 inches long.   In general, root ends not disturbed produced more new roots than those cut back but differences were small.

Methods of Installation. The technique used to install the first fabric containers was to excavate a hole and as effectively as possible fill the container with soil as well as back fill around the outside. This was awkward, labor intensive and did not provide a good ball shape at time of harvest.

An auger of the same diameter as the fabric container works well for making the hole. This provides support for the fabric while filling and in turn, makes harvesting easier. A smooth side wall also makes a more attractive package to market (Figure 4.9).

When planting with an auger, the question arises regarding circling roots in clay soils. This does not happen with the fabric container even if there is glazing of the hole sidewall. The reason is that the fabric, which is pressed firmly against the glazed soil surface by the fill soil, traps and holds new root tips in such a position that they cannot circle and therefore penetrate the soil beyond the fabric. Planting when clay soils are too wet should be avoided not because of glazing, but because of soil compaction and large air spaces from the resulting clods.

One complication can occur when an auger is used on heavy clay. If the depth of the augered hole is below the depth of the parpared soil, a "bathtub" effect can occur and suffocate roots, especially of sensitive species such as redbud, dogwood, and some conifers (Figure 4.10). Subsoiling as described in Chapter 7 can reduce or eliminate this problem.

A depth gauge or leg on the auger between the back of the tractor and the vertical shaft will insure that all holes are the same depth (Figure 4.11). Locate the depth gauge as near the auger shaft as possible without interfering with its function. This will give more accurate depth control than if the gauge is located nearer the tractor. The depth gauge should have a flat plate on the bottom to prevent sinking into the prepared soil.

Fill the fabric container with the field soil augered from the hole. This allows for natural movement of water through the fabric. The fabric does not restrict water movement. Very little water "wicks" out of the soil by the fabric since the fibers are solid as opposed to burlap strands which are porous and provide a much greater opportunity for water loss when exposed.

Figure 4.9. This river birch was grown for one year in a 16-inch fabric container. Since the original planting hole was made by a 16-inch auger, the sides of the harvested root ball is smooth and straight. Notice the exposed fabric of containers in the background to prevent roots from "escaping" over the top.

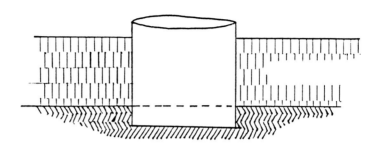

Figure 4.10. If the RootBag is installed below the depth of the prepared soil and the soil is heavy or compacted, the bottom may act as a "bath tub" and accumulate water to the extent to cause problems. Under these conditions, a subsoiler or ripper run down the center of each row solves the problem (see Chapter 7).

Figure 4.11. By installing a depth gauge on the auger frame assembly, all holes will be the same depth. This simplifies harvesting, prevents root escapes over the top and makes all root balls about the same weight. The sleeve (left) is used to hold the fabric container open while filling. It is then removed and used again.

105

Soil management, fertility and weed control systems are the same with this technique as with conventional field production. Soil building crops to aid in soil tilth and structure are very helpful not only in soil management but in plant growth as well (see Chapter 7 on rebuilding nursery soils).

Since many roots of plants grown in the fabric containers extend far beyond the fabric wall, (see Figure 4.16) and water and nutrient absorption proceeds normally, fertility of the entire field should be maintained. The fabric provides little, if any, restriction to the translocation of water and nutrients from the root tips, through the fabric wall, and up to the leaves. This is because this occurs in the xylem or central core of the root (Figure 4.12). On the other hand, energy returning from the leaves is translocated downward primarily in the phloem or outer sheath of the root and is blocked by the fabric. As a result, the **root tips beyond the fabric wall contribute substantially to plant health, growth, and stability, yet received little energy from the leaves in return.**

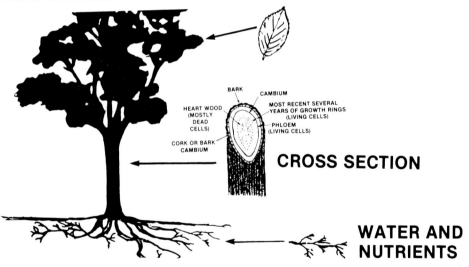

CROSS SECTION

WATER AND NUTRIENTS

Figure 4.12.   Translocation of water and nutrients to the leaves is through the most recent several years of growth rings inside the cambium (xylem).   Energy from the leaves is transported downward by the living cells outside the cambium (phloem).   As a result, the constriction of the roots by the fabric causes an accumulation of energy at that point.

Nitrogen fertilizers may be broadcast over the soil surface, banded in the rows of trees, injected into the drip irrigation system or a combination of all three. However, phosphorus should be added and incorporated into the soil prior to planting to be most effective. Any adjustments in soil pH or liming should also be done prior to planting. Further information is provided on soil fertility in another chapter.

Rototilling strips in the field as deep as possible where the fabric containers will be installed aids in making the soil easier to handle during the filling process (Figure 4.13). A loose friable soil will leave fewer air voids and can be compressed to prevent excessive settling much easier than soils with coarse clods.

A filler tube or sleeve is necessary to hold the fabric container open during the filling process. Sleeves of metal, fiberglass, and plastic have been used successfully (Figure 4.13). If the height of the sleeve is the same as the depth of the planting hole, after placing the sleeve and fabric container combination into the hole, the soil removed by the auger can be moved horizontally to fill the hole. This avoids having to lift or shovel the soil. During the filling process, the top of the fabric container will be folded over into the planting hole. However, if the sleeve has been made with finger holes for removal, when filling is complete and the sleeve is removed, the top of the fabric container will be drawn above the soil surface to prevent roots from escaping. It is important to firm the soil in the fabric container to prevent settling and remove air spaces that will restrict root growth and moisture relationships with the surrounding soil.

The Hollofil method of installing fabric containers consists of an apparatus fitted around a conventional auger. As the hole is augered, the soil is retained in a surrounding band. The auger is then lifted and the fabric container is placed in the hole with a filler sleeve in place. The auger is lowered again and a trip lever is moved to allow the lifting of the outer ring of the apparatus. This deposits all of the soil from the hole back into the fabric container (Figure 4.14). This makes certain that the containers will be filled to the proper depth following settling. Fertilizers added to the ring during the digging process will be incorporated somewhat when the container is filled. Time and

107

motion studies show that to install 18-inch fabric containers using this system requires about one minute each, with a crew of three.

Figure 4.13. A cover crop was planted over the entire field then strips were rototilled for the rows of containers. This provides a friable soil for backfilling the containers while leaving the cover crop undisturbed between the rows for erosion control. Below, a fabric container with a filling sleeve inside. Note, the fabric must remain above the soil surface to prevent roots from escaping and to make harvesting easier. In this case, the plastic sleeve is coiled, placed inside the New Generation RootBag and released. After filling, the sleeve is removed and assumes a flat position. This makes planting trees three feet or more in height much easier.

The major disadvantage to this method is that bare root or larger container-grown plants cannot be planted while the fabric containers are being filled. This must be done as a second process whereby a portion of the soil is removed again for planting. On the other hand, where container-grown plants are small enough that only a dibble hole is required for planting, the method is excellent.

Figure 4.14. The Hollofil system installed on the three-point hitch of a tractor.

Figure 4.14 (cont'd). Above, the auger is lowered into the opening in the center of the apparatus. Below, soil removed by the auger is held by the flexible band between the inner and outer rings.

Figure 4.14 (cont'd). Above, while the hole is being made one person adds fertilizer to the soil if desired while another person fits a fabric container over a filling sleeve. Below, the auger is raised to expose the planting hole. The fabric container and filling sleeve are placed into the hole.

111

Figure 4.14 (cont'd). Above, with the fabric container and sleeve positioned in the hole, the auger is lowered again and a trip lever is pulled to adjust the chain lengths. Below, with the trip lever pulled, the entire assembly is raised which returns all of the soil into the fabric container.

112

Figure 4.14 (cont'd). The fabric container is filled and ready for planting. About one minute is required for the complete installation of an 18-inch fabric container.

The HoleStar system works by augering a hole, retaining the soil around the auger in a steel sleeve. The auger and sleeve are raised, a RootBag is placed in the hole with a filler funnel. The auger is then reversed which places the soil in the RootBag (Figure 4.15).

Figure 4.15. The HoleStar system for filling fabric RootBags.

Bare Root Liners. In order to determine the performance of bare root whips as lining out stock in the field with various production systems, the following study was conducted:

    a) with or without root-pruning,

    b) with or without top-pruning at planting time and

    c) with or without fabric containers.

The best procedures for handling bare root nursery stock at planting time remain somewhat in question for many people in the nursery industry. The common practice of cutting back the tops of four- to six-foot bare root trees at planting time was not supported by the experiments with several species by Shoup, Reavis and Whitcomb (6). However, the trees they used experienced only limited shipping conditions. When trees are shipped cross-country, neither seller nor buyer has control of conditions.

The question also arises regarding pruning of the roots when planting bare root whips. Research by Shigo (5) has shown that when an above-ground branch or limb is removed, the plant reacts by compartmentalizing or walling-off the damaged tissues from the adjacent healthy wood. This probably occurs in damaged roots in a similar manner. If this is true and the ends of roots cut during the digging process begin to wall-off the damaged tissue during the typical storage of bare root stock, then any cutting back of roots at planting time would force the plant to begin the walling-off process again and provide a fresh open wound in the soil for possible entrance of disease organisms. On the other hand, the roots of many machine-dug bare root trees may be long and awkward to handle at planting, especially in the limited volume of a fabric container.

The third part of the study addressed the question of performance of bare root trees in the fabric RootBag containers as opposed to conventional field production. Some root pruning is essential when planting bare root whips in the limited volume of the containers. All of the early studies with the fabric containers were done using air-root-pruned seedlings grown in bottomless milk cartons. The air-root-pruned tree seedlings have a very fibrous root system which complements the fabric containers. On the other hand, all fine fibrous roots on the bare root trees are lost and only the larger roots remain functional to re-establish the tree.

Five species of unbranched, bare root whips were obtained from Oregon and planted in April. Bloodgood London planetrees (*Platanus acerifolia* 'Bloodgood') and Champaign County white ash (*Fraxinus americana* 'Champaign County') were four to five feet tall. Sunburst honey locust (*Gleditsia triacanthos* 'Sunburst') were seven to eight feet tall and redmond linden (*Tilia americana* 'Redmond') and northern red oak (*Quercus rubra*) were approximately three feet tall.

The treatments were as follows:

a) root-pruned approximately one-third of the length of the large roots or roots not pruned;

b) top-pruned approximately one-third of the height or tops not pruned (except that the seven- to eight-foot whips of honey locust were pruned back approximately six inches to stimulate branching);

c) trees planted into 18-inch, fabric containers or trees planted conventionally.

All trees were spaced on four-foot centers in the row with eight-foot rows. All treatments were replicated nine times. Soil was a sandy loam with good internal drainage. Supplemental watering was by drip irrigation as needed. Fertilization was approximately 200 pounds of nitrogen per acre per year with a base level of phosphorus approximately 65 to 80 pounds of available P_2O_5 and 200 pounds of K_2O per acre. No further pruning was done following planting. During the following July, (after 1.5 growing seasons) all trees were given a visual quality rating where 1 = poor overall form, appearance and salability, 4 = fair, 7 = good, 10 = excellent. Plant height and stem diameter were measured during October.

All trees were of similar height and stem diameter regardless of the top or root pruning treatments or presence or absence of the fabric containers. However, the visual grade of the treetops showed a response to treatments with considerable differences among species as follows:

Bloodgood London planetree: visual quality 7.7 with no root or top pruning, but only 4.4 with top pruning with or without root pruning.

Champaign County white ash: visual quality 1.0 with any top pruning (since a double leader occurred in all 36 plants), and 8.8 with no top pruning, regardless of root pruning treatment.

Sunburst honeylocust: visual quality 6.8 with top pruning, and 9.2 with no top pruning.

The reason for the lower visual quality of the London planetree, white ash, and honeylocust, was crooked stems caused by the top pruning. By contrast, nearly all trees without top pruning developed straight stems with good branching patterns. All trees of these three species survived.

Northern red oak: visual quality was 6.4 to 6.8 regardless of root or top pruning. Likewise, survival was not related to top or root pruning as 16% or 22% (three or four of 18 trees) died with all root or top pruning treatments.

Redmond linden: insufficient plants survived to determine a trend. However, like the red oak, survival was not related to root or top pruning.

Evaluation of 360 trees after two growing seasons shows the fabric containers neither enhance nor restrict tree growth and visual quality of the top during this length of time.

As earlier noted by Shoup, Reavis and Whitcomb in 1981 (6), "There was no advantage to the indiscriminate pruning of tops of bare root deciduous trees at planting time". These data suggest that root pruning may be included in that statement as well. However, root pruning may be practical on these species, with no restriction of growth or quality of the top, if necessary to aid planting in the fabric containers. Conditions in the tree when dug, along with proper shipping and prompt planting into a good soil, are probably the key factors involved in survival, good subsequent growth, and quality of bare root trees. The indiscriminate pruning of tops and/or roots is not necessary and, in some cases (ash and London planetree), is detrimental to overall tree quality without considerable additional labor for pruning.

Root Growth Comparisons. In an attempt to better understand the root growth and development of trees, an assortment of two-year-old ash and sycamore trees with 2.0 to 2.5 inches in stem caliper were dug the following ways:

    a) with a 30-inch tree spade,

    b) with a backhoe to retain most of the roots,

    c) in 18-inch fabric containers using a shovel, and

    d) in 18-inch fabric containers, only using a backhoe in order to try to retain the roots outside of the fabric container as well.

The fewest roots consistently were on those trees dug with the 30-inch tree spade. The 30-inch tree spade-dug ball weighed about 350 pounds, whereas, the 18-inch fabric container weighed about 150 pounds, yet many more roots were present in the fabric container (Figure 4.16). The tremendous difference in roots on trees dug with the tree spade and dug with the backhoe supports the findings of Watson and Himelick (7) who concluded that up to 98% of the roots of trees may be lost when harvested in the nursery (Figure 4.16).

The trees that had been grown in the 18-inch fabric containers for two years had many long slender roots beyond the fabric wall. These roots function in absorbing water and nutrients as well as holding the plant upright. However, when the tree is dug and the fabric is removed, the loss of these 'nurse roots' is of minor consequence to the tree since they have received only limited supplies of energy from the leaves (Figures 4.12 and 4.16). Following transplanting, it is the numerous small roots inside the root ball plus the rapid development of new roots from the swollen root ends that establish the tree.

Trees dug with a tree spade have several large roots with open wounds. Before new roots can develop, some wounding reaction occurs followed by callus development back from the cut surface and finally new roots are produced but mostly at the surface of the cut. This process may take two to four weeks or more, depending on the season of the year, condition of the plants, and conditions on the site. On the other hand, the roots of trees grown in the fabric containers can begin extending new roots into the surrounding soil almost immediately following transplanting. The distribution of root tips around the face of the soil ball provides anchorage from stresses in any direction (Figure 4.8) In addition, because of the secondary root branching inside the fabric containers, there are many more roots inside the soil ball to sustain the tree until roots grow into the surrounding soil.

Roots that develop outside the fabric wall are an asset to the tree during production in the field nursery but represent only a limited liability when lost at the time of transplanting. In contrast, the roots left behind when trees are dug B & B or with machines represent a traumatic loss.

Figure 4.16. Above, roots of white ash (**Fraxinus americana**) grown for two years with or without 18-inch fabric containers. Left, with most of the roots, next, dug with a 30-inch tree spade, next, grown and dug in an 18-inch fabric container and right, dug to retain most of the roots on the outside of the fabric. Below, a close-up of a representative root system dug with a 30-inch tree spade (left) and grown in an 18-inch fabric container (right).

119

Harvesting and Holding. From the various studies conducted and the thousands of trees harvested, held, and established from the fabric container system, several points are clear:

a) Trees may be harvested and transplanted as soon as growth hardens in the fall. River birch and pine, which have reputations for being difficult to transplant, perform well when fall-dug and transplanted using this method.

b) Trees may be harvested and transplanted anytime during the dormant period.

c) Some species of trees may be harvested and transplanted after bud break in the spring with excellent root development. However, how late and how long the new growth can proceed in the spring and still have successful harvest and transplant, depends on the species involved, the geographic location and associated weather factors. Care the tree receives before, during and after transplanting also plays key roles. It may also be that what was successful one year may not be successful another year because of vast but subtle differences in plant response to the season.

There is a definite time when trees grown in the fabric containers should **NOT** be dug. When active new growth is present and spring temperatures increase and in some areas become sufficiently high so as to suppress relative humidity, digging should not be attempted. If moisture stress on the new shoots and leaves is sufficient to stop all extension and leaf activity, the continuing chemical signal from the new growth will be partially or completely eliminated and further root growth following transplanting will probably not occur (Figure 4.17). This **unfavorable** condition for digging **extends until** all new growth has ceased. This may be in late summer when all leaves are fully expanded and buds on the current flush are mature. However, with flush-type growers, after one flush of growth has matured and before another flush of growth begins, generally the trees may be successfully harvested and transplanted (Figure 4.18).

Once the leaves and shoots are all mature and the buds fully matured, trees grown in the fabric container can generally be dug and transplanted. With conventional field production and B & B or tree spades, one technique that aids late summer transplanting is to strip off all leaves just before or immediately following digging. This does two things: a) greatly reduces the moisture loss to the air and b) following transplanting, the mature buds begin to swell, sending a strong signal to the roots to resume

120

growth. This technique generally works better in the South where the growing season is long. Since the plant may be forced to make a flush of growth out of sequence with the normal seasonal conditions, more winter injury is likely to occur, especially in more northern areas or when practiced too late in the growing season.

Figure 4.17.   The dieback in the top of this Chinese pistache is due to leaf and branch dessication following a harvest date of August 8.   Leaves near the tip were only partially expanded, whereas, the leaves at the base were fully matured.   Note the dieback stopped at the point where mature leaves and buds were present.

Figure 4.18. The current flush of growth of this oak has hardened; that is, all leaves are full size and axillary and terminal buds are mature or nearly mature. This tree can be harvested in the fabric containers with good success even though it may be early summer. On the other hand, when leaves are present that are not fully expanded, harvesting is not encouraged.

The practice of leaf-stripping will probably not aid earlier fall (or late summer) digging when the fabric containers are used since the buds at the ends of the current season flush of growth must be mature or nearly mature before it is effective. Rapid root growth into the surrounding soil after late summer digging and transplanting of trees grown in the fabric container occurs without the labor of leaf stripping. This also avoids a late summer or early fall flush that may weaken the plant overall since a substantial amount of energy in the plant would be used and would not be available for aiding winter survival and the flush the following spring.

The unfavorable "window" or time unfavorable for harvesting trees grown with the fabric container is difficult to define as it varies with many seasonal and cultural factors. For example,

122

successful late summer digging and transplanting will be later (mid September as opposed to late August) if the trees are growing under very high nitrogen levels and drip irrigation or where natural rainfall and abnormally warm weather are sufficient to extend the growing season. Trees grown with grass sod will generally mature more quickly in late summer than trees grown with clean cultivation, especially without irrigation. By reducing or eliminating drip irrigation in drier climates, maturity of trees can be hastened for successful early fall transplanting.

The fabric container allows rapid growth of new roots following transplanting later in the spring and earlier in fall (or under some conditions, late summer). As more experience using this technique for growing and transplanting trees is gained, the length of the unfavorable "window" when transplanting should **not** occur, can be better defined for the various regions and environmental conditions in the country.

Unlike trees grown conventionally and dug B & B or with tree spades, trees grown in the fabric containers retain their quality above-ground. Conventional techniques of mulching harvested trees with sawdust, bark, straw or similar materials work well during late fall and winter. However, if the mulch is left around the fabric container when spring bud swell occurs, many new roots will extend into the mulch. When the tree is moved and the fabric removed for planting, these roots are lost and the tree suffers. On the other hand, if the mulch is removed after the severe winter weather that may injure roots is past but before spring bud swell, the new roots produced in conjunction with the spring flush will be within the fabric container. This reduces the stress on the tree and makes planting easier. Since the fabric will not decompose, there is never the need to re-ball as so often occurs with trees dug B & B and held for more than a few weeks.

Trees harvested in fabric containers may be tied with twine or other cord to secure the top of the fabric over the exposed soil at the surface. Such tying should **never** include the stem of the tree where girdling could occur if the cord is not removed at planting (Figure 4.19). In some cases there is no need to do anything to the root ball with loss of only a very small amount of soil from the surface.

Trees may be harvested during the favorable periods, fabric removed and placed in various types of above-ground containers for sale at times when they should not be dug (Figure 4.20). A key factor to remember here is the size of the root ball relative to the size of the container. If the root ball contacts the interior sides of the container above the drain holes, 50% or more of the soil will remain saturated following watering and a major portion of the root system may be lost by suffocation. The same thing will occur if the container is large enough but field soil is used to fill in the space around the root ball. **On the other hand, if space exists between the root ball and container and a porous mix suitable for plant growth in the particular depth of container is placed around the root ball, the plant will remain healthy** (Figure 4.21).

Some argue that to place a tree grown in a fabric container into a conventional above-ground container is impractical. However, consider a) the selling season can be extended, b) the trees increase in value because of the market for container-grown trees and the fact that the trees continue to grow if the container is large enough, c) loss of trees between harvest and sale (shrinkage) is virtually eliminated and, d) the cost of the container and mix is short-term and is recovered with the tree is sold.

Trees grown with the fabric container system have better top size, branch development, stem diameter and root systems than trees grown in above-ground and conventional containers. In addition, trees can be overwintered in the field with no root injury, blow-over, mulching or watering problems. If the trees are dug in winter or early spring, and placed in containers, only a few weeks are required for root establishment in the container (see Figure 4.8). If the trees sell quickly, all is well, but if the trees are held a month or more, their value increases and there are no complications of rooting out into mulch or other mess at time of sale. In short, it is the best of both techniques.

Figure 4.20. Above left, this loblolly pine was dug before spring bud break and placed in a large container. It was planted in the landscape in early August with little or no stress. Below right, if the tree remains in the container too long, the roots will begin to circle in round containers and may quickly become "root bound". Wooden boxes are better, but still create root entanglement problems. The RootBuilder container described and shown at the end of the previous chapter is a good alternative.

125

Figure 4.19. This cherry was dug B & B, wrapped with "no-rot" burlap and tied around the stem. When the tree died four years later, the plastic twine and "no-rot" burlap were still intact. Note the growth of the top of the tree above the point of girdling by the plastic twine. This is due to the blockage of downward movement of energy from the leaves. The plant died because the roots were starved.

One objection to placing trees grown in fabric containers into conventional above-ground round containers is the wrapping and circling of the roots as they grow out and contact the container sidewall. Wooden boxes such as shown in Figure 4.20 are better. than round plastic containers, but still much root entanglement exists. A solution to this problem now exists. It consists of a container made of sections or modules 19 inches long and 14 inches tall that lock together with air-root-pruning depressions throughout the sidewall, such that no root circling occurs (Figure 4.22). To remove the container from the tree, simply unlock any section. This is also the technique used if the tree needs a larger container. Simply unlock and add one or two modules and fill in with mix. One interesting aspect of this container is the fact that when it is removed (opened), few roots are visible. This is because the root tips are air-root-pruned at

126

the tips and root-branching occurs back in the mix and not against the container wall. Because the roots are directed horizontally, tree establishment is very rapid following planting into the landscape. The side wall of this container is vertical (no taper), thus blow-over is much less troublesome than with conventional tapered containers. This container design is shown and discussed in more detail in the previous chapter, see especially Figures 3.23, 3.24, 3.25.

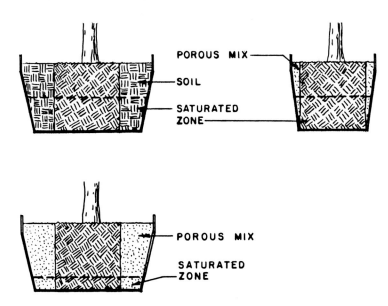

Figure 4.21.   When placing a root ball of soil in a container, be sure there is at least one inch of space between the side of the soil ball and the side of the container. If space is present and if a porous mix is used to fill in the space, the porous mix controls drainage and the plant will remain healthy.   However, if the space is filled with soil or the soil ball contacts the sides of the container (above), the saturated zone will be much deeper and many roots will likely be suffocated.

Figure 4.22. The RootBuilder container in use in a retail nursery. These are three units locked together to make 18-inch, 15-gallon containers.

Fabric Removal and Planting. The fabric should be removed when planting into the landscape unless a dwarfing or bonsai effect is desired. If the fabric is cut vertically every eight to ten inches around the circumference of the root ball, the sections can generally be removed with difficulty with the old (black) fabric and much easier with the fabric used in the New Generation RootBag. With heavier soils and species with more fibrous root systems, the fabric may be removed above the ground, then the root ball positioned in the hole (Figure 4.23). However, when the trees are grown in sandy soils or when the trees have been in the container only a short period of time, it may be best to place the tree in the planting hole **before** removing the fabric. In this case, cut the fabric vertically as before, and pull the fabric downward. This puts pressure on the bottom of the ball which is supported by soil. The fabric strips can be cut free of the bottom which may be left in the of the hole. Since water moves in soil by capillarity, not gravity, the plastic bottom will not impair normal water movement in the soil.

Figure 4.23.   Above, a tree harvested in a fabric container, ready for planting.   If the soil is heavy, the fabric may be removed before placing the root ball in the hole (below).   However, with sandy soils, place the root ball in the planting hole before removing the fabric.   Then cut the fabric every six to eight inches around the perimeter and pull the fabric down.   This puts pressure on the bottom of the root ball which is supported by the bottom of the planting hole.

129

Backfill with the existing soil unless a large area can be changed to a better soil. Soil amendments are of no benefit except under very unique conditions. This topic is covered in detail in the book, *Establishment and Maintenance of Landscape Plants* by Carl Whitcomb.

Fabric Container Size/Tree Size Relationships. Success in transplanting relatively large trees with small root balls raises the question of fabric container size vs. tree size and grades and standards. Clearly, this technique is very different from B & B and tree spades. The root system is not only more fibrous but also primed with energy for rapid growth of new roots following transplanting. But how small can the root ball be for a given size of tree? The answer lies in the conditions and care when the tree is grown and harvested, time of year, care after planting, tolerance of the species and other factors (Figure 4.24). What will work successfully in Pennsylvania or Georgia may not work in Oklahoma or Kansas. In areas of Europe where the climate is very mild and soils are good, much larger trees can be transplanted with greater ease than can be done in much of North America.

Even within limited geographic areas, striking differences in tolerance of the same species have been noted. Trees grown, harvested and transplanted in eastern Oklahoma do not endure the level of stress as the same trees planted 100 miles west where the rainfall and humidity are lower and the dehydrating effect of the wind is greater.

Interestingly, there is no difference in actual soil/root volume between an 18-inch fabric container and a 24-inch Vermeer tree spade which meets American Association of Nurserymen Grades and Standards for a two-inch caliper tree. The cone shape of the soil ball with the tree spade contains about two cubic feet of soil while the 18-inch fabric container 14 inches deep contains the same volume (Figure 4.25).

Figure 4.24. This loblolly pine was about 13 feet tall with a 4-inch caliper stem when harvested in a 22-inch fabric container. The root ball appears very small proportionate to the top of the tree. However, it is not the size of the root ball that determines transplant success, but rather what is in the root ball and the capacity to produce new roots following transplanting. Many trees have been transplanted successfully in central Oklahoma with similar root ball-top proportions by harvesting at the most favorable times.

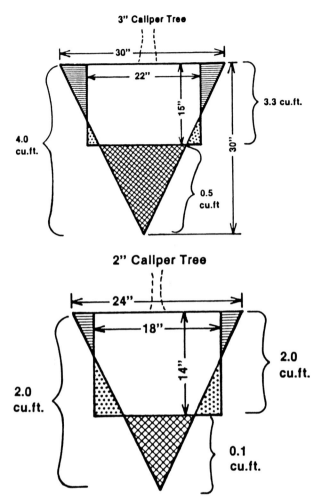

3" Caliper Tree

30"

22"

15"

30"

3.3 cu.ft.

4.0 cu.ft.

0.5 cu.ft

2" Caliper Tree

24"

18"

14"

2.0 cu.ft.

2.0 cu.ft.

0.1 cu.ft.

Figure 4.25. The actual volume of an 18-inch fabric container, 14 inches deep, is the same as a 24-inch Vermeer tree spade which meets American Association of Nurserymen grades and standards for a two-inch caliper tree (below). The actual volume of a 22-inch fabric container 15 inches deep does contain 0.7 cubic foot of soil less than a 30-inch Vermeer tree spade (above). However, 0.5 cubic foot of soil dug by the tree spade is below the active root zone of the tree and contributes nothing to transplant success. Therefore, with a three-inch caliper tree, the effective root ball is about the same volume for both techniques.

132

In the case of a three-inch caliper tree, the grades and standards call for a 30-inch soil ball. At first, a three-inch tree in a 22-inch fabric container looks out of proportion. However, when the soil depth in the 22-inch fabric container is 15 inches deep, it contains 3.3 cubic feet. A 30-inch Vermeer tree spade contains 4.0 cubic feet but 0.5 cubic foot is below the 15-inch soil depth and contains few, if any, functional roots. In comparing the functional root zone, the soil volumes are about the same (Figure 4.25).

When these comparisons are related to the improved root branching and capacity to produce new roots following transplanting, the "small" fabric containers are reasonable.

How the System Works. This unique system works because of the tremendous physical strength of the fabric to resist expansion by the roots and the reaction of the roots to the restriction. As roots grow outward and downward following the initial planting, they contact the fabric wall. Roots that reach the bottom of the container first are directed horizontally by the impermeable plastic-coated bottom so they, too, contact the fabric sidewall.

The surface of the fabric is easily penetrated by roots. This prevents root circling by forcing them to grow through the container wall. Since the root is very small at this point, there is little or no restriction by the fabric. However, as the root grows further into the surrounding soil and increases in diameter, the fabric begins to constrict or girdle the root.

At some point in the girdling process of the root by the fabric, the apical dominance of the root tip begins to decrease. The tip of a root has an apical dominance or control over lateral root developments just as the tip of a stem above-ground has an apical dominance over side branch development. When the apical dominance (on an above-ground stem) is removed by pruning, many side branches grow from dormant buds in the stem tissues. The same thing happens with the root system (Figure 4.26). This is why air-root-pruning is so effective in stimulating fibrous roots on tree seedlings. The restriction by the fabric on the root has a similar, but more subtle effect. Because the root pruning effect is gradual, trees must be left in the fabric containers long enough for the root restriction and root branching to occur or little benefit is gained. As additional root branching occurs, those will also grow outward through the fabric and be restricted and produce further root branching (Figure 4.27). The larger the diameter of the fabric container, the greater the time required to build an excellent root system since the roots must grow further before contacting the fabric.

Figure 4.26. Root development inside a fabric container. In this case the tree was dug, the bottom removed, and the soil washed away while leaving the fabric-root complex undisturbed. Trees grown conventionally and dug B & B have only a fraction of the fibrous roots in their root ball.

Figure 4.27. A root of an ash tree that grew through the fabric and was restricted (large arrow) then developed a root branch that was also restricted by the fabric (little arrow).

Water and nutrients are absorbed almost exclusively at the root tips and are translocated to the leaves through the xylem or central core of the root. The downward movement of energy from the leaves is mostly in the phloem or outer ring of tissues. **It is this transfer process that allows the restriction of the fabric to cause energy accumulation within the container.**

As the roots, both outside and inside the fabric, continue to function, the energy production of the leaves increases. The more energy the leaves produce, the more energy there is for flowers, fruits, stems, and roots. The increase in stem diameter of a tree is the result of energy from the leaves above the quantity needed by flowers, fruits, leaves and developing buds. Stem diameter increase and root growth occur primarily when there is energy available in the plant above that needed by the crown. Since the fabric blocks most energy from the leaves as it moves downward, the energy level in plant tissues inside the fabric containers is increased. This restriction by the fabric on the downward flow of energy is what causes the swelling or nodule on the roots on the inside of the container (Figure 4.28). The smaller swelling of the root outside the fabric wall is probably due to growth regulating chemicals produced by the root tip that have been blocked at this point.

These nodules are quite firm as a result of many small cells with very thick walls. Consequently, they are not easily damaged in handling and are probably more resistant to dehydration than other root tissues. Microscopic examination of these nodules and root tissue just behind the nodule shows vast quantities of starch (Figure 4.29). This is the stored energy source that supports the tremendous burst of new root growth following transplanting. It is uncertain whether or not root primordia (dormant root buds) are present in the nodules and adjacent root tissue. However, the extremely rapid production of new roots following transplanting suggests this (Figure 4.28). New root production from the end of a cut root on a plant grown conventionally takes several weeks. The much more rapid root development with this technique shows that a very different and more responsive root production system has been created (Figure 4.30).

At some point, growth of a tree or shrub in a given size of fabric container will be restricted. However, the restriction is quite different from a "root-bound" plant in a conventional above-ground container. In a conventional container the plant becomes stunted and internally starved. On the other hand, in the fabric container the plant eventually becomes dwarfed, but internally it has an abundance of energy. This is reflected in fullness and overall thrifty appearance of the top and the continued increase in stem diameter long after further height growth has slowed to a fraction of its earlier rate. It is not surprising then, that trees that have been dwarfed by considerable periods in fabric containers resume normal growth following digging, removal of the fabric, and transplanting. In some cases, where landscape plants tend to overgrow the space available, leaving the fabric container on at planting time may be desirable and is under study at the present time.

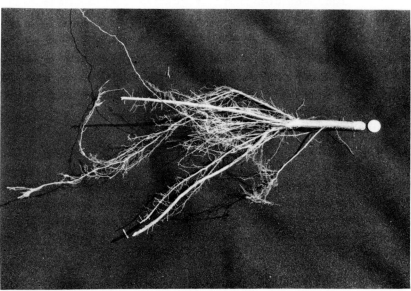

Figure 4.28. The pine root (above) shows the nodule formed on the inside of the fabric by the physical restriction which causes an accumulation of energy in the root at that point. Following transplanting, a tremendous number of roots develop very quickly from these nodules (below).

*Figure 4.29.   Roots of sycamore (**Platanus occidentalis**) grown conventionally (left) and restricted by the fabric container (right).   The ends of the two roots were about the same diameter, yet show vast differences in starch stored in the tissues.   These sections were made, then treated with iodine which turns dark when it reacts with starch.*

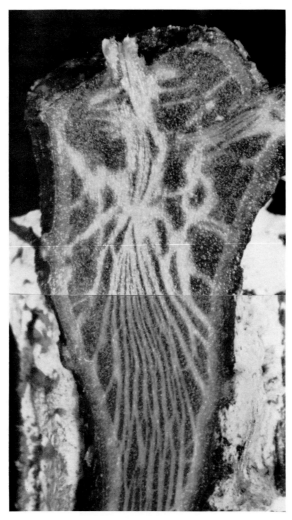

Figure 4.30. The root modification caused by the fabric restriction. The small stub at the top of the photo is where the original root penetrated the fabric. A branch root developed at the upper right. Notice the convergence of xylem vessels (light strands) caused by the restriction. Since water and nutrients from the root tips beyond the fabric wall moves in through these vessels, little restriction occurs. However, the downward movement of energy in the outer gray sheath of tissues (phloem) is mostly blocked.

The extensive root system with the capacity to establish quickly in a limited volume of soil, allows a much larger tree to be harvested and transplanted successfully with a smaller and lighter ball than is required using conventional techniques. It is not the size of the root ball, but rather what is in the root ball that counts. The combination of more roots and more energy to produce new roots sets this system apart from all others (Figure 4.31).

Figure 4.31.   Roots of an ash tree grown in a fabric container. Notice how each restriction of a primary root stimulated secondary root branching which, in turn, were restricted.   In addition, the nodules at the ends of the roots contain vast quantities of energy to support new root growth following transplanting.

The unusually fibrous permanent root system in the landscape means no one root will be critical to the health of the tree. Many have observed the death of a tree on the fringe of construction, while others nearer the construction lived. Investigation and excavation of some of these trees have revealed

140

the disturbance or loss of a major root. The loss of one major root by a tree in marginal health may make the difference between life and death. On the other hand, with hundreds of roots of similar size providing the tree's needs, no one root becomes critical.

During 20 years of research and experimentation by the author, it has been found that every technique which stimulates root branching has increased plant growth and health. This technique is no exception.

The Permanent Root System. In August 1982, three river birch, loblolly pine and green ash trees (all having calipers of about two and one-half inches) were dug and planted two days later on a site 35 miles away. The river birch and green ash had been grown in 20-inch, and the loblolly pine in 16-inch, fabric containers. The fabric containers were completely removed at planting time.

Two full years had gone by and the trees had grown well. By digging these trees, the question regarding the root development of trees grown in fabric containers following transplanting into the landscape could be answered. A pine and a river birch were dug using an 80-inch tree spade. The soil was removed by shaking and washing. Both had trunks in excess of four-inch stem caliper by this time. For comparison, a river birch and loblolly pine of similar size but grown conventionally were also dug for root evaluation.

Following digging, soil was easily removed from the roots of the trees grown conventionally. On the other hand, extensive efforts of shaking and washing were required to expose the root systems of both trees grown in the fabric containers. Comparisons of the root systems provide a striking contrast (Figure 4.32).

Since water and nutrient absorption occur almost exclusively at the root tips, a larger number of root tips will increase the growth and overall health of the top. Anchorage by many small roots should be equal to or greater than that of a few large roots.

Figure 4.32. Roots of two loblolly pines five years old (above) and a four-year-old river birch (below) grown with (left) or without (right) benefit of the fabric container. Both trees began as seedlings in small bottomless containers for the first three months, then were transplanted into two-gallon containers for the remainder of the first growing season. The pine and birch on the left were grown in the fabric containers in the field for two years then dug, fabric removed, planted, and allowed to grow for two more years. The control trees on the right were planted directly from one-year-old two-gallon containers into the field and allowed to grow four years (pine) and three years (birch) before being dug.

142

The fibrous root system created by the fabric container may provide long-term benefits to tree health in addition to the obvious advantages of ease of transplanting and rapid establishment. Evidence continues to mount as to the detrimental effect of twisted and distorted root systems on long-term tree health. In this case, with species grown in the fabric containers, the likelihood of root girdling or strangulation is remote, since water and nutrient absorption is accomplished by a mass of small roots as opposed to a few major roots. In addition, roots from trees grown in the fabric containers are unlikely to get as large as when the same species are grown conventionally, reducing the likelihood of damage to sidewalks, driveways or foundations. The fibrous and compact root systems of the trees from the fabric containers also lend themselves readily to planting pits and other landscape situations where horizontal root development is restricted. Anchorage of the trees from the fabric containers should be equal to or better than conventional trees since the many small roots act much like the many fine strands of steel in a cable vs. a solid steel rod of the same diameter (Figure 4.33).

Trees grown in the fabric containers then transplanted and grown to a larger size would be better candidates for large trees to be moved either conventionally or with large tree spades. The root systems in Figure 4.33 and the effort required to dislodge the soil from both root systems emphasize their greater tolerance for moving than that of trees grown conventionally.

Figure 4.33. Roots of a loblolly pine that had been grown in a 16-inch fabric container for two years before being transplanted into the landscape and allowed to grow for two years with the fabric removed. Because of the tremendous numbers of roots, no one root will ever become as large as with trees grown conventionally. These many small roots act like strands in a cable and provide tremendous anchorage as well.

Problems With the Old Bag and Sorting Out the Answers. Since the introduction of the first fabric containers, the reviews have been mixed. Fuller and Meadows (1) observed increases in root mass density of from 32% to 159% for five species over conventional B & B even though the root ball size was 17% smaller. Yadav, Ingram, and Reese (13) studied transplant performance of five species of trees grown in fabric containers and concluded that survival was excellent and the harvest period could be extended over B & B. Reese (4) noted increased stem diameter growth and crown development of trees grown in fabric containers in Florida. He also found the smaller root ball to be an advantage in handling and shipping. Jones (2) observed that fabric containers allowed extended harvesting, better inventory control and space

144

utilization. Langlinais (3) concluded that trees in fabric containers were less subject to blow-over, the lighter root balls were easier to handle, trees re-established faster and overall production cost was lower.

On the other hand, there were problems with the original version of the fabric container. Jones (2) noted that the major problem was root escape at the seam where fabric side wall was sewn to the plastic bottom (Figure 4.34). Whitcomb (11) concluded that if three or four roots escape either through the bottom or side wall of the bag, the plant stress was similar to B & B.

One of the frustrating aspects of the old bags was the fact that one nursery would report problems while another, growing the same species and in some cases nearby, would report no problems and they were pleased with the system. Two factors slowly surfaced, 1) bare root liners tend to produce more roots near the bottom of the bags, thus putting a great deal of pressure on the poly bottom and seam and in some cases roots were jabbed through the poly during planting, and 2) root-bound container stock used as liners generally have active roots only at the very bottom, thus this also put pressure on the poly bottom and seam. **Clearly, the better the root system on the plant installed in the bag, the better the system works since it is a root-multiplying process.**

Major escape roots through the side wall of the old bags made from six-ounce Phillips Supac or Duon is the result of initial root contact with the side wall and failure to penetrate the fabric. Roots would either turn and grow parallel to the side wall or branch. The near 90-degree root branches from the original root would then grow parallel to the fabric wall. When these roots penetrated the fabric while growing nearly parallel, they often grew between the layers of fibers and escape with little or no pruning (Figure 4.34). This is because Supac is made of "staple" fibers, i.e., the fibers are cut, spread in layers and stapled together again via needle-punching and heat bonding.

Figure 4.34. In this case (above) roots escaped at the poly bottom/fabric junction or seam. In the process of harvesting, the poly bottom was further stressed and torn. This is a very undesirable situation. The tree must now be burlapped or tied in order to prevent soil loss during shipping and handling. Roots would sometimes "escape" through the old fabric (below) by growing nearly parallel to the fabric, then when penetration occurred, the root would force the layers apart and escape with little or no restriction.

146

During the summer and fall of 1988, numerous fabrics were evaluated for their ability to allow easy root penetration, yet quickly begin root-pruning as the root increased in diameter. Likewise, an assortment of materials were evaluated at that time for making a much stronger bottom. It was felt that the bottom of the fabric container must not only be strong enough to prevent root escape but also strong enough to stand sliding the root ball across a truck bed during loading or across gravel on a holding site.

The New Generation RootBag. The results of these studies led to the New Generation RootBag. This fabric container is made from the best fabric available, which is a continuous fiber without layers (Figure 4.36). Roots penetrate the fabric easily, regardless of the angle of entry (Figure 4.35). As the roots increase in diameter they are consistently pruned. The fabric is much easier to remove at planting time and the root system is more fibrous with a RootBag made of continuous fibers. Escape roots through the side wall should not occur unless the fabric is cut or damaged.

The bottom of the New Generation RootBag is made of the same fabric as the side wall. This allows double-sewing of common materials at the side wall/bottom junction so the seam is stronger than the fabric. If a root grows through a needle hole, it is pruned with the same effectiveness as if it had grown through the side wall. The inside surface of the fabric bottom is coated with polyethylene to make it impenetrable to roots to aid harvest (Figure 4.36). When old style containers with the sewn or glued 8-mil poly bottom were stressed, the poly or the seam were easily torn. By contrast, the coated fabric bottom withstood a 200-pound load as well as a "drag-over-gravel" test. The New Generation RootBags were filled with field soil and drug over gravel for 20 feet. The fabric and seam remained intact whereas the poly bottoms of the old bags either sewn or glued were in shreds before sliding three feet.

The New Generation RootBags solve the problems of the old style fabric containers. With the superior root-pruning fabric and stronger bottom, nurserymen can now get the full benefit of my original root-pruning concept.

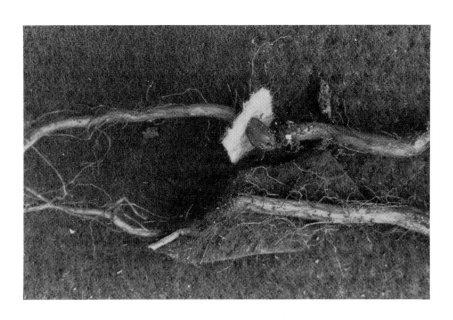

Figure 4.35. Studies with special Polyfelt vs. Phillips Duon showed that oak roots consistently grew through the Polyfelt (light material) and were pruned (above), whereas they became entangled in the Duon (black material). In this study, 15 of 15 oak roots penetrated the special Polyfelt and were pruned, whereas, 14 of 15 oak roots grew into the Duon at one point and emerged on the other side after 1/2-inch to 3 inches of entanglement in the fabric. This very important difference means easy removal of the fabric at planting instead of a great deal of difficulty.

Figure 4.36. The New Generation RootBag is made of a fabric with continuous fibers (above). There are no layers for roots to separate and escape. The sidewall is double sewn to the same fabric on the bottom, but the inside surface of the bottom has a poly coating (below).

149

Literature Cited

1. Fuller, Don and Warren Meadows, 1987. Root and top growth response of five woody ornamental species to fabric field-grow containers, bed height and trickle irrigation. Proc. SNA Res. Conf. 32:148-153.

2. Jones, B., 1987. Experiences in growing and marketing trees and shrubs in grow-bags. Proc. Int. Plant Prop. Soc. 37:532-533.

3. Langlinais, Kent, 1987. Pros vs. cons in using root-control field-grow containers. Proc. Int. Plant Prop. Soc. 37:529-531.

4. Reese, Bill, 1987. Mass production of tree in gro-bags. Proc. Int. Plant Prop. Soc. 37:526-528.

5. Shigo, Alex 1977. Compartmentalization of decay in trees. USDA Bulletin #405. 73 pg.

6. Shoup, Steve, Rick Reavis and Carl E. Whitcomb. 1981. Effects of pruning and fertilizer on establishment of bare root deciduous trees. Jour. of Arboriculture 7:155-157.

7. Watson, Gary and E.B. Himelick. 1982. Root distribution of nursery trees and its relationship to transplanting success. Jour. of Arboriculture 8:225-229.

8. Whitcomb, Carl E. 1969. Effects of root competition between trees and turfgrass. Ph.D. Dissertation, Iowa State University, 196 pages.

9. Whitcomb, Carl E., 1985. Innovations and the nursery industry. J. Environ. Hort. 3:33-38.

10. Whitcomb, Carl E., 1987. *Production of Landscape Plants*, Lacebark Publications Inc., Stillwater, Ok. 487 pages.

11. Whitcomb, Carl E., 1989. Harvesting, holding, and planting trees grown in fabric containers. Fla. Nurseryman 36(4):49-53.

12. Whitcomb, Carl E., Eliot C. Roberts, and Roger Q. Landers. 1969. A connecting pot technique for root competition investigations between woody plants or between woody and herbaceous plants. Ecology 50:326-329.

13. Yadav, U., D. Ingram, and B. Reese, 1987. Observations on transplanting from field-grow containers in Florida. Proc. SNA Res. Conf. 32:162-163.

CHAPTER 5

PLANT NUTRITION, SOILS AND FERTILIZERS

PLANT NUTRITION, SOILS AND FERTILIZERS

A Practical Summary of Fertilization Practices for Field Nursery Stock. Good field soil is an asset often unappreciated and overlooked in the routine management of nurseries. In an array of studies of soil additives and amendments covering more than 20 years, there is nothing that can be added to a poor soil to make it a good soil. Adding organic matter and any deficient nutrient elements to a soil will substantially improve the productivity of the soil, however.

There are four basic steps in improving field soils.

1) **Soil Test.** Soil samples may be taken using a soil probe six to eight inches deep until approximately one pint of soil is accumulated from an area. Spade slices also work well (Figure 5.1). Remove any surface debris and remove a normal spade volume six to eight inches deep. Take another spade slice one-half to one inch down the face of the previous spade hole for the soil sample. Three or four spade slices from an area should be taken and mixed together to give a representative sample. Dry the soil sample(s) at room temperature, then send to a laboratory with instructions for the desired analysis.

Most state universities and many private laboratories conduct tests of soil samples to determine the levels of available nutrients. The nutrient elements generally checked are:

nitrogen (sometimes expressed as nitrates, ammonia or organic matter level, since the breakdown of organic matter releases nitrogen for plant growth)

phosphorus,

potassium (sometimes called potash),

calcium,

magnesium and

sulfur.

Rates may be expressed in pounds per acre or ppm (parts per million). To convert ppm to pounds per acre, multiply times two for most soils. Laboratories generally give the pH of the soil and on special request, check for the levels of iron, manganese, copper and zinc. Levels of boron and molybdenum are determined by only a few laboratories.

154

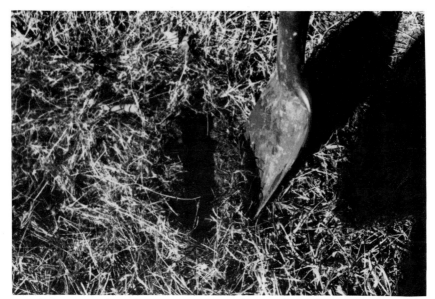

Figure 5.1.   Spade slices six to eight inches deep work well for soil tests.   Remove any surface debris and remove a normal spade volume six to eight inches deep.   If the area is in an existing lawn or bed, insert the spade and push it forward to create an opening.   Take another spade slice one-half to one inch thick down the face of the opening as the soil sample.   Three or four spade slices should be taken and mixed together to represent an area. Simply step on the soil originally pushed forward to close the hole.

The pH of a field soil is useful information.   A high pH, above 7.0, generally reflects the presence of substantial quantities of calcium, magnesium, sodium, or bicarbonates since these elements are strong bases or alkali materials.   On the other hand, a low pH, below 5.0, generally reflects a low to moderate level of calcium, magnesium, or sodium, **or** a moderate to high level of some acid-forming agent such as sulfur, sulfate, ammonium, or hydrogen.

For most woody nursery crops, in most soils, the "ideal" pH is in a range from 5.0 to 6.5, however, if the pH of your soil is higher or lower, there are practical adjustments that can be made. If your soil has a pH below 5.0, the soil test may reveal rather low levels of calcium and magnesium available for plant growth.

Even if the levels of these two elements are not low, it is probably desirable to lime the soil to raise the pH to about 5.0 to 6.0 **but no more**. Lime is calcium carbonate and will raise the pH of the soil by adding calcium and carbonate. For an estimate of the quantity to add per acre, check with your county agricultural agent or state university. They should be knowledgeable of your specific soils. Otherwise, use the rough estimates in Table 5.1.

Table 5.1. Approximate quantity of limestone needed to raise the pH of various soils. No two soils are the same and only a rough estimate can be offered here. In many, if not all cases, magnesium is needed as well as calcium, therefore dolomite, which contains magnesium, should be used as the lime source.

- -

Current	Desired		Limestone, pounds per acre		
pH	pH	Sand	Sandy loam	Silt loam	Clay loam
4.0	6.0	2000	4000	6000	8000
4.5	6.0	1500	3000	4500	6000
5.0	6.0	1000	2000	3000	4000
5.5	6.0	500	1000	2000	3000

The primary reason for liming is to raise the soil pH. Even when adequate levels of calcium and magnesium are present, raising the pH will reduce the solubility of aluminum and manganese, since these are the major problems that accompany very acid soils. On the other hand, if the pH of the soil is above 6.5 to 7.0, it may be desirable to add elemental sulfur to lower the pH. Granular elemental sulfur is the most effective and safest material to use (Figure 5.2). **Do not use aluminum sulfate** since aluminum is toxic to most plants. Rates of granular sulfur should be from 30 to 60 pounds per 1000 square feet (1000 to 2000 pounds per acre), depending on the pH and internal drainage characteristics of the soil. In order for moderate to high rates of sulfur to be effective, the internal drainage of the soil must be such that the calcium, magnesium or sodium displaced by the sulfur can be leached below the root zone of the crop.

Figure 5.2. Granular elemental sulfur is clean and easy to spread, whereas powdered sulfur can be a nightmare. Conventional rotary spreaders work well with most granules. Granular sulfur should be incorporated for best results.

2) Expressions of Soil Test Results. Soil test values should be adjusted to the following areas or general ranges:

pH: 5 to 6.5 with allowance for the species to be grown and the geographic area.

Nitrogen: 5 to 50 pounds per acre, depending on species involved, type of fertilizer used, desired growth rate of the plant and time of year.

Phosphorus: 60 to 120 pounds per acre. Levels above 150 pounds may suppress growth of some species.

Potassium: 150 to 300 pounds per acre.

Calcium: 600 to 2000 pounds per acre.

Magnesium: 200 to 1000 pounds per acre.

Iron: 40 to 150 parts per million (sometimes also expressed as milligrams per liter, which is the same)

Manganese: 15 to 40 ppm

Sulfur: 40 pounds per acre or more.

Copper: 3 to 8 ppm

Boron: 0.4 to 0.8 ppm

Zinc: 2 to 4 ppm

Plants may grow well with soil test values above or below these general ranges primarily due to the nature of the specific soil, soil test procedure used, and species involved. However, when problems occur or are suspected, adjusting soil nutrients to these levels will generally aid plant growth.

3) Build Reserves of Phosphorus and Potassium. Many soils are very deficient in phosphorus and unless the level of phosphorus is raised, plant growth will be poor, despite all other fertilizers added and cultural practices used. Unlike nitrogen, which moves readily in the soil, **phosphorus does not** move in any soil, even the pure sands of central Florida. Because of this, phosphorus applied to a soil is more effective when incorporated into the plant root zone. Once the level of phosphorus in the soil is raised to an adequate level, no additional phosphorus needs to be added for several years.

On the other hand, excessive levels of phosphorus in the soils should be avoided. Not only is phosphorus the most expensive fertilizer element, but if an excess is added to the soil, it will tie-up or make unavailable some of the micronutrients necessary for plant growth. There is no practical way to remove excess phosphorus from a field soil.

For most nursery crops, a level of phosphorus expressed in pounds of available phosphorus (P_2O_5) per acre, should be between 60 and 120 pounds. No two soils are the same in terms of fixing phosphorus. For example, if a soil test shows 10 pounds of phosphorus per acre and 60 to 100 pounds is needed, adding 50 pounds of phosphorus per acre (110 pounds of 0-46-0, triple superphosphate) will, in most cases, raise the level of available phosphorus for plant growth only to 25 to 50 pounds per acre. The reason for this is the fixing capacity of the soil for phosphorus. Consequently, on most soils add enough phosphorus to raise the level near the highest recommended level (100 pounds per acre). After fixing, the available level of phosphorus will be near the lower level (60 pounds per acre). Therefore, in the example of 10 pounds currently in the soil, add 90 pounds of actual phosphorus (about 200 pounds of 0-46-0, triple superphosphate or use 200 pounds of 18-46-0 to also provide nitrogen if planting will soon follow). After fixing in the soil, the level of phosphorus will be around 50 to 60 pounds per acre on most soils. To convert pounds per acre to pounds per 1000 square feet, divide by 43.5 since there are 43560 square feet per acre.

Potassium is most economically purchased as potassium chloride, KCl (58% to 62% K_2O). For maximum productivity, a field soil should contain between 150 and 300 pounds of available K_2O per acre. Since potassium is not fixed to the same degree as phosphorus, if a soil test showed 80 pounds of available potassium, by adding 120 pounds of potassium (200 pounds of potassium chloride, 0-0-60, using a 200- pound level as the target) the level of available potassium would be raised to the 150-pound level or above in most soils.

4) Managing Nitrogen. Nitrogen may be added infrequently using various slow-release forms such as sulfur-coated urea, Osmocote or ureaformaldehyde, or frequently using soluble forms such as ammonium nitrate (33-0-0) or urea (46-0-0). **Frequency and rate of nitrogen application are more influenced by the porosity and leaching of the nitrogen below the root zone than by any other factor.** Heavy clay or silt soils may require limited nitrogen, whereas sandy soils require more frequent applications and, in extremely sandy soils, the expense of slow-release nitrogen sources can easily be justified.

In the spring and fall, applications of urea (46-0-0) every six to eight weeks work well. However, during the summer, with greater soil temperatures, the frequency may need to be increased to every three to four weeks and the rate per application lowered, if maximum growth is to be achieved. Again, however, no two soils react and hold nitrogen the same. Therefore, some adjustments will be necessary on each soil and site. If the field nursery stock is drip- or sprinkler-irrigated, the level applied during the summer will be higher than without irrigation. With most soils, 150 to 400 pounds of actual nitrogen per acre per year is necessary for maximum plant growth. A practical application in many geographic areas, for example, would be 50 pounds of nitrogen per acre in early spring, just after leaves emerge, followed by another 50 pounds six weeks later and the same rate again six to eight weeks later and again in late September if a soil test shows a nitrogen level below 20 to 30 pounds of available nitrogen per acre.

The use of slow-release fertilizer in the field is relatively new. In clay loam and sandy clay loam soils, slow-release fertilizers have provided little benefit in Oklahoma. However, in sandy soils of Florida, the addition of Osmocote or other slow-release fertilizer, either to the planting hole or in a dibble hole on either side of the tree following planting or after the initial fertilizer application is depleted, has been effective. Check with your fertilizer distributor for specific rates in your area.

A Word of Caution: soils are extremely variable, not only between geographic areas or states, but frequently within the same field. These recommendations should be considered as very general guidelines only. Your soil may require more or less than the levels suggested here. Check with persons knowledgeable in your area for more specific fertilizer recommendations for your soil. On the other hand, **do fertilize, but not without knowing the specific needs of your soils.**

Leaf Analysis. Leaf analysis shows what the plant actually absorbed from the soil. However, there are some major factors to consider:

1) take a large enough sample of leaves to give a true picture of the nutritional conditions;
2) leaves recently reaching mature size are generally the preferred sampling point;
3) keep in mind that nitrogen, phosphorus, potassium and magnesium are mobile in the plant. These elements can be removed from old leaves and transferred to new leaves, giving a false reading of the quantity actually taken up by the plant. For example, if magnesium deficiency is suspected, take leaf samples from **old** leaves and **young** leaves about the time the last leaves of the season reach full size and analyze them separately. This procedure is also useful when toxicities of nutrient elements are suspected. For example, boron deficiency can best be detected by sampling new leaves, whereas excess boron accumulates in old leaves. On the other hand, calcium, sulfur and the micronutrients are not mobile in the plant and are more easily detected in an analysis of recently matured leaves.

With tree or shrub species, where desired nutrient ranges for leaf analysis have been established through extensive research and testing, this is a valuable diagnostic tool. However, for the many species for which no desired nutrient ranges have been established, a leaf analysis is like looking at a road map printed in an unfamiliar foreign language; it may be telling you where you want to go, but you generally won't be able to figure it out until an interpreter comes along. With most of the landscape plants, no interpretation exists.

In some instances, a clue to diagnosing plant problems can be obtained from leaf analysis of a healthy and a deficient specimen, especially if the two plants arc relatively close together and growing in the same general soil conditions.

Even with this information, often a clear diagnosis of a problem cannot be made. For example, if the healthy plant has 500 ppm manganese and the unthrifty plant has 50, it is very tempting to conclude that manganese is needed. This is probably not the case since the level of manganese can vary over a wide range in many species with no apparent detrimental or beneficial effect. If the root system of the plant has been damaged by gophers, disease, a high water table that suffocated part of the roots, or other similar factors, leaf analysis may suggest very low levels of available nutrients when such is not the case. A final word of caution: do not draw hasty conclusions.

Plant Nutrition and Fertilizers. In order to grow healthy plants of excellent quality, a production system must be maintained that keeps all factors near the ideal. Only under such favorable conditions can the nutritional program be most effective in stimulating growth. The nutritional factors presented in the next section assume reasonable growing conditions so that maximum response to nutrition can be obtained.

The meshing or synchronization of all nutritional elements in the proper rates and ratios can best be likened to a fine automobile: all the factors can be there (wheels, pistons, starter, carburetor, generator, etc.), but it only takes a malfunction of one of these components to stop the entire machine. Plant growth is not normally affected so abruptly. However, the greater the synchronization among the nutrient elements, the more strong and vigorous the growth of the plants. Strong growth with a proper balance among the nutrient elements reduces the likelihood of disease or insect problems. Figures 5.3, 5.4, 5.5, 5.6 dramatize the wooden barrel theory as it relates to plant nutrition and growth. The barrel can hold water only to the level of the lowest stave (the wooden strips making up the barrel). As each stave is raised, the barrel can hold more, likewise, as the level of the most deficient element is raised, plant growth improves.

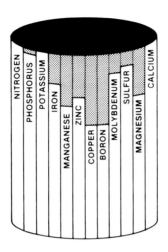

Figure 5.3. For many years, plants grown in the sandy soils of Florida suffered from numerous deficiencies of varying degrees. In this example, copper and boron were most deficient. Therefore those were the symptoms observed most, but the moderate deficiencies of manganese, magnesium and iron also played a role in restricting plant growth.

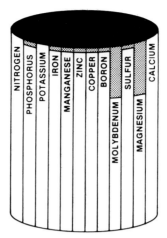

Figure 5.4. With improvements in micronutrient fertilizers, especially the balance or ratio between iron, manganese, zinc, copper, and boron, plant growth improved but restrictions remained. These restrictions were later diagnosed as deficiencies of both molybdenum and magnesium.

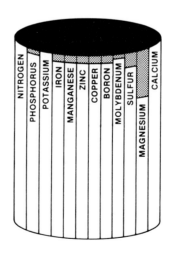

Figure 5.5. With improvements in the level of molybdenum, either alone or in micronutrient fertilizers, plant growth improved only to find magnesium deficiency symptoms more and more common.

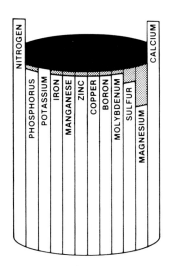

Figure 5.6. A common error in the management of nutrient elements is the excess of nitrogen and calcium. The excess nitrogen is added in an attempt to further stimulate growth. The excess calcium is added under the false information that the pH of the soil must be 6.8 to 7.0. The most common limiting factor of plant growth presently is the excess of these two elements and the deficiency of magnesium.

Nutrient Absorption and Energy Distribution. All plants have a distinct distribution system for the energy manufac-tured by the leaves (various carbohydrates, proteins and starches). In order to better understand the needs of the plant and the sequence of events involved, consider the following over-simplification of the nutrient absorption, food manufacture and distribution system:

A) Fertilizer is applied or is otherwise available to the root system.

B) If adequate moisture **and** aeration are available around the roots and temperature conditions are favorable, the roots will absorb the water and nutrients and the translocation from the roots to the leaves begins (Figure 5.7). Aeration is a key ingredient in this process. Without adequate aeration, the root system cannot carry on the necessary respiration, which is the energy-supplying process, necessary for water and nutrient absorption. Nutrient absorption mostly is an active process in that the plant must spend energy. It is not a passive or energy-free process as was once believed.

164

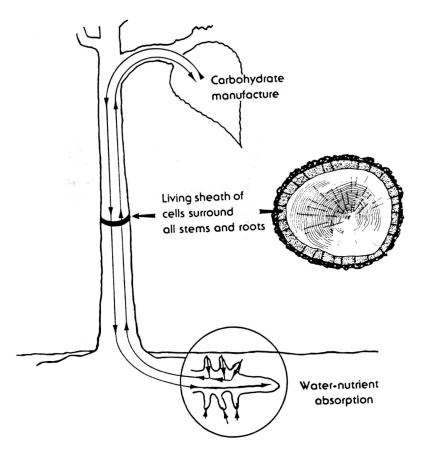

Figure 5.7. Root growth is a rather indirect, roundabout process. Nutrients and water are absorbed by the roots and transferred to the leaves where energy (carbohydrates) is manufactured. Roots can grow only if some of the energy is returned to the root tips. If there is a shortage, the roots are the first to suffer.

C) When the water and nutrients arrive in the leaves (or other green parts of the plant) most of the water is lost by the leaves, mainly through the stomates, as transpirational cooling. A small portion must be retained in the plant to maintain cell turgidity and a very small fraction is utilized in the manufacture of energy (carbohydrates). The various nutrients are combined with carbon dioxide and water in the chloroplasts (green disc-like structures) in the leaves and capture the energy (sunlight) to form various simple sugars or carbohydrates that comprise the basic energy for all living cells in the plant.

D) The many cells within the leaves are closest and therefore have easy access to this energy. However, they do not necessarily have first priority.

E) Within the plant, there is a distinct energy priority of distribution or "peck-order". In very broad general terms, it is: **flowers, fruits, leaves, stems, and roots.** In other words, if flowers or fruits are developing on the plant, they take precedence over the needs of other plant parts, especially if the plant is under stress. It has been well documented that trees under stress will frequently develop more flowers and fruits than trees with little or no stress. Likewise, it is not uncommon to observe the leaves on either side of a citrus or other fruit develop an off-color while the fruit is rapidly developing, whereas leaves further away from the fruit retain their normal green color. Once the fruit reaches maturity, these leaves will also return to their normal color. For ease of further discussion, assume no flowers or fruits are present, only leaves.

The quantity of energy manufactured determines the quantity available for distribution. If all is ideal, there is plenty of energy for all cells within the plant as well as some for storage within the stems and roots. However, what if there is not enough energy to go around? A restriction in energy production may be due to many factors. For example, too much or too little of any one or several of the essential nutrient elements, not enough or too much light, water, or carbon dioxide, or perhaps insect or disease injury or spray damage has affected the leaves and thereby reduced their functional capacity.

Regardless of why the leaves are restricted in their energy manufacturing capacity, if they are restricted, the priority distribution system dominates. The living cells in the leaves will retain the energy they need before transfer to the stems or roots begins. Likewise, when a leaf reaches the point where it cannot manufacture more energy than it needs, it will be dropped, in the case of most woody and many herbaceous plants. For example, if a leaf is shaded by other leaves or has been damaged

166

by disease or suffers from a nutrient deficiency to where the energy manufactured does not exceed the energy required, it will be dropped. The break-even situation in which the amount of energy manufactured by the leaf just equals the amount used in respiration is referred to as the compensation point.

When energy manufactured by the leaves is restricted for any reason, the roots are first to be affected. For example, when azaleas were grown under varying levels of shade (15), 30% shade was ideal for growth of tops and roots. However, when plants were grown under 45% shade, the weight of the plant top was unaffected while the root weight was restricted. The same condition occurs when a nutrient deficiency or water stress develops.

Research by Gordon and Larson (6, 7) showed that with red pine, which holds needles for two years, the one-year-old needles were the prime supplier of energy for current shoot development and growth of the terminal bud, whereas the two-year-old needles were the prime supplier of energy for the roots. When a nutrient deficiency of nitrogen, phosphorus, potassium, or magnesium develops or drought occurs, the older leaves are lost first. Therefore, the roots are most affected. This phenomenon probably holds true for all woody plants.

F) Roots are the key factor in plant vigor. If the energy production by the leaves is restricted for any reason, root growth is restricted before any other plant part. It seems ironic that root growth is restricted by a lack of energy from the leaves when the top of the plant is deficient in nutrient elements that can only be supplied by the roots. In short, the plant hastens its own demise by failing to provide energy to that part (roots) that could best help overcome a nutrient element deficiency by expanding into additional soil.

On the other hand, if the energy manufactured by the leaves is sufficient to meet all requirements of the above-ground parts and the living cells in the stem, the roots receive appreciable quantities of energy from the leaves and grow vigorously. With vigorous root growth, more soil is contacted to supply water and nutrients and add stability to the plant's physical location (keeps trees upright) and growth is further accelerated.

Roots cannot maintain water and nutrient absorption capabilities and grow without energy from the leaves. In short, **as the root system goes, so goes the plant!** Also remember that increased plant stress, for any reason, means an increased

167

likelihood of disease and insect problems and, conversely, reduced stress means increased resistance to problems.

Sources of Nutrient Elements. The discussion here will be on the various sources of nutrient elements, their solubility and how they are normally used. The following section will deal with various methods of fertilizer application and the plant response in various situations.

Nitrogen:
Nitrogen is available in several soluble forms:
urea - 46% nitrogen
ammonium nitrate - 33% nitrogen
calcium nitrate - 15% nitrogen
potassium nitrate - 14% nitrogen, 44% potassium
monoammonium phosphate - 12% nitrogen, 48% phosphorus
diammonium phosphate - 21% nitrogen, 52% phosphorus
sodium nitrate - 16% nitrogen
ammonium sulfate - 20% nitrogen
Most liquid nitrogen fertilization is done with ammonium nitrate or if potassium is needed, with potassium nitrate in a 2 to 1 up to a 5 to 1 ratio of the two nutrient elements, which provides both ammonium (NH_4) and nitrate (NO_3) nitrogen. Calcium nitrate is sometimes used as a foliar spray but seldom for soil applications, due to the much higher cost. Urea has the highest nitrogen concentration and is generally the least expensive of the granular sources and has the lowest salt index per unit of nitrogen. However, urea provides only ammonium nitrogen initially and under cool conditions, the conversion to nitrate is slow. This may be an advantage or disadvantage depending on the immediate plant needs and the species involved.

Nitrogen is also available in several slow-release forms:
ureaformaldehyde - 38-0-0 sold as Blue Chip, Nitroform or Uramite in the U.S.A.
sulfur-coated urea - urea 46-0-0 is coated with molten sulfur which restricts water entrance into and out of the coated granule. In some cases the sulfur coating is further treated with a wax or resin to further slow the nutrient release. Final analysis is generally 32% to 40% nitrogen.

Osmocote -- several formulations: 19-6-12, 18-6-12, 17-7-12, 24-5-9, 38-0-0 (coated urea), 16-38-0 (coated diammonium phosphate), and others.

IBDU (isobutylene diurea) - 30-0-0

various organic materials including sewage sludge and various animal manures.

Phosphorus:
Phosphorus is generally available in several forms:
diammonium phosphate, 21-52-0 or 18-46-0 and
monoammonium phosphate, 12-48-0 are water-soluble.

Slow-release sources of phosphorus include:
single superphosphate, 0-20-0 which also includes 12% sulfur and 18% calcium as calcium sulfate.
triple superphosphate, 0-46-0 which includes 12% calcium as calcium phosphate but almost no sulfur.
magamp, 7-40-6, is magnesium ammonium phosphate.

Sierra Chemical Co. is using the Osmocote resin coating on diammonium phosphate creating an analysis of 16-38-0. The various coating thicknesses allow for varying release rates and provides a good slow-release source under conditions very subject to leaching.

sulfur coating of diammonium phosphate has also been successful.

Potassium:
Potassium is widely available in three forms:
potassium chloride (KCl), 0-0-60, is very soluble and has the highest salt level of any fertilizer material.
potassium sulfate (K_2SO_4), 0-0-53, plus 18% sulfur, is very soluble.
potassium nitrate (KNO_3), 13-0-44, is frequently used in liquid fertilizer systems in combination with ammonium nitrate

Other sources of potassium include:
sulfate of potash magnesia (K_2SO_4 $2MgSO_4$), 0-0-26 plus 15% sulfur and 10% magnesium, frequently sold as K-mag.

Sierra Chemical Co. used the Osmocote resin coating on potassium sulfate to create an analysis of 0-0-39 or 0-0-42, depending on the thickness of the coating and release rate.

sulfur coating of potassium sulfate has also been accomplished to minimize release.

Calcium:

Calcium is available in three principal forms but is also present in nearly all irrigation water. Calcium in the water supply is soluble and available for plant growth and must be considered in planning a nutrition program. In some cases, no calcium other than that in the water supply is needed.

calcium carbonate, lime, ($CaCO_3$), - 40% calcium

calcium sulfate, gypsum, ($CaSO_4$), 29% calcium, 23% sulfur, is sometimes used, however, extra calcium without magnesium is generally undesirable.

dolomite, also referred to as dolomite lime. Analysis varies but generally 20% calcium and 9% to 10% magnesium from calcium carbonate and magnesium carbonate. Dolomite is a widely used source of calcium and magnesium.

calcium oxide (CaO), 70% calcium

some calcium is also available from single and triple superphosphate, 18% and 12%, respectively. Calcium nitrate is sometimes used in liquid fertilization programs and contains 22% to 37% calcium, depending on the source.

Magnesium:

Magnesium is sometimes present in irrigation waters and should be considered in the nutritional program. However, there is generally only a small proportion of magnesium relative to calcium in the water. Sources include:

dolomite, calcium and magnesium carbonates (see under calcium).

magnesium sulfate, ($MgSO_4$), 10% magnesium, 20% sulfur, may be broadcast and incorporated or watered-in. It is very water-soluble and may be injected into irrigation water, however, it is difficult to keep in suspension during cool weather.

magnesium oxide (MgO), 58% magnesium. This is very insoluble (see Table 5.3) and, unless finely ground, may not supply enough soluble magnesium for crop growth unless the soil is acid, thus increasing the solubility. Martin-Marietta Corporation and Kaizer Chemicals produce a magnesium oxide, 120-mesh, that is helpful in preventing magnesium deficiencies.

sulfate of potash magnesia (K_2SO_4 $2MgSO_4$) is 10% magnesium, 15% sulfur and 26% potassium. It is soluble and may be used as a general incorporation into the soil (see Tables 5.2 and 5.3).

Sulfur:

Sulfur is an impurity or associated element with several other nutrient elements. However as fertilizers become more refined, it may be necessary to add sulfur to the soil to maintain a sufficient supply. Sources of sulfur include:

ammonium sulfate,

sulfur coatings used on urea and other elements,

potassium sulfate,

sulfate of potash magnesia (also sold as K-mag),

calcium sulfate,

magnesium sulfate,

the various sulfate forms of micronutrients used in some micronutrient fertilizers, and

elemental sulfur, (S_2) which is generally 96% sulfur, may also be used. It is slowly oxidized to form sulfuric acid and therefore provides the sulfate (SO_4) needed for plant growth.

The Micronutrients:

The micronutrients are available in several forms, but most common are the sulfates of iron, copper, zinc, and manganese, and sodium forms of boron and molybdenum. These are readily soluble in water. Oxide forms of iron, copper, zinc and manganese are also available, but are, in general, very insoluble and of minor importance.

Several of the micronutrients can exist in various valence states or levels of electrical charge. For example, iron and manganese are readily available with two or three electrical charges, ++ or +++. Both elements are primarily absorbed as the ++ form with little, if any, benefit to the plant from the +++ form. Because the electrical state of the micronutrient element is critical as are the rates and ratios among the micronutrients, be cautious when adding specific micronutrient sources to the soil. The safest and most practical approach is to lower the soil pH to release the natural complex of micronutrients in the soil, or use a manufactured micronutrient fertilizer that has been thoroughly researched and tested.

Why a Fertilizer Burns. It is important to understand why a fertilizer burns. Soluble nitrogen fertilizers, if applied properly, can be just as effective as a slowly soluble nitrogen source in providing the plant with the nitrogen it requires. The risk of burn may be minimized if the factors that contribute to a burn are understood (8).

Fertilizers are salts. These salts are not unlike table salt, except that they contain various plant nutrients. When a salt is added to water, the osmotic pressure of the solution is increased. Osmotic pressure is, in a sense, a measure of how tightly water is held in a solution. When a fertilizer, either as a solid or a liquid, is applied, the fertilizer salts must sooner or later enter and become a part of the soil solution before the nutrients can enter the roots and be used by the plant. The increase in the osmotic pressure of the soil solution associated with the application of a fertilizer may determine whether the plant will survive or suffer from moisture stress from excess fertilizer.

For a plant's root system to take in water, the water must pass through a root cell membrane. Water can pass through this membrane only when the osmotic pressure of the solution inside the cell is higher than the osmotic pressure of the solution outside the cell. Water moves from a solution with low osmotic pressure into a solution with higher osmotic pressure. If the osmotic pressure of the soil solution becomes higher than that of the solution inside the cell, water cannot enter the cell and, under severe conditions, may move out. This results in damage to, or death of, the cell. When root cells die, the whole plant may die. The end result is termed "fertilizer burn".

An understanding of the potential salt effect of the various fertilizer materials can help prevent possible fertilizer burn. Salt index values are a measure of a material's relative tendency to increase the osmotic pressure of the soil solution as compared to the increase caused by an equal weight of sodium nitrate (12). The salt index of sodium nitrate is 100. The higher the salt index, the greater the potential of a material to increase the osmotic pressure of the soil solution, and thus the greater potential for burn (Table 5.2.)

The potential for burn is not totally dependent upon the salt index of the fertilizer material. The moisture status of the soil and the plant is also important. If the level of soil moisture is low, a fertilizer will have a greater effect on increasing the osmotic pressure of the soil solution. When a fertilizer is "watered in", the volume of the soil solution increases and thus the osmotic pressure is reduced. In well-drained soils, however, heavy applications of water, while having the beneficial effect of reducing the osmotic pressure of the soil solution, may also have the harmful effect of leaching nutrients past the root system.

The water status of the plant is affected by both the air temperature and the humidity, which is the amount of water in the air surrounding the plant. These factors to a large degree affect the plant's water requirements. The plant requires more water as the air temperature increases and as the humidity decreases. As the osmotic pressure of the soil solution increases, less and less water is available to the plant. Watering-in a fertilizer material may increase the water available to the root system by decreasing the osmotic pressure of the soil solution, and may also aid in reducing the plant's water requirements by cooling the plant and increasing the humidity of the plant's micro-environment.

Fertilizer Salts and Salt Index. In areas where poor water quality is a problem in field production and soils are sandy, slow-release fertilizers should be emphasized as an effective mechanism of nutrient delivery to the plant with virtually no salt effect to add to the salt from the water. If the soil has a limited water-holding capacity, the problem is further compounded. If a soil has a total salt reading of 500 parts per million at field capacity (the maximum water the soil will hold after watering), then later dries down to some point approaching the wilting point of the plant, the salt concentration will be much higher because the quantity of soluble salts remains the same while the water quantity has been reduced substantially. Therefore, the water-holding capacity of the soil and/or watering frequency has a great influence on the salt concentration experienced by the roots.

The total salt effect of a fertilizer is dependent upon the rate applied and the nature of the fertilizer. For example, if ammonium nitrate is applied, both the ammonium and nitrate is used by the plant. On the other hand, if potassium chloride is applied, the potassium can be used but the chlorine is not. The same would be true of the sodium in sodium nitrate. These extra elements (chlorine and sodium) contribute to the total salt content of the soil while contributing nothing to plant growth. When water quality is good, unwanted elements are of little or no consequence. However, when water quality is poor or there is some other factor affecting the total salt level in the soil, these unnecessary elements carried along with the desired fertilizer element may be the proverbial straw that breaks the camel's back, especially on sensitive species.

Table 5.2 shows the classical salt index of various fertilizers (12). In addition, there has been added a salt index per unit of fertilizer which gives a more accurate view of the salt effect of a fertilizer. For example, urea with a classical salt index of 75 appears moderately high. However, the salt index per unit of nitrogen is only 1.6, which is much lower that of nitrogen from ammonium nitrate which is 105 in the classical expression but 3.0 units of salt per unit of nitrogen. By contrast, with potassium nitrate, has a salt index of 75 in the classical expression, but 5.4 per unit of potassium. Assuming that both the potassium and nitrogen are needed for plant growth (in other words, the high potassium would not be in excess over and above plant needs) the values for potassium nitrate should be 13.8 + 46.6 = 60.4, divided into 74 = a salt index per unit of both nitrogen and potassium of 1.2.

In general, materials with classical salt indexes above 20 or on a unit of element above 0.5 should be added to a soil and incorporated pre-plant or in moderate levels to the soil surface before rainfall or irrigation. On the other hand, the fertilizer materials with a very low salt index can be likened to hard candy. They very slowly dissolve and release a small portion of their contents. Dolomite, calcium carbonate, gypsum and single and triple superphosphates are the most widely used examples. These are naturally occurring slow-release fertilizers (dolomite, calcium carbonate and gypsum) or manufactured products with slow-release characteristics (single and triple superphosphates).

174

Table 5.2. Chemical content and salt index of several fertilizer carriers (12).

	Analysis of fertilizer tested	Salt index	Salt index per unit of fertilizer element
Nitrogen carriers:			
ammonium nitrate	35.0%	105	3.0
monoammonium phosphate	12.1	30	2.5
diammonium phosphate	21.2	34	1.6
ammonium sulfate	21.1	69	3.3
calcium nitrate	11.9	53	4.5
potassium nitrate	13.8	74	5.4
sodium nitrate	16.5	100	6.1
urea	46.6	75	1.6
Potassium carriers:			
potassium chloride	60.0	116	1.9
potassium nitrate	46.6	74	1.6
potassium sulfate	54.0	46	0.8
sulfate of potash-magnesia	21.9	43	2.0
Phosphorus carriers:			
monoammonium phosphate	61.7	30	0.5
diammonium phosphate	53.8	34	0.6
single superphosphate	20.0	8	0.4
triple superphosphate	46.0	10	0.2
Miscellaneous:			
calcium carbonate	56.0	5	0.09
dolomite	20.0	1	0.05
magnesium sulfate	16.0	44	2.7
gypsum	32.6	8	0.3

----

*Fertilizer analysis means % nitrogen in nitrogen carriers, % potassium oxide in potassium carriers and % magnesium oxide in magnesium carriers including dolomite, and % calcium oxide in calcium carbonate and gypsum.
**Salt index compared against equal weight of sodium nitrate, which was assigned a value of 100.
***Adjusted salt index per unit of fertilizer. (For example, divide salt index of 100 for sodium nitrate by 16.5, the number of fertilizer units, and the salt units per fertilizer unit is 6.1)

175

The solubilities of several commonly used fertilizer sources are listed in Table 5.3. In the case of the less soluble materials, assume the particle size is extremely small, a fine powder. Therefore, these values would be decreased if the particle size were increased. Using the hard candy analogy again, several small pieces of hard candy will dissolve faster than one large piece of equal size and weight, because the smaller the particles, the greater the surface area.

During the late '60s and '70s some of the research with agronomic crops grown in field soils suggested that the concern about the ratio of calcium to magnesium was unfounded. With fibrous rooted annual crops in field soils, where the plate-like or lattice structure of the clay colloids can adsorb many nutrients and the plant root system is unrestricted, this may be true. However, a point to keep in mind when considering plant establishment and growth in the field, is that **woody plant requirements are different: their root systems, in comparison, are very sparse and soil conditions are often marginal.** Before the discussion of nutrition and fertilizers progresses, the reader is reminded that several materials provide more than one essential element, making it difficult to distinguish between the benefit of one or both, or the benefit from one and detrimental effect of the other during evaluation of plant responses. For example, single superphosphate contains 20% P_2O_5, or about 9% actual phosphorus, but it also contains about 20% calcium and 12% sulfur and numerous micronutrients in small quantities as impurities. If phosphorus and calcium are both low, the plant response may be from both elements. However, calcium is rarely lacking, so if single superphosphate is added, the phosphorus may be beneficial while the calcium is detrimental.

Dolomite is the major source of both calcium and magnesium. However, because it is a naturally occurring mineral, it also contains various impurities, especially micronutrients, depending on the specific source.

Table 5.3. Solubilities of various nutrient elements.

Material   Solubility gm./100 gm. water

    calcium carbonate (lime)   0.0014
    calcium sulfate (gypsum)   0.209
    calcium oxide   0.131

    magnesium sulfate (Epsom salts)   26.0
    magnesium oxide   0.00062
    magnesium carbonate   0.176

    potassium nitrate   13.3
    potassium sulfate   12.0
    potassium chloride   23.8
    sulfate of potash magnesia   19.6
    superphosphate, single and triple   0.0316 (about)

    ammonium phosphates   22.7 or greater
    ammonium sulfate   70.6
    ammonium nitrate   118.3
    calcium nitrate   121.2

Nutrient Elements: Plant Response and Use. Nitrogen. More nitrogen is required for plant growth than any other fertilizer element (5). In addition, nitrogen has the greatest effect on plant growth (10). This is both the good news and bad news. The good news is that additional nitrogen will generally stimulate additional plant growth (increase in size) up to some point which is controlled by other limiting factors such as light, water, temperature, etc. The bad news is that nitrogen is often misused or over-used at the overall expense of plant quality and health. There appears to be a favorable ratio among **all** of the nutrient elements that provides good growth and ample internal storage of carbohydrates and other energy reserves as well. A disproportionate or excess level of nitrogen relative to one or all of the other essential elements will provide additional growth but the tissues will be weak, and because the levels of stored energy (carbohydrates and other storage compounds) are low, resistance to disease, insects and environmental stress is also low.

177

The ideal level of nitrogen depends on many environmental factors, levels of the other essential nutrient elements as well as the basic growth potential of the particular species or cultivar (9). An African violet (*Saintpaulia* spp.) requires a very low level of nitrogen compared to a chrysanthemum or sweetgum (*Liquidambar* spp.).

Nitrogen requirements of the many species of plants are so varied under the vast array of environmental and cultural conditions that no specific level or generalization can be made at this point. The preferred nitrogen rate or level on a specific site with a specific crop at a particular stage of growth can only be determined on that site. Experimentation with several levels of nitrogen on the major plants grown at a nursery or present in a landscape is a wise investment. However, don't fall for the trap that bigger is always better. Excessive growth, due to excess nitrogen, especially at high temperatures, may be false prosperity, resulting in bigger plants but of poorer quality and a lowered resistance to problems.

Nitrogen is absorbed by plants both as nitrate (NO_3) and ammonium (NH_4) (10). Once inside the plant, the nitrogen is transformed into the amine form (NH_2) and combines with soluble carbohydrates to form amino acids which are then translocated to the shoots in the xylem sap (2, 3, 4) and used in the formation of proteins. Most of the proteins are used in the protoplasm of new cells.

Phosphorus. Phosphorus may interact with other elements both directly and indirectly. Excess phosphorus may combine with calcium and several of the micronutrients to form insoluble compounds, thereby depriving the plant of these elements. Single superphosphate, 0-20-0, generally contains 20% PO_5 or 8.8% actual phosphorus plus 20% calcium as calcium sulfate and 12% sulfur. On the other hand, triple superphosphate, sometimes called concentrated superphosphate, 0-46-0, generally contains 46% P_2O_5, or 20.2% actual phosphorus plus 14% calcium, but only 1.4% sulfur. Therefore, when either single or triple superphosphate is added to the soil, the calcium added should be considered in the overall nutritional program. **Excess phosphorus and calcium can suppress growth** (14) (Figures 5.8 and 5.9).

178

It is important to emphasize that slow-release sources of all elements must be evaluated carefully to determine not only the rate to be used but how much of the nutrient is released over what period of time.

Figure 5.8. Effects of no additional phosphorus other than that in Osmocote 17-7-12 (left), 4 pounds per cubic yard of 0-20-0 (left of center), and 1.5 pounds per cubic yard of 0-46-0, with or without gypsum (right) on growth of Fosters holly. Note the strong stem development and branching of the two plants on the left as opposed to the more shrubby growth of the plants on the right where excess calcium and phosphorus were present. This same plant response occurs in field soils.

*Figure 5.9. Osmocote 24-5-9, 12- to 14-month-release formulation was used in the mix with a constant rate of nitrogen but with phosphorus levels of 0.6, 1.2 and 1.8 pounds P_2O_5 per cubic yard. Note that the shore juniper (**Juniperus conferta**) is fuller and has many more branches at the 1.2 pound rate as opposed to either higher or lower levels of phosphorus.*

Potassium. Potassium may be applied either as potassium chloride or potassium sulfate, which are both very soluble. Slow-release fertilizer such as Osmocote 18-6-12, 17-7-12, 24-5-9, Scotts SREF 24-4-10, or others also work well on sandy soils.

The quantity of potassium required for excellent plant growth and quality is generally lower than the common levels used. There is no additional benefit in terms of increased cold tolerance or disease resistance from excessive levels of potassium, as has been proposed from time to time. In three different studies over a period of 11 years, plants with excessive levels of potassium were equally damaged by cold as plants with low levels of potassium. Only if the plant was severely deficient was cold hardiness affected.

In one of the studies reported under phosphorus, potassium and phosphorus combinations at various rates were studied (1). As long as a moderate level of potassium was supplied, and the other nutrient elements were at the proper levels, growth was excellent.

180

Excessive potassium can suppress growth. This has occurred in several studies over several years, reducing the emphasis on potassium. Some of the potassium levels listed as ideal for tissue levels in various species are fiction. Some of these are based on potassium levels of plants grown in solution culture (hydroponics), which is quite different from practical plant production in the nursery or landscape.

Sulfur. Sulfur is an impurity in single superphosphate (0-20-0) amounting to about 12%, whereas triple superphosphate 0-46-0) contains less than 2% sulfur. Calcium sulfate (gypsum) and magnesium sulfate (Epsom salts) are also common sources of sulfur. In some cases the irrigation water contains dissolved calcium sulfate or other sources of sulfate in sufficient quantity to provide the plant's requirements.

The exact level of sulfur necessary for excellent plant growth when all other factors are at or near the ideal level is not well known. However, if a source of phosphorus without sulfur is used and dolomite is the calcium and magnesium source, sulfur deficiency symptoms may eventually appear in sandy soils. Under these conditions, broadcasting granular sulfur, (96% S) is an economical and effective source. Do not try to spread sulfur dust.

Calcium and Magnesium. Excess calcium can strongly interfere with magnesium nutrition in several ways (Figure 5.10). It should be noted that the reason the magnesium cation with two electrical charges is not as strong as the calcium with two electrical charges is probably due to the fact that water is always associated with the magnesium. This water of hydration prevents the magnesium from attaching as closely and, therefore, as strongly as the calcium.

Observations, experiments and experience have gradually increased awareness of the importance of water quality on calcium and magnesium levels and the growth of plants.

Figure 5.10. Excess calcium suppresses both top and root growth primarily by reducing the availability of magnesium and micronutrients. The plant on the left was grown with a moderate level of calcium, whereas the one on the right was grown with a high rate of calcium.

In one water quality study conducted in containers, shortly after the study began, calcium deficiency symptoms began to appear on the new growth of geraniums which had no dolomite in the soil mix and received only pure water. Geraniums grown to salable size with no dolomite and either pure water or water with 40 ppm (parts per million) calcium and 20 ppm magnesium showed calcium deficiency symptoms, while plants grown with the medium-hard water showed no deficiency symptoms. Geraniums grown with the medium-hard water and no dolomite were as attractive as any treatment in the study. Plants grown with the very hard water were somewhat less attractive. Geraniums grown with two pounds of dolomite per cubic yard developed calcium deficiencies with the two best quality water sources.

Geraniums grown with four pounds of dolomite per cubic yard were of similar quality regardless of the water quality used, except for the very hard water, which reduced flower size.

Geraniums grown with eight pounds of dolomite per cubic yard were generally smaller and of poorer quality with all water sources showing the growth suppression of an excess (Figure 5.11).

Figure 5.11. Geraniums grown with pure water (all minerals removed) and eight pounds of dolomite per cubic yard (left) were full and attractive, whereas plants receiving the same level of dolomite but increasing quantities of calcium in the water supply were progressively restricted (left to right). This emphasizes how great the effect of dissolved minerals in the water supply can be. The same effect occurs in soils, only the symptoms are slower to appear because of the soil's buffering capacity.

Gardenias were more sensitive to the poor quality water used than were geraniums. In general, the gardenias grew poorly with the very hard water. On the other hand, they grew similarly with two or four pounds of dolomite and pure water or two pounds of dolomite and good quality water, or no dolomite and the moderately hard water. This shows that the soluble calcium and magnesium in the water is substituting for the calcium and magnesium normally provided by the dolomite.

It is difficult to determine precisely the quantities of calcium and magnesium a plant needs. If the irrigation water has even moderate quantities of soluble calcium and magnesium, the plant is being fertilized with these elements in the water just as is commonly done with nitrogen, phosphorus and potassium. Most of the calcium and magnesium in the water is adsorbed by the soil since they are readily exchanged cations (they have a positive electrical charge). The roots can exchange hydrogen for these ions as needed during the growth of the plant. Calcium levels continue to increase with time when calcium is present in the irrigation water because calcium can displace other elements such as potassium, magnesium, and sodium.

Although the example above deals with plants in containers, similar changes in the soil occur from irrigation water. Since most soils are highly buffered (resistant to change), the changes occur over a period of years instead of months and, unfortunately, go undetected until plant problems arise.

Water quality is a major factor influencing the proper calcium and magnesium nutrition of plants. A good water quality test is an inexpensive investment. Remember that any time a change occurs in the water source, an additional water quality test should be done and pH of the irrigation water tells **nothing** about the level or proportion of dissolved minerals in the water.

The Micronutrients. In most cases, micronutrients are sufficiently available and in reasonable proportions in good field soils that there is no benefit from adding them as fertilizers. There are exceptions, however, especially in the sandy soils of Florida and in the arid Southwest. Plant nutrition in containers is entirely a different story. In 1957, Matkin, Chandler and Baker (11) wrote, "Since micronutrients are required in such minute amounts by plants and are natural components of peat, soil, fertilizer, and water, it is improbable that a soil mix would develop micronutrient deficiencies." Since that time, many studies have been conducted to improve the physical and chemical aspects of container growth media and nutrition. In general, with each improvement in the conditions in the container (i.e. total pore space, air space, carbon:nitrogen ratio, and media structure and components), plant growth and quality improves. Likewise, with each advancement in the understanding of container nutrition, growth has improved. These improvements in plant growth and quality have come in steps as successive limiting factors have been removed. There are probably many more limiting factors to be discovered and removed before maximum plant growth in containers can be achieved.

In 1969, it was shown that as nitrogen, phosphorus, and potassium rates increased, rates of Perk (a micronutrient fertilizer manufactured by Wilson & Toomer Fertilizer Company, Jacksonville, Florida) also had to be increased to achieve maximum growth with the physical and cultural conditions imposed on the plants at that time (13) (Figure 5.12).

*Figure 5.12. Effects of Perk micronutrients at rates of 0, 1, 2, 4, 6, 8 pounds per cubic yard (left to right) on wax leaf ligustrum (**Ligustrum japonicum**). The bare stems on the tops of the plants are old flower stalks. It is important to note that all of the leaves were of similar size, dark green and apparently healthy even though plant size was vastly different. Just because no chlorosis is visible does not mean that a plant is making maximum growth.*

185

Deficiency symptoms of micronutrients are often difficult, if not impossible, to distinguish from toxicity symptoms. In addition, when the suspected deficient micronutrient element is provided to the plants and no response occurs, it may be because there were actually:

a) more than one deficient element,
b) already a toxicity of one or more elements,
c) a deficiency of one element and a toxicity of another, or
d) some other combination of deficiencies or toxicities.

The tendency is to assume a single deficiency. In reality, there may be several deficiencies or near-deficiencies but perhaps only the most severe deficiency is reflected in foliage symptoms on the plant.

One of the striking aspects of this research with micronutrients was the root growth response, especially with azaleas. When the "ideal" combination of micronutrients was provided in the container medium, the root growth was excellent, whereas, if one or more of the micronutrients was out of synchronization, root growth was limited (Figure 5.13). This occurred with the same mix, watering and other nutrient additives.

The reason for this improved root growth is the improved micronutrient formulation which greatly increases the capacity of the leaves to utilize other nutrients and manufacture energy (carbohydrates) for use in various aspects in plant growth. The greater the energy manufacturing capacity of the leaves, the greater the quantity of energy transferred to or stored in the stems or roots. Since root growth is dependent upon energy from the leaves, this increased leaf capacity is reflected in additional root growth, which in turn improves nutrient uptake and leaf energy manufacturing capacity, thus growth is accelerated.

Figure 5.13. The azaleas above were grown with the high rate of copper and boron and low manganese. Azaleas grown with low iron (left), medium iron (center), and high iron (right) are shown. Leaf retention and color, flower numbers, and overall plant quality were increased by increased rates of iron, but only if manganese, boron and copper were at the correct level. The azaleas below reflect the difference in both top and root development as a result of proper micronutrient nutrition when all other factors were held constant.

Micromax is a unique formulation of water soluble micro-nutrients (16). It is not a slow-release formulation initially. However, when Micromax is incorporated into a soilless medium or soil, with the first wetting, the micronutrients react with the components of the mix and create a slow-release micronutrient fertilizer. The advantage of this process over other slow-release micronutrient products is that the threshold level of micronutrients in the growth medium or soil (whereby micronutrients are available for plant growth) is reached immediately. Micromax is recommended for incorporation only. This is because the fertilizer salts used in the manufacture of Micromax are soluble and, if allowed to remain on plant foliage for any period of time, may cause burning. In addition, some of the iron sulfate may oxidize if top-dressed, thereby altering the important ratio of iron to manganese and copper. However, Micromax has been successfully top-dressed on plants showing micronutrient deficiencies where contact with the stem or foliage is avoided, and where it is watered-in well and very soon. As work progresses, effects of micronutrient fertilizers on all aspects of plant growth become more clear. Preliminary studies with several species of shrubs and trees suggest that the micronutrient level in the parent plant, and/or increased plant growth and vigor associated with improved parent plant micronutrient nutrition, affects rooting of cuttings and subsequent growth. Micromax has, in some situations, provided increased plant growth and improved foliage color in field nursery and landscape situations. Unfortnuately, defining the desired soil level of micronutrients is difficult, so proceed with caution.

Relationships of Plant Nutrients. Plant growth is most vigorous and problem-free when all the nutrient elements and environmental conditions are synchronized. An excess of one nutrient element frequently influences the availability and absorption of other nutrients. There are several key element relationships that must be considered (Table 5.4). For example, the ratio of calcium to magnesium available for plant growth is important. If calcium is in excess, magnesium absorption is depressed or vice versa.

Table 5.4. Important Ratios of Nutrient Elements
- -

Elements	Ratio
calcium to magnesium	2-1 to 6-1
nitrogen to sulfur	20-1

- -

An excess of...	may cause a deficiency of...
nitrogen	potassium
potassium	calcium and/or magnesium
sodium	potassium, calcium, and magnesium
calcium	magnesium
magnesium	calcium
calcium	boron, iron, manganese, copper, zinc
iron	manganese
manganese	iron
iron	molybdenum
phosphorus	iron and/or manganese

- -

When soluble sources of nitrogen are used, they must be applied frequently in order to maintain a reasonable level available for plant growth at all times. Nitrogen, potassium and magnesium are the elements most readily leached. Therefore, they are the most difficult to manage and require the greatest attention or monitoring. Phosphorus, calcium, magnesium, sulfur, and the micronutrients are best added to the soil at time of planting. The reason these elements can be incorporated is related to either the low solubility and low salt index, or the mechanism of binding with the soil.

The ideal quantity of any one nutrient element is not a specific level, but rather a range (Figure 5.14). In the case of soluble nitrogen fertilizer applications, maintaining the ideal range can be difficult. For example, when soluble nitrogen is applied, the maximum quantity is generally provided (short of root or top damage) so that the interval between applications can be longer. At the same time, unless nutrient levels are closely monitored, the level of nitrogen can drop below the ideal range before the next application. If a heavy rain occurs shortly after an application is made and the soil is sandy, the nitrogen is partially or entirely leached out. **The porosity of the soil has a greater effect than any other factor on how much nitrogen must be applied for good plant growth and the frequency of application.**

189

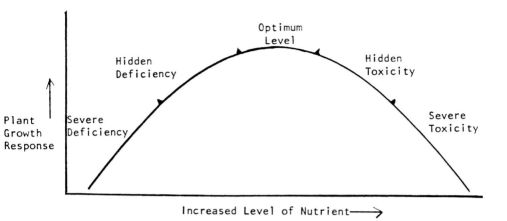

Figure 5.14. The optimum level of a plant nutrient is probably a limited range rather than a specific level. However, it should be noted that hidden deficiencies or toxicities occur long before either deficiency or toxicity symptoms appear. Just because there are no deficiency symptoms does not mean that all elements are near optimum.

Slow-release fertilizers are especially useful on salt-sensitive plants such as azaleas, rhododendrons and blueberries. When slow-release sources of elements are used, an important aspect is the rate of release per unit of time. For example, if Osmocote releases the three nutrient elements over a period of six months, there will be a given quantity available for plant growth at any one time. On the other hand, if the Osmocote releases its nutrients over a period of four months instead of six, the quantity of nutrients available at any one time during the four-month period will be 33% greater. Consequently, knowing the length of release time for a slow-release fertilizer in a given situation is very important in determining when to re-apply. The slow-release mechanism simply maintains the nutrient availability in the ideal range for a longer time between applications (Figure 5.15). Unfortunately, slow-release fertilizers are applied and forgotten, people often forget that they will supply nutrients for only some predetermined period of time under the specific environmental conditions. There is an easy way to determine if all the fertilizer has been released from the Osmocote granule. Break a capsule between the fingers and taste the liquid, if it is salty, fertilizer remains, but if it is not, all has been released. The failure to re-apply the slow-release fertilizer at the proper time is a management error. Unfortunately, slow-release fertilizers are often blamed for poor performance when it is really poor management.

Figure 5.15. Osmocote granules magnified several hundred times. Note the complete resin coating around the dry fertilizer granule. Because the fertilizer has an attraction for water, water is drawn into the resin-coated granule and creates a "water balloon" effect. When the fertilizer salt concentration outside the "balloon" is lower than inside, the nutrient elements slowly move out. Because this movement is slow, a heavy rain leaches out only the small amount of fertilizer outside the "balloon" that has not been absorbed by the plant. The result is an effective slow-release delivery system for nitrogen and potassium.

Slow-release fertilizers are most beneficial, relative to the cost, on sandy soils where nitrogen is readily leached and the buffer/nutrient holding capacity of the soil is less than with heavier soils. Osmocote with a thin coating, for example three-

191

to four-month 19-6-12, will last much longer under field soil conditions because of the soil temperature. The three- to four-month release duration time is based on 70 degrees F container temperatures and not field soil temperatures. In general, temperatures of field soils are much lower than containers during the growing season, **unless** the soil is dark and the Osmocote is placed on the surface.

Given all other factors are equal, slow-release sources of nutrients will provide for plants of equal or greater size and quality than dry chemical fertilizers. Dry chemical fertilizers must be applied more frequently in order to effectively promote plant growth, thus increasing labor costs. Osmocote (Sierra Chemical Co., Milpitas, Ca.) is a slow-release fertilizer containing nitrogen, phosphorus, and potassium, produced by coating various water-soluble fertilizers with plastic resins. Isobutylidene diurea (IBDU) (Swift Agricultural Chemical Corp., Chicago, Il.) is a synthetic organic nitrogen (31-0-0) containing 27.9% water-insoluble nitrogen. Variations in release rates are obtained through particle size and hardness and rainfall or irrigation water application. Sulfur-coated urea (SCU) is manufactured by Lesco (Lake Shore Industries) and others and contains 36% to 42% nitrogen. The O.M. Scotts Company has a modified sulfur-coated urea sold under the trade name SREF.

Literature Cited

1. Babcock, Frank E., Bonnie L. Appleton and Carl E. Whitcomb. 1982. Phosphorus nutrition of nursery stock. Okla. Agri. Exp. Sta. Res. Rept. P-829:44-48.

2. Barnes, R.L. 1963. Nitrogen transport in the xylem of trees. Jour. of Forestry 61:50-51.

3. Barner, R.L. 1963. Organic compounds in tree xylem sap. Forest Sci. 9:98-102.

4. Bollard, E.G. 1957. Translocation of organic nitrogen in the xylem. Aust. Jour. Biol. Sci. 10:292-301.

5. Epstein, E. 1972. Mineral Nutrition of Plants: Principles and Perspectives. John Wiley & Sons, New York.

6. Gordon, J.C. and P.R. Larson. 1968. The seasonal course of photosynthesis, respiration and distribution of carbon in young *Pinus resinosa* trees as related to wood formation. Plant Physiol. 43:1617-1624.

7. Gordon, J.C. and P.R. Larson. 1970. Redistribution of C-labeled reserve food in young red pines during shoot elongation. Forest Sci. 16:14-20.

8. Knoop, W. 1976. Why a fertilizer burns. Weeds, Trees and Turf, 12:14-15.

9. Kramer, P.J. and T.T. Kozlowski. 1960. Physiology of Trees. McGraw Hill, New York.

10. Kramer, P.J. and T.T. Kozlowski. 1979. Physiology of Woody Plants. Academic Press. New York.

11. Matkin, O.A., P.A. Chandler and K.F. Baker. 1957. Components and development of mixes. In: The U.C. System for producing healthy container-grown plants. Calif. Agri. Exp. Sta. Manual 23.

12. Rader, L.F. Jr., L.M. White and C.W. Whitaker. 1943. The salt index--a measure of the effect of fertilizers on the concentration of the soil solution. Soil Science 12:201-218.

13. Whitcomb, Carl E. 1970. Response of four container-grown woody ornamentals to rates of Perk and Osmocote. The Florida Nurseryman 15:7, 36, 37.

14. Whitcomb, Carl E. 1988. *Plant Production in Containers*. Lacebark Inc. Stillwater, Ok. 640 pages.

15. Whitcomb, Carl E. and L.K. Euchner. 1979. Effects of shade levels on growth of container nursery stock. Nursery Res. Jour. 6:1-11.

16. Whitcomb, Carl E., Allan Storjohann and William D. Warde. 1981. Micromax--micronutrients for improved plant growth. Proc. Int. Plant Prop. Soc. 30:462-467.

CHAPTER 6

THE ESSENTIAL NUTRIENT ELEMENTS:
FUNCTION, DEFICIENCY AND TOXICITY

THE ESSENTIAL NUTRIENT ELEMENTS: FUNCTION, DEFICIENCY, AND TOXICITY

The 12 essential nutrient elements are generally referred to as macro (needed in relatively large quantities) and micro (needed in relatively small quantities). The macro-nutrients and their chemical symbols are: nitrogen (N), phosphorus (P), potassium (K), magnesium (Mg), sulfur (S), and calcium (Ca). The micronutrients are: iron (Fe), manganese (Mn), copper (Cu), boron (B), zinc (Zn), and molybdenum (Mo). All but three of the elements are absorbed as the elemental ion (the element without an accompanying element or group of elements). For example, you may apply potassium sulfate, K_2SO_4. However, if the potassium is absorbed, it is as K^+ not as K_2SO_4. The exceptions are: sulfur, which is absorbed as sulfate, $SO_4^=$; phosphorus, which is absorbed as phosphate, $PO_4^=$; and nitrogen, which may be absorbed either as nitrate, NO_3^- or ammonium, NH_4^+.

The elements: carbon, hydrogen and oxygen, are also needed by plants, however, the carbon is obtained from carbon dioxide, CO_2, in the air and the oxygen and hydrogen from water. The following is a general discussion of each of the nutrient elements. When considering nutrient deficiency symptoms, keep in mind that a deficiency of one element rarely occurs, but varying degrees of deficiencies of several elements are more common. Quite often the symptoms of deficiencies we see are the most deficient element. See Figure 5.14 as a reminder of hidden deficiencies.

The Macro Elements. **Nitrogen.** Large quantities of nitrogen, generally from 1.5% to 4.0% on a dry weight basis, are required for rapid plant growth. When nitrogen is deficient, growth is generally slow and the lower leaves are pale or sometimes mottled because nitrogen is mobile in the plant and can be taken from older tissues and translocated to new growth. In rapid growing herbaceous and foliage plants, the lower leaves may become lighter green or yellow in color. On many woody plants, however, a nitrogen deficiency is reflected mostly as a reduced growth rate, and only under severe conditions do the lower or older leaves become pale green or yellow. In some instances, where a plant experiences an abrupt nitrogen deficiency and no new growth occurs, the entire plant will remain green, giving no clue to the problem. Only if bud break and new growth occurs will the classical lower leaf-yellowing symptom develop. Nitrogen can be supplied as nitrate such as calcium nitrate, $Ca(NO_3)_2$, from either ammonium or nitrate, as in ammonium nitrate, NH_4NO_3, or just from ammonium, as in diammonium phosphate (18-46-0). Nitrate, NO_3^-, has a negative charge and consequently is not attached as strongly to the soil as is ammonium. This means that the likelihood of leaching of nitrate from heavy rainfall or excess watering is greater. Ammonium, NH_4^+, has a positive charge and is held more strongly by the adsorptive capacity of the soil. Ammonium is usually converted to nitrate by bacterial action after a few days to a few weeks, depending on soil temperature and other factors. Once nitrogen is absorbed as either nitrate or ammonium, it is transformed in the plant to the amine form (NH_2) and combines with soluble carbohydrates to form amino acids and proteins.

Because nitrogen is required in large quantities by the plant and is so subject to loss by leaching, it is generally the most difficult nutrient element to manage. The management of nitrogen is very dependent on soil type and drainage. On very sandy soils, especially in areas of high rainfall and high temperatures such as Florida and some areas of the Gulf Coast, nitrogen is quickly converted from ammonium, which has a positive charge and is strongly held by the soil, to nitrate with a negative charge and is weakly held. This conversion factor, which is primarily dependent upon temperature, in conjunction with high rainfall and sandy soils that allow rapid percolation of water downward through the soils means frequent applications of nitrogen or the use of slow-release nitrogen sources. Where drip irrigation is used, nitrogen may be added to the water with each application to maintain a moderate but constant level of nitrogen available for plant growth. Slow-release fertilizers are also very useful on sandy soils. Osmocote (a plastic resin-coated fertilizer), sulfur-coated urea (where a molten sulfur-coating surrounds otherwise soluble urea nitrogen fertilizer making it slow-release), or compounds such as ureaformaldehyde and IBDU, which are only slowly soluble, are very useful under these conditions.

Where soils are clays, managing nitrogen is much easier, especially in cooler climates with moderate rainfall. For example, the heavy clay loam soils of eastern Iowa need only infrequent nitrogen applications for good plant growth. This is because of
a) the adsorptive capacity of the soils,

196

b) the limited percolation or leaching of water through the soil which leaches the nitrate nitrogen below the root zone,

c) the moderate rainfall which further limits leaching and,

d) since the soils are generally cooler, the conversion of ammonium to nitrate is slower.

No two soils are the same and when coupled with climatic conditions, it can be easily seen that nitrogen management must be considered relative to each specific site. Add to this the unique aspects of various field soils and factors such as irrigation systems that may encourage more leaching, unusual soil depths, textures, and drainage systems and nitrogen management becomes much more complex. The important thing to remember is never allow the plant to become more than mildly nitrogen-deficient during the production phase. Because nitrogen has a profound effect on plant growth, it is sometimes used in excess. There is probably an ideal balance or proportion among all the nutrient elements required for plant growth. When an element is in excess or deficient, growth is restricted. However, excess nitrogen frequently stimulates additional soft, succulent growth that is slow to mature. These soft tissues are much more vulnerable to disease organisms than are tissues developed with a more favorable combination of all nutrients.

Another nitrogen-related management factor deals with shade and leaf color. Plants grown with moderate levels of nitrogen and under moderate shade levels are very dark green. This is frequently assumed to be a very good situation. However, this "false prosperity" is actually restricting growth and may make the plant more vulnerable to other problems. If the same plants are grown with a higher level of nitrogen and less shade, the leaves may appear slightly lighter green in color. However, the total energy production of the leaves and in turn the health and vigor of the root system will be improved and the plants can tolerate more stress.

Phosphorus. Phosphorus is tightly held in field soils, even those that are nearly 100% sand. Phosphorus is sometimes applied as phosphoric acid, H_2PO_4, or as mono- or diammonium phosphates as part of liquid fertilizer. More often, however, part or all of the phosphorus requirement of the plants can be met by incorporating either single or triple superphosphate (0-20-0 or 0-46-0) or diammonium phosphate (18-46-0) into the soil prior to planting. **Because these materials have a low salt index and are very slowly soluble, they can be safely incorporated without danger of a salt buildup or injury to developing roots of new plantings.** Soils with phosphorus levels of 60 to 100 pounds per acre (expressed as P_2O_5 will need no further phosphorus fertilizer for several years).

Phosphorus deficiency causes stunting long before the classical deficiency symptoms of reddening of the lower leaves (Figure 6.1). Plants mildly deficient in phosphorus have a dull appearance or lack of luster, especially on the older leaves. Because phosphorus is mobile in the plant, the older leaves show the symptoms first and most severely.

Phosphorus is used in the plant in several ways. However, the high energy organic complexes, ATP (adenosine triphosphate) and ADP (adenosine diphosphate), provide the energy for several chemical reactions within the plant. A phosphorus deficiency, even though very mild, will reduce this energy transfer system and slow growth functions of the plant. It is therefore very important to supply the proper amount of phosphorus. However, **excess phosphorus is equally detrimental to plant growth.** Excess phosphorus combines with calcium, iron and other micronutrients to form insoluble complexes of these elements. Thus, **excess phosphorus generally is observed as stunting and deficiencies of several micronutrients.** Phosphorus is normally found in plant tissues at only about one-tenth to one-eighth the level of nitrogen, comprising 0.14 percent to 0.32 percent of the dry weight of leaves.

Figure 6.1. Phosphorus deficiency on chrysanthemums. The leaf on the right is a normal leaf, whereas the leaf on the left has severe phosphorus deficiency symptoms. The darker areas on the upper portion of the leaf are reddish-purple, whereas the center and lower portions of the leaf are identical to the normal leaf.

Potassium. Leaves of healthy plants generally contain from one to four percent potassium. Potassium is very mobile in the plant tissues and is not bound into organic chemical complexes as are nitrogen and phosphorus. Simply dipping a leaf into a container of water a few times will remove 25 percent or more of the potassium. Potassium is leached from leaves during rains and probably is absorbed by the roots and recycled many times in the life of a large tree.

Deficiency symptoms always occur on older leaves due to the mobility of potassium within the plant. There is generally no chlorosis or leaf color change associated with potassium deficiency, but rather a death of the leaf margins (Figure 6.2). On some species, irregular spots or lesions develop on the leaves that, at first, look like a disease. These spots are most severe on the older leaves and may be various shades of tan, light brown, or gray, depending on the plant species. On one occasion in Hawaii, foliage plants grown in a soil of volcanic ash with some peat added had severe potassium deficiency symptoms that had been misdiagnosed as various diseases (Figure 6.3). The confusion was accentuated in this case because:

a) 3:1:2 nitrogen, phosphorus, potassium ratio fertilizer was used, thus the managers thought there was little likelihood of potassium deficiency, however, the rate was low,
b) it was supplemented with additional nitrogen through the irrigation system,
c) the volcanic ash soil has the capacity to bind large quantities of phosphorus and potassium,
d) when a plant becomes weakened from a severe deficiency, it is more susceptible to various diseases, and
e) as soon as the lesions form on the leaves, secondary organisms begin a further attack on the dead and damaged tissues, making it difficult to distinguish between the primary cause and the secondary effects.

Potassium may be added as potassium chloride, potassium sulfate, or other sources. The needs of plants for potassium in field soils is difficult to define, in part because of the mobility and recycling of potassium. In general 150 to 300 pounds of potassium (expressed as K_2O) is sufficient for good plant growth. When soils contained potassium at this level, adding potassium **restricted** plant growth in a series of studies over several years in central Oklahoma. As with most nutrient elements, more is not better. Add nutrients only when the soil test shows a need, do not arbitrarily apply a 10-10-10 analysis fertilizer when only nitrogen is needed.

*Figure 6.2. Potassium deficiency on southern magnolia (**Magnolia grandiflora**). Note that the margin of the leaf is dead and dark brown to dark gray, while the inner portion of the leaf appears normal except for a few small dark spots just in from the dead leaf margin.*

*Figure 6.3. Potassium deficiency on **Dracena fragrans**. In this case the symptoms appear only as spots on the leaves until the deficiency becomes severe, and the lower leaves begin to die along the margin and finally collapse entirely. The leaf spots are frequently misdiagnosed as various diseases and make these foliage plants unsalable.*

Magnesium. Magnesium is a key element in the formation of chlorophyll and plays a vital role in several other plant processes. Magnesium is very mobile in the plant. Therefore, the symptoms develop first on the older leaves. However, **magnesium deficiency symptoms rarely develop the striking visual characteristics on woody plants as were noted for nitrogen, phosphorus and potassium, and the symptoms vary among species.** On most woody species, a slight yellowing of the outer margin of the older leaves is the extent of the visual symptoms. In most cases, the leaves drop before any further chlorosis develops (Figure 6.4). However, after some experience, the absence of older leaves on the plant and the more open appearance also become clues (Figure 6.5).

Magnesium deficiency on pittosporum *Pittosporum tobira* shrubs causes a slight yellowing of the margin of the older leaves near the center. As the deficiency becomes more severe the entire center portion of the leaf becomes chlorotic (Figure 6.6). *Podocarpus* spp. also show rather unusual magnesium deficiency symptoms. At first a faint loss of green color occurs in the center of the leaf followed by a progressive yellowing which eventually affects all but the tip of the leaf just prior to dropping (Figure 6.7).

Magnesium deficiency on flowering dogwood (*Cornus florida*) develops an interveinal chlorosis that is somewhat similar to iron and manganese deficiencies on this species, except the affected tissues remain light green to almost greenish white, whereas iron and manganese deficiencies cause a distinct yellowing and the symptoms are on older leaves as opposed to younger leaves. Magnesium deficiency on poinsettia also causes an interveinal chlorosis.

Figure 6.4.   The slight chlorosis or yellowing near the tip of the leaf is the only visual clue to magnesium deficiency on **Pyracantha coccinea** *(above) and* **Ilex cornuta** *'Burfordi Nana' (right two leaves).   The leaves drop soon after developing the symptoms. Therefore, there are few clues to magnesium deficiency.   The new leaves of the same holly (below, left) appear normal because magnesium is mobile in the plant and is shifted from the older leaves to the new growth.*

Figure 6.5.   The faint yellowing of the outer narrow margin of a southern magnolia (**Magnolia grandiflora**) leaf is the only visual symptom of magnesium deficiency before the leaf drops (top).   A magnesium-deficient magnolia is barren of internal leaves as the result of the early leaf drop.

Figure 6.6. Magnesium deficiency on **Pittosporum tobira**. *Note the slight yellowing of the sides of the leaf in the upper right hand section, whereas the entire center of the leaf to its left has yellowed. It is also important to observe that the young leaves in the lower portion of the photo are normal*

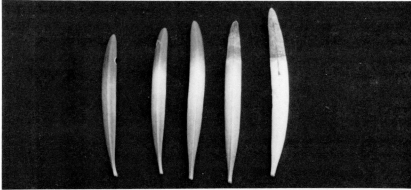

Figure 6.7. **Podocarpus** *spp. with magnesium deficiency progressing from the first visually detectable symptom on the left to the most severe symptom on the right. The earliest deficiency symptom is simply a reduction of the intensity of the green color in the center of the leaf.*

205

On some herbaceous plants, especially monocots such as dracenas and palms, the leaves are not dropped since no abscission (separation) layer is formed at the base of the leaf as on the dicots or woody plants. With these species, the leaves become more and more pale developing a yellow to yellow-green chlorosis, and finally tissues of the outer portion of the leaves begin to die.

With container-grown greenhouse and nursery stock, magnesium deficiency symptoms may be more dramatic and may appear very similar to severe iron deficiency. With the development of Micromax micronutrients, numerous cases of severe magnesium deficiency were misdiagnosed as iron deficiency, especially in some areas of Europe where little, if any, magnesium is normally added to the growth medium. When a mildly magnesium-deficient plant or seedling, that is also borderline deficient in one or more of the micronutrients, is planted in a growth medium with an abundance of micronutrients in the proper ratio, the magnesium deficiency abruptly becomes so severe that all leaves are affected, young and old alike. The leaf chlorosis symptoms in this case are nearly identical to iron deficiency and their appearance on young leaves makes diagnosis very deceptive. The answer becomes clear when a magnesium sulfate drench provides a response, whereas iron sprays have no effect.

Magnesium deficiency in plants is relatively slow to correct, compared to a deficiency of iron or manganese. Likewise, plants growing in containers are more responsive to supplemental magnesium than plants growing in the field or landscape. Once leaves have developed even mild magnesium deficiency, applying magnesium to the roots or spraying directly on the leaves is slow to provide a visual plant response. The new leaves continue to be green while the old leaves showing symptoms are unaffected. Only after the old leaves drop or are removed and sufficient new growth has occurred to provide a new plant canopy, are the symptoms eliminated (Figure 6.8). Another key factor on woody plants lies in the energy supply and distribution from the leaves to various plant parts. Gordon and Larson (4) showed that the carbohydrates from the young leaves were directed principally to the new shoots and developing buds, whereas carbohydrates from the older leaves provided the primary source of energy for the roots. Taking this one step further, any deficiency that affects the older leaves, especially if the old leaves drop, will have a great effect on root activity. Since magnesium deficiency is slow to correct and probably affects the root system most, the best advice is to plan a nutrition program to **prevent** a magnesium deficiency from developing rather than to try to correct the deficiency once it becomes visually apparent. Nurseries that prune frequently and severely tend to create greater problems with magnesium than nurseries that prune lightly. The reason is that with frequent pruning, much of the magnesium is removed in the new growth. Then, with further growth, the magnesium is translocated to the new growth from the older leaves, diluted even farther, and so on. Also keep in mind that a nutrient deficiency generally causes stunting long before visual symptoms appear.

*Figure 6.8.   Magnesium deficiency on schefflera (**Brassaia actinophylla**) causes an irregular blotching of the older leaves. These leaves will never regain their normal green color. Only after magnesium is supplied and sufficient growth has occurred to cover these leaves, or after the affected leaves are removed, will the symptoms disappear. By contrast, if this had been an iron or manganese deficiency, the leaves showing the symptoms would have regained their normal color quickly after the deficient element was provided*

The elements covered: nitrogen, phosphorus, potassium, and magnesium are **mobile** in the plant. Therefore, deficiency symptoms generally appear **on the older leaves.**

The elements following: sulfur, calcium, iron, manganese, copper, boron, zinc, and molybdenum are **not mobile** in the plant. Therefore, deficiency symptoms generally appear **on the new growth.** However, toxicity symptoms, especially boron, may appear on the older leaves.

Sulfur. Sulfur deficiency appears similar to nitrogen deficiency except the symptoms appear on the new leaves instead of the old leaves. Leaves become pale and, with severe conditions, develop a yellowing with the veins remaining darker than the leaf tissues between the veins. Sulfur is absorbed as $SO_4^=$ instead of elemental sulfur. There appears to be a relationship or balance between nitrogen and sulfate of approximately 20 to 1. When single superphosphate 0-20-0, $(N-P_2O_5-K_2O)$ was readily available and widely used, the 8% to 10% sulfate was more than adequate for all plants. More recently, however, with the use of triple superphosphate (0-46-0) and diammonium phosphate (18-46-0) in most fertilizers little or no sulfate is carried as impurities. Granular elemental sulfur (92% sulfur) provides a good semi-slow release source for most uses. Sulfur deficiencies on plants grown in containers are relatively common (Figure 6.9). Once sulfur is applied as a topdress to the growth medium, the symptoms disappear within a few days.

Micronutrient products such as Micromax and Perk, that are based on sulfate forms of micronutrients, generally supply enough sulfate to meet the 20 to 1 ratio with the nitrogen supply. Likewise, if a liquid fertilizer program is used where potassium sulfate or ammonium sulfate is part of the fertilizer program, adequate sulfur will be provided. Sulfate toxicity is highly unlikely but large quantities of sulfate would create a very low pH in the soil. With the paranoia regarding pH, no one has studied the effect of excess sulfate on plant growth.

Figure 6.9. Sulfur deficiency symptoms on geranium. The leaf on the left is from the newest growth and has the most severe symptoms while the leaf on the right is from the oldest part of the plant and shows only a slight off-color and loss of luster compared to a non-deficient plant. Nitrogen deficiency could appear very similar, except that the location of the symptom on the plant would be reversed because sulfur is not mobile in the plant, whereas nitrogen is very mobile.

Calcium. Calcium is rarely deficient since some calcium source, generally calcium carbonate or dolomite (which is calcium and magnesium carbonate), is widely used to adjust the pH of soils. In addition, most soils contain sufficient calcium for plant growth even when soil pH is relatively low. However, as plant nutrition becomes more precise to further accelerate growth, specific calcium levels may be required. The **excess** calcium added to raise the pH of soils may actually suppress plant growth in many instances. Because no visual symptoms occur from the excess calcium, or if chlorosis does occur, it is blamed on the high pH or micronutrient difficiencies and not the calcium; the high levels of calcium are generally ignored or thought to be acceptable. About 600 to 1000 pounds of available calcium per acre is sufficient for most plants. Likewise, the "ideal" pH for most woody plants is between 5.0 and 6.0. this is lower than many publications suggest. This is covered in greater detail elsewhere in this book.

Since most irrigation waters contain calcium, many plants are constantly being supplied with this element. Calcium is a strong cation and attaches readily to the exchange sites on the soil. This gradual accumulation of calcium slowly raises the pH of many irrigated soils.

Calcium is not mobile in plant tissues, therefore, if a deficiency develops, it will be noticeable first and most severely on the new growth (Figure 6.10). Applications of calcium will eliminate the deficiency symptom in a few days. On woody plants the terminal buds on the uppermost branches may die when calcium is severely deficient, with or without any chlorosis pattern. The older leaves may be brittle and will cup or curl upwards on some species.

Figure 6.10. This young geranium plant was grown in a mix of peat and perlite with no calcium added. Even under these conditions and no calcium in the water, the first leaves appeared normal. Then slowly the symptoms began to appear. The photo was taken looking down on the top of the plant. Note the dark older leaves and progressive symptoms with the newer leaves. Dolomite was applied to the surface of the medium and within four days, all symptoms had disappeared.

The Micro Elements.   Iron. Iron deficiency is common on many species grown in alkaline soils.   Iron deficiency is also common where high levels of calcium from calcium containing materials such as lime, dolomite, the water source, bicarbonates, or some component in the soil ties up the iron in insoluble compounds. High levels of phosphorus, either alone or in conjunction with calcium, may also tie up iron in insoluble complexes.

Iron is not mobile in the plant, therefore, symptoms are generally   most severe   on new   growth.   Iron deficiency first appears as pale green in the leaf tissues between the veins, then progresses to yellow-green to yellow (Figure 6.11).

*Figure 6.11.   Iron deficiency of Chinese hibiscus (**Hibiscus rosa-sinensis**).   Note that the veins in the leaf are darker while the areas of the leaf blade farthest from the veins are most affected.*

The symptoms are virtually identical to manganese deficiency symptoms on most species.   Iron and manganese react similarly to calcium and phosphorus or high pH situations.   In many cases what is diagnosed as an iron deficiency may be a manganese deficiency or even more likely, a moderate deficiency of both elements (Figure 6.12).

*Figure 6.12. Azaleas (**Rhododendron** X 'Hinodegiri'), grown with a low level of iron (left) and a low level of both iron and manganese (right). Interestingly, the overall size of the plants was about the same as plants with adequate levels of both elements. However, the number of flower buds were greatly reduced on the deficient plants.*

Iron is most noted for its presence in the chlorophyll of the leaves. In the chloroplasts, iron plays a role in the synthesis of proteins. Iron also plays a role in the function of other enzymes. Iron can be supplied to plants by foliar sprays, root zone treatments or quite often simply reducing the pH of the soil will release enough iron from the complexes with calcium to meet the plants' needs.

Manganese. Manganese is not mobile in the plant and reacts similarly to iron in many respects. It is also essential in the synthesis of chlorophyll and is similarly affected by calcium and phosphorus. Therefore, the deficiency symptoms of manganese and iron are virtually identical. Only the foolish or the very knowledgeable try to distinguish between visual iron and manganese deficiency symptoms on most species. There are, however, some distinct differences on some species. Mouse-ear disease on pecan is caused by a deficiency of manganese, but in this case, no chlorosis occurs, only the distortion of the leaflet from the normal pointed or oval shape to an unusual blunted end (Figure 6.13). **Ixora coccinea** is apparently a poor absorber of manganese so it is most often the deficient element causing the chlorosis of this otherwise very attractive shrub (Figure 6.14).

*Figure 6.13. A pecan (**Carya illinoinensis**) leaflet with manganese deficiency. Because of the deformity of the leaflet, which normally has a pointed tip, it has been dubbed mouse-ear disease. Because manganese availability is affected by soil temperatures, it is most common in early spring when soils are cold and may disappear with warmer weather. Generally no chlorosis is visible*

Manganese solubility is affected by the temperature of soils. As the temperature of soils decreases, so does manganese solubility. Therefore, deficiencies are most likely to occur during low soil temperatures. The ratio of manganese to iron is quite specific. An excess of either frequently causes a deficiency of the other.

*Figure 6.14.   Leaves of **Ixora coccinea** showing typical manganese deficiency. Deficient plants also flower poorly.*

Copper. Copper plays a key role in several enzymatic systems. The most common deficiency symptom is the stunting of overall growth (Figure 6.15) followed by leaf stunting, a loss of leaf luster and leaf size, leaf distortion (Figure 6.16), and on some species, rosetting of buds on the branch terminal after the terminal bud has died (Figure 6.17).   There is generally no chlorosis or leaf discoloration symptoms associated with either copper deficiency or toxicity.   However, copper deficiency on roses (*Rosa* spp.) sometimes gives a general mottled or flecking pattern that appears like damage from a heavy population of mites (Figure 6.18).   Copper deficiency is most likely to occur on high organic soils and plants in landscape beds with high levels of organic matter.

214

*Figure 6.15. Japanese holly (**Ilex crenata** 'Convexa') with copper deficiency (left), and a normal plant (right). Note the dull leaf surface on the deficient plant compared to the healthy plant.*

*Figure 6.16. Leaf distortion of waxleaf ligustrum (**Ligustrum japonicum**), caused by a mild copper deficiency. A normal leaf of this species is waxy, glossy green and smooth with no undulations on the leaf surface.*

*Figure 6.17. Severe copper deficiency on natal plum (**Carissa grandiflora** 'Boxwood Beauty'). Note the clustering of buds where the terminal bud should be and the very small leaves compared to the older normal leaves. In this case, a young plant was placed in a mix of Florida peat and sand with no micronutrients added. The result was an abrupt and very striking copper deficiency.*

*Figure 6.18. Copper deficiency on rose (**Rosa** spp.). Note the fine flecking pattern similar to damage from a severe infestation of mites.*

216

Zinc. Zinc deficiency is common in pecans but uncommon with other species. Unlike iron, manganese and copper, as the soil pH changes, zinc solubility is affected slightly or not at all. Zinc toxicity is also rare.

Boron. Boron deficiency is not common, even in the synthetic or man-made "soil" mixes for containers. It is difficult to create a boron deficiency even when adding no boron but all other micronutrients at the normal rates and growing the plants for two growing seasons in the same growth medium. This is probably due to the minute amounts required and the fact that most irrigation water contains some boron. Dickey et al. (1) noted that boron deficiency symptoms caused an abnormal thickening of leaves and, in some cases, stems became shorter and abnormally thick and stiff and the terminal buds sometimes died or aborted.

Boron toxicity, on the other hand, is much more common (2, 3). **Excess boron tends to accumulate in the older leaves** of a plant and causes a faint yellowing or chlorosis of the leaf margin followed by necrosis or death of the leaf tip and margins (5) (Figure 6.19). Boron toxicity is frequently caused by excess boron in irrigation waters or in micronutrient fertilizers. Improving the copper to boron ratio and iron to copper ratio may reduce injury. In one case, where a micronutrient fertilizer with high boron caused injury, adding another micronutrient fertilizer with high iron and copper eliminated the boron toxicity symptoms. However, this is not a recommended practice.

Figure 6.19. Boron toxicity on chrysanthemum. Note the faint yellowing of the leaf margin and death of the leaf tips of the older leaves. Old leaves may show severe toxicity symptoms while the new growth appears normal.

Molybdenum. Molybdenum is required in very small quantities in plants, but nonetheless is very essential. Molybdenum is required for the transformation of nitrate nitrogen into amino acids. Therefore one of the key symptoms of a molybdenum deficiency is a pale green color of the plant that at first appears as nitrogen deficiency. Deficiency symptoms generally appear on the youngest leaves, but may appear on older leaves as well. Molybdenum deficiency on chrysanthemums causes a lighter-than-normal green color at first, but as the deficiency progresses, leaves become pale green and lighter along the margins of the youngest leaves (Figure 6.20). The light margin color is white to cream, not yellow as in boron toxicity, and generally the tips or margins of the leaves do not die.

Molybdenum deficiency on Chinese hibiscus (*Hibiscus rosa-sinensis*) was, at one time, very common in Florida landscapes, especially on the very sandy and marl soils of south Florida. The deficiency, dubbed strap-leaf disease, caused the normally oval leaves to become narrow, rough-surfaced, thick and leathery.

Superphosphate and many sources of dolomite contain minute quantities of molybdenum as an impurity. As nutritional programs for phosphorus, calcium and magnesium become more precise, molybdenum deficiency may become more common.

Figure 6.20. Molybdenum deficiency on chrysanthemums. Note the pale color of the leaves and lack of sheen. Symptoms appear on some of the older leaves, but the younger leaves are most affected. The leaf margin becomes white or cream-colored, not yellow, as in boron toxicity.

Literature Cited

1. Dickey, R.D., E.W. McElwee, C.A. Conover and J.H. Joiner. 1978. Container growing of woody ornamental nursery plants in Florida. Fla. Agri. Exp. Sta. Res. Bulletin 793.

2. Eaton, F.M. 1944. Deficiency, toxicity and accumulation of boron in plants. Jour. Agri. Res. 69:237-277.

3. Gilliam, C.H. and E.M. Smith. 1980. Sources and symptoms of boron toxicity in container-grown woody ornamentals. Jour. of Arboriculture 6:209-212.

4. Gordon, John C. and P.R. Larson. 1970. Redistribution of C-labeled reserve food in young red pines during shoot elongation. Forest Sci. 16:14-20.

5. Kohl, H.C. and J.J. Oertli. 1961. Distribution of boron in leaves. Plant Physiol. 36:420-421.

CHAPTER 7

REBUILDING FIELD NURSERY SOILS

REBUILDING FIELD NURSERY SOILS

Ideal nursery soils for field production are generally described as deep friable soils of good tilth. Unfortunately, the ideal does not exist in many locations and if a near-ideal soil existed when the nursery was begun, it is a different story after a few years of production.

The problems of soil management in a field nursery are related to several factors:

a) Many nursery operations must be done while soils are wet, thus soil compaction becomes a major problem.

b) In nursery operations where tree spades, fabric containers or B & B techniques are used, the removal of soil with each plant also removes some of the top soil containing the organic matter, the portion responsible for good soil tilth.

c) Normal farming operations and crop removal deplete various nutrient elements in the soil and influence nutrient availability.

Subsoiling. Water, aeration and nutrition are the greatest factors limiting plant growth. If roots function deeper in the soil as a result of improved aeration, more moisture and nutrients are available in the expanded volume of soil. On the other hand, when soils are compacted and roots are especially shallow, the moisture and nutrients available are limited. One very effective, yet little used technique to aid in soil aeration and root function at greater depths, is subsoiling. A subsoiler consists of one or more vertical shanks 18 to 24 inches long that can be attached to a tractor and pulled through the soil. Subsoilers designed with a lifting toe at the bottom are the most effective. In some cases, additional weights may be needed to get penetration into the compacted subsoil (Figure 7.1).

To be most effective, the subsoilers should be four feet apart. Make two passes across the field, the second at roughly a 60 degree angle to the first. Subsoiling should be done between each crop or every two to three years with most soils. Even sandy soils will be more productive when subsoiling is practiced every two or three years since normal plowing, cultivation or discing and other nursery operations on the surface compact the soil.

222

Figure 7.1. This single-shank subsoiler is equipped with a lifting toe to enhance loosening of the soil (above). An effective subsoiler should cause a distinct ridge on the soil surface as a result of the lifting and loosening of the soil (below).

223

Soil Building Crops. Green manure crops have long been used to add organic matter and maintain good soil tilth. The incorporated organic matter also serves as a reservoir for nutrients and water in the soil. Unlike many farming operations, many field nurseries do a poor job of soil management, particularly in the utilization of green manure crops.

In 1972, two fields were cleared of overgrown nursery stock and a soil rebuilding study began. The soils were of two types: a heavy clay loam and a sandy loam. Both soils were very compacted from years of repeated discing for weed control and since nothing had been added back to the soil, the organic matter content was very low. Plants could only be dug B & B during a brief period following a rain. Plant roots were shallow and poorly branched, indicating very low soil oxygen levels.

During the 1973 and 1974 growing seasons, soybeans and hybrid sudan (also known as Sudex, 'Hay Grazer', or 'Good Grazing') were used as green manure crops. All crops were planted in mid May and made good initial growth, however, by late July the soybeans were fully grown and ready to be turned under. This left the soil exposed and subject to weed growth until fall planting in late September.

The hybrid sudan reached a height of five to six feet by mid June and began developing seed heads (Figure 7.2). At that time, it was mowed at a height of approximately eight inches and allowed to sucker from the crowns for a second flush. Following the second mowing, regrowth was slow due to drought conditions but nonetheless, regrowth resulted in four mowings during the season. Because of the mat of organic matter on the soil surface and competition from the sudan, weeds were not a problem. (The thick growth shaded out most weeds since they are mostly high light-requiring plants.)

Since that time, other soil-building crops such as yellow clover and German millet have been studied. An assortment of tree and shrub species have been grown in soils with residue from all four of these crops without complication or measurable growth restriction.

Figure 7.2. Hybrid sudan grows very fast under warm soil conditions with good fertility and moisture. Mow just before the seed heads appear to avoid the pollen and/or seed when mowing. Each time the plants are cut, they will tiller (develop secondary shoots) and become thicker than before, providing a tremendous amount of organic matter in one growing season.

Using a rotation of three years nursery stock and one summer soil building crop, both soils are now manageable and productive. The following six-step approach appears most productive:

1) Subsoil as described earlier.
2) Soil test before planting the green manure crop.

225

Phosphorus should be between 60 and 100 pounds per acre (30 to 50 ppm). Potassium should be between 150 and 300 pounds per acre (75 to 150 ppm). If either of these elements are low, they should be added using the most economical source (generally 0-46-0, triple superphosphate and 0-0-60, potassium chloride also called muriate-of-potash). If the soil pH is below 5.0, add dolomite lime to raise the soil pH to 5.6 or 6.0. If the soil pH is above 7.0, add elemental sulfur to drop the pH to about 6.0. Any materials added for phosphorus, potassium or soil pH adjustment should be incorporated into the soil by plowing, discing or rototilling.

3) Add nitrogen **just before** planting the green manure crop. Unless the soil test for nitrogen is 50 or higher, 100 to 200 pounds of nitrogen per acre should be added using the most economical source (urea, 46-0-0 or ammonium nitrate, 33-0-0). If soil moisture is not generally a mid summer growth-limiting factor and if labor is generally available during late June or July, the nitrogen application can be split into a planting application and a mid summer application for better utilization of nitrogen and a greater production of organic matter.

4) Plant the hybrid sudan (Sudex) as soon as the soil is warm (when tomatoes are growing well in the garden). Use a seeding rate of approximately 30 pounds per acre. Because the soil fertility is high and you want to produce the maximum organic matter, both by the tops and the roots, the higher-than-normal seeding rate is needed. The dense stand also shades out most weeds, including perennial pests such as bermudagrass.

5) Mow the sudan whenever seed heads appear (three to five times during a season). Generally, this will be when the plants are five to six feet tall. If mowing is done before the seeds mature, there will be no "weed" problem with the sudan seed the following season. Also, if it is mowed at the first sign of seed heads, the pollen level will not aggravate the tractor operator.

6) Prior to frost, mow again and plow under the organic matter to a depth of 8 to 12 inches. One-, three- and five-gallon container-grown trees of many species have been successfully fall-planted into this soil in October. No complications or stunting could be measured when compared with adjacent areas of the fields without the sudan treatment. However, **if** the sudan is grown without adding nitrogen during the spring or summer **and** no nitrogen is added at the time of fall planting, newly planted trees and shrubs may suffer from nitrogen deficiency, particularly

for a period following plowing of the organic matter unless 50 to 100 pounds of nitrogen per acre is applied.

7) The following spring an additional soil test should be done. Any phosphorus or potassium deficiency should be corrected to bring phosphorus and potassium levels up to levels noted in step 1. Remember that you now have a slow-release nitrogen and other nutrient sources in the organic matter, thus the rate of nitrogen used the following year can be somewhat lower than normal.

This system provides for maximum growth of the green manure crop. The large quantity of organic matter added to the soil, both from tops and roots, will improve soil tilth for up to three years. Every time the tops of the plants are cut, a substantial portion of the root system dies. However, with the tillering (branch development) of the crown, and new top growth, new roots expand into new soil areas. It is the combination of roots growing through the soil, dying and regrowing along with the organic matter added from both the tops and roots that makes this program so effective (Figure 7.3). A crop rotation such that every third or fourth year a green manure crop is grown will aid in the improved nursery stock growth and quality while also improving the root system and thereby reduce the time and complication associated with digging. If a field is cleared of nursery stock in the spring, the field can be prepared and the hybrid sudan program completed in time for fall planting of container stock. This eliminates the loss of a growing season in the overall production scheme.

It should be noted that the procedure just described is providing a soil amendment. **This is a very desirable process as long as** the entire field is amended. This is in direct contrast to much published data by this author and others showing soil amendments in the planting hole to be **undesirable**. The difference is the soil amendments used most in landscape plantings are "hard" organic matter in that they are highly weathered (peat) or biproducts of woody plants (bark). By contrast, the residue from the sudex or other crop is "soft" organic matter and contains the entire nutrient complex used in growing that plant, **plus** the distribution is throughout the soil profile vs. only a narrow band around a newly planted tree or shrub in the landscape.

227

Figure 7.3. Root growth of hybrid sudan in a sandy loam soil. In this case, when the field was plowed in the spring it turned over in chunks the size of sofa cushions. Once over with a disc still left a very rough field. The seed was broadcast using a rotary fertilizer spreader/seeder then disc again to provide some incorporation and about 150 pounds of nitrogen per acre was also broadcast. At the end of the growing season when the field was plowed it was mellow and friable.

Interplantings. Another procedure that works very well is to interplant a soil-building crop between rows of nursery stock. If nursery stock is planted on 10- to 12-foot rows, the opportunity exists to grow a soil-building crop between the rows. For example, if rows are on 10-foot centers, a 5-foot strip down the center between rows could be planted to a soil-building crop and still leave a 2.5-foot clear zone on either side. This clear zone could be cultivated or maintained vegetation-free with herbicides. This technique is especially useful on land subject to erosion. It provides a cover over part of the soil surface yet the growth/ competition restriction of the crop is minimal (Figure 7.4).

Figure 7.4. A sloping field (right to left) of erodible soil using interplantings. To the left is a roadway of K-31 fescue, then open soil, a row of young crapemyrtle shrubs, open soil, alfalfa as an intercrop, open soil, young crapemyrtles and so on up the slope.

After a crop is harvested, the field should be subsoiled if necessary, plowed, fertilized if needed, and prepared for the next crop. When the next crop is planted, the rows should be shifted so that they are located over the previous soil-building crop. A new planting of the soil-building crop would then be made between the rows...in the space previously occupied by the trees or other nursery stock. This shifting process would be reversed again with the next crop.

Various nitrogen fixing legumes have been tried. Red clover, crimson clover, alfalfa, white Dutch clover, and arrowleaf clover have been studied. Alfalfa is a deep-rooted perennial with good soil-loosening/building capacity, but it does not remain dense enough to restrict weed invasion without the assistance of herbicides. Red and crimson clover produce seed that becomes a weed in the rows of nursery stock and do not provide much soil cover during the major portion of the growing season since they are winter annuals. Perennial white Dutch clover does not have sufficient drought tolerance and tends to die out in the summer. Arrowleaf clover is too tall and invasive to be acceptable and since it is also a winter annual, leaves the soil exposed during summer and early fall. Of the various species tested by the author, alfalfa has performed best. However, the search for a better intercrop legume will continue. Under current study is Korean lespedeza. Grasses such as K-31 fescue and orchard grass have been tried. Grasses that do not creep by stolons and thus stay put are much preferred for intercrops. However, all grasses are very competitive and restrict the growth of woody plants.

CHAPTER 8

SPRING VS. FALL PLANTING

SPRING VS. FALL PLANTING

There is a distinct advantage to fall planting of container-grown nursery stock in the field in hardiness zones 6 and southward. Further north, the timing of fall planting is more critical but the concept still has merit. Knowledge of plant root and top functions relative to the growing season suggests fall planting may have advantages over spring planting (Table 8.1). In addition, fall planting has the advantage of utilizing field space in the fall after spring harvest and sales. By clearing a field in the spring and planting in the fall, a convenient time exists for a soil building crop such as hybrid sudan (see the chapter on rebuilding nursery soils). If container-grown plants are to be planted into the field, it is much better to have them developing roots in the field than potentially losing roots to cold temperatures above ground while waiting for spring planting.

Table 8.1. Contrasting spring vs fall conditions supports fall planting of container-grown nursery stock, where the root system is not disturbed at time of planting.

- -

	Spring	Fall
Day length	increasing	decreasing
Air temperature	warm-increasing	cool-decreasing
Soil temperature	cool/cold	warm
Soil moisture	good to excessive	fair-good
Soil oxygen level	low to moderate	moderate to good
Leaf water loss	new leaves-high	old leaves-low
Stored energy level in the plant	low, after spring flush	very high

----

Fall planting of container-grown nursery stock can provide a tremendous advantage over spring planting for some species (1). For example, eighteen two-year-old plants of each of the following species on November 6 and 7 in a field of clay loam soil:

Chinese pistache, *Pistacia chinensis*
Japanese black pine, *Pinus thunbergiana*
cluster pine, *Pinus pinaster*
bur oak, *Quercus macrocarpa*
dwarf burford holly, *Ilex cornuta* 'Burford Dwarf'

bur oak, *Quercus macrocarpa*
dwarf burford holly, *Ilex cornuta* 'Burford Dwarf'
pfitzer juniper, *Juniperus chinensis* 'Pfitzeriana'
sawtooth oak, *Quercus acutissima*

At the same time, 12 plants of similar size and quality were heavily mulched with ground pine bark in their original containers and held for spring planting. Container sizes were one-gallon for the pfitzer juniper, dwarf burford holly, Chinese pistache and Japanese black pine; and three-gallon for the cluster pine, bur oak and sawtooth oak. The growth medium for all species had been a 2:1:1 mix of ground pine bark, peat moss and sand.

No soil amendments or fertilizers were used in the planting holes and all plants were watered in three times by hand. Rainfall was very limited during the winter period with only 4.2 inches occurring between November 6 and March 19 when one-third of the fall-planted trees and shrubs were dug.

The winter period during this study had minimum temperatures of minus three degrees Fahrenheit on two occasions. However, it was a mild winter by central Oklahoma standards, and the soil did not freeze below about three inches.

On March 19, six plants of each species that had been fall-planted were selected at random to evaluate root growth during the dormant period. There were no leaves present on the deciduous species when planted and at the time of evaluation no new top growth had begun. All species had developed some new roots during the dormant period (Figure 8.1). Sawtooth oak, bur oak, cluster pine, Japanese black pine and pfitzer juniper developed the most roots with some roots extending as far as ten to twelve inches beyond the original face of the container ball. Fewer roots were observed on the Chinese pistache (a tree known for its growth during hot, dry weather) and dwarf burford holly. One interesting factor observed was that all roots extending beyond the original container ball were not "new roots" but were extensions of roots that were in the container at the time of planting the previous fall. That is, new roots in the surrounding soil could be followed back to the container and around, or into, the container ball. New roots had branched very little, although tremendous quantities of root hairs were present. This shows that roots of container-grown plants in soilless mixes will readily grow into the surrounding soil during the winter period. It also suggests that the new roots growing around the container when it was

233

planted were not fixed in that position, as has been previously theorized and readily grew into the surrounding soil (1 and 2). Root growth was aided by the **absence** of soil amendments. Whitcomb et al. (7) and Schulte and Whitcomb (6) reported that when soil amendments were used in the back fill when planting trees or shrubs, the root growth beyond the amended back fill soil was restricted.

Figure 8.1. Typical root growth of bur oak from a container. Photo taken March 19, following planting November 7. The broken black line is the end of the original container ball. No leaves were present at time of planting and bud swell had not yet occurred in the spring when this photo was taken.

Following excavation of 1/3 of the fall-planted plants in the spring, the 12 plants of each species that were mulched-in over the winter were planted in the same field. All plants were fertilized with one pound 10-20-0 per 25 square feet (175 pounds of nitrogen per acre). On October 21, six spring- and six fall-transplants were selected at random, dug and evaluated for further root growth after one full growing season. Top growth, stem caliper and number of branches, were taken from all 12

234

replications. All plants were dug at approximately the same depth with a backhoe with a 24-inch wide bucket. In all cases, many roots were still in the shape of the original container, providing an easy separation point for roots in the container from those developed in the surrounding soil, hereafter referred to for brevity, as old roots and new roots.

After one growing season (seven months after spring planting and 11 months after fall planting), Japanese black pine, bur oak and sawtooth oak had more new roots, old roots, total roots, top weight, stem caliper and height when fall-planted, than when spring-planted (Figure 8.2). Stem caliper and height of bur oak was strikingly favored by fall planting (Figure 8.3). Pfitzer junipers had slightly more roots when planted in the spring, however, top weight was greater when fall-planted. Cluster pine and Chinese pistache responded similarly to the juniper, in that there was no advantage to fall planting for these species, but there was no damage or injury.

All plants of all species survived fall planting except the dwarf burford holly. Survival of the dwarf burford holly in this study was poor. Of the 18 planted in the fall, nine died during the winter. In addition, in the open field with no supplemental irrigation during the summertime, several of the fall- and spring-planted dwarf burford holly died prior to termination of step two of the experiment in the fall of the following year. The location of this study was such that a portable irrigation system could not be utilized and only hand watering was possible. In an adjacent field with similar soil, 45 of 47 fall-planted dwarf burford holly survived in a separate experiment using plants from the same uniformly grown container material. The difference was due to about one inch of water applied by irrigation sprinklers on two occasions following planting of this container material. Thus the contrast in survival at the two locations was probably due to soil moisture and not the winter conditions or planting time.

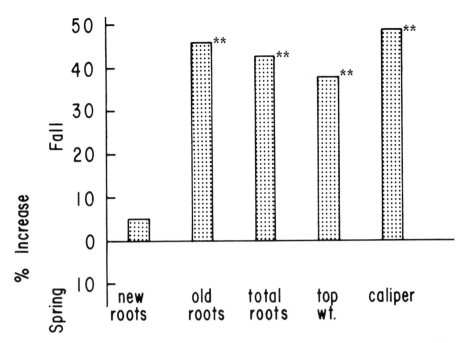

*Figure 8.2. Comparison of fall vs. spring planting expressed as percent increase for sawtooth oak (**Quercus acutissima**). Japanese black pine and bur oak responded similarly. Had more roots developed as a result of spring planting, the bar would have been below the 0 line.*

In another fall vs. spring planting study, only top growth at the end of one growing season was evaluated and no complex root examinations were done (8).

Uniform plants of river birch (*Betula nigra*), deodar cedar (*Cedrus deodara*), shumard oak (*Quercus shumardi*), mugo pine (*Pinus mugo*) and pyracantha (*Pyracantha* X 'Mojave') in two-gallon containers were planted in the field on October 28. Plants of identical size were held in an unheated polyethylene-covered greenhouse and planted on April 16. Plants were evaluated on November 20 for survival, height, stem caliper and in some cases, the number of branches. The summer had been quite hot and dry and the plants received **no** supplemental irrigation following planting. Spring rains were accomodating through June 28, but no meaningful rainfall occurred again until September 28 in north central Oklahoma where the study was done.

236

Figure 8.3. Bur oak stem caliper, fall-planted (left) and spring-planted (right). The fall-planted trees had better developed root systems for support the following summer and experienced less stress which especially favored stem caliper increase which occurs mostly in the fall.

The results can best be summarized by two photos (Figures 8.4 and 8.5). Every river birch, deodar cedar and shumard oak survived, regardless of treatment, although growth differences were sizeable. The only pyracantha that died were from those planted in the spring. All mugo pine eventually died, however, the sequence of death supported the concept of fall planting. In late July a few of the spring-planted mugo pines began to show severe moisture stress. By August 10, all spring-planted mugo pines were dead. At that time, all of the fall-planted mugo pines looked thrifty. By August 24, several of the fall-planted mugo pines began to show severe moisture stress and all were dead by the September 15 evaluation date.

Figure 8.4. River birch planted in the spring (left) and planted in the fall (right). All plants survived the summer with no irrigation, however, the growth and visual appearance of the trees clearly emphasize the benefit of fall planting.

Figure 8.5 Pyracantha planted in the spring (left) and fall (right). The spring-planted shrub on the left is dead, the fall-planted one has dense foliage at the end of the summer drought and showed no symptoms of moisture stress.

238

Two additional studies have been conducted by the author with several species and different seasons. The results have consistently supported fall planting or if there was no advantage, there was certainly no disadvantage or injury.

These data suggest that with most species, there is a decided advantage in terms of root growth, top growth, and, in some cases, stem caliper, to planting in the fall versus spring-planting identical plants grown in the same conditions and containers. Species such as juniper, cluster pine, and Chinese pistache are very heat-tolerant and this probably explains why there was no particular advantage to fall planting. Growth of some species was strikingly greater when fall-planted as opposed to planting in the spring (Figure 8.3).

Most plants could be developing roots during the winter in the field or landscape if fall-planted instead of being held in some type of overwintering apparatus. In addition, the overwintering apparatus is expensive and difficult to construct and maintain.

It is important to re-emphasize that these plants were all grown in containers prior to planting in the field. In addition, the roots that developed during the wintertime were extensions of roots that were already present in the container at the time of planting and thus grew out into the surrounding soil. **A great deal depends on the condition of the plant. Fall planting of container-grown nursery stock that is root bound would no doubt be less than satisfactory!**

With bare root plants and, to some degree, balled and burlapped plants, initiation of new roots must come from the cut ends of older, larger roots and this process is very dependent on a chemical signal from the terminal buds. Richardson (5) reported that after silver maple had been dug bare root, no new roots developed until the buds expanded in the spring. This has been observed by the author many times. Because of this factor, **bare root trees and shrubs should not** be planted in the fall.

The prime reason roots developed readily into the surrounding field was due to the high energy level in the plant. This was provided by a slow-release fertilizer system in the growth medium in the container (5). In addition, the **absence** of soil amendments incorporated into the back fill around the trees or shrubs enhanced lateral root development (5, 6).

239

It is also important to note that these studies were done with trees and shrubs started in the spring so they were in prime condition in the fall or the following spring. If plants were prime for planting in the fall or spring and held over until the next fall, to compare spring vs. fall establishment, the fall planting would be poor, not because of the conditions in the fall but because of the severe root bound and stunted condition of the plants.

A recent study conducted in Kentucky with only southern magnolia showed no advantage to fall planting (3). They did not reveal the planting conditions or condition of the roots and root ball at planting time, therefore no firm conclusions can be drawn from such a limited study.

Mulching of the soil surface adjacent to the newly fall-planted tree or shrub, to retard the cooling of the soil and assist moisture and temperature relationships would probably stimulate further development of roots during the fall and early winter period. This author has studied 16 species over four growing (winter) seasons and firmly endorses fall planting of container-grown nursery stock.

Literature Cited

1. Dickinson, Sancho and Carl E. Whitcomb. 1977. The effects of spring vs fall planting on establishment of landscape plants. Nursery Res. Jour. 4:9-19.

2. McGuire, John J. 1972. Growing ornamental plants in containers: a handbook for the nurseryman. Univ. of Rhode Island Ext. Bulletin. 197. 39 pages.

3. McNeil, Robert, David Hensley, and Richard Sundheim. 1989. Magnolia grandiflora. Nursery Manager 5(2):62-66.

4. Reisch, K.W. 1957. Propagating plants directly in containers by means of hardwood cuttings. Proc. Int. Plant Prop. Soc. 7:78-81.

5. Richardson S.D. 1953. Root growth of *Acer pseudoplatanus*, L. in relation to grass cover and nitrogen deficiency. Meded. Landbouw. Wageningen. 53:75-07.

6. Schulte, Joseph R. and Carl E. Whitcomb. 1975. Effects of soil amendments and fertilizer levels on the establishment of silver maple. Jour. of Arboriculture. 1:192-195.

7. Whitcomb, Carl E., Robert L. Byrnes, Joseph R. Schulte and James D. Ward. 1976. What is a $5 planting hole? Amer. Nurseryman 144(2):14, 22.

8. Whitcomb, Carl E. 1984. Another look at fall planting. Okla. Agri. Exp. Sta. Res. Rept. P-855:28-29.

CHAPTER 9

WATER RELATIONSHIPS OF CONTAINER-GROWN PLANTS

WATER RELATIONSHIPS OF CONTAINER-GROWN PLANTS

Large liners in one-gallon or larger containers have appeal and are widely used when establishing field plantings in the South. The assumption is made by some that a container-grown liner is "better". In general, the plant does experience less stress during the transplanting/establishment process, especially if it is planted in the fall and **is not** root-bound, but it is important to understand the benefits and risks.

Plants grown in containers, if handled properly, have 100% of the roots retained at transplanting. In theory this should mean minimal plant stress since none of the roots are either disturbed or lost. Unfortunately the water-air relationships in a container growth medium and the restrictions imposed by the limited root volume make plants grown in conventional containers less than ideal, especially when planted during late spring or summer when the rate of water loss from the top is high.

Water Movement in Soils. One of the basic principles of soil physics is that **water will move from a coarse-textured material (or soil) to a fine-textured material (or soil) but it will not move from a fine-textured material to a coarse-textured material until it is saturated.** This is due to capillarity, the adhesive forces (attraction of water to the surfaces of soil particles) and cohesive forces (the attraction of water for water). (This is why it is possible to fill a glass with water above the top of the rim). Because of the perched water table in the bottom of every container*, the mixture of materials or growth medium in the container cannot be soil. Water drains through normal field soils via capillary action and percolation and the greater the porosity and depth of the soil, the more rapid the movement of water downward. Even in heavy soils, if the soil depth is several feet, the movement of water occurs at a moderate rate. **On the other hand, since the growth medium in the container is more coarse in texture than the surrounding soil in the field or landscape--any surrounding soil--water is quickly drawn away from the container growth medium and the plant suffers from drought, even though the surrounding soil may be adequately moist to support plant growth.**

*Perched water table defined: In the field or landscape, nearly all soils have a water table at some depth. A perched water table is one abnormally high or "perched" above the normal water table. The abrupt textural difference between the mix in the container and the open drain hole prevents the water from exiting. Water will flow out of the drain holes in the bottom of the container only when the weight of the water above is sufficient to force out the water at the bottom against the adhesive and cohesive forces that hold the water. Even after part of the water exits, considerable water will remain in the bottom of the container. As soon as the weight of the water on top is no longer enough to force water out the bottom, drainage stops. As soon as the container is removed and the plant is placed in field soil there is no perched water table and the water is drawn out of the container growth medium very quickly.

The situation becomes even more complicated when the alternative condition occurs. If an abundance of moisture is applied to the surface of the container growth medium following planting, root suffocation is likely to occur, especially when soils have a moderate to high clay content (Figure 9.1). Since the container growth medium is more coarse in texture (has larger pores or openings) than the surrounding soil, water percolates into the container growth medium more quickly and creates a "bathtub" effect, whereby the roots may be suffocated if a) watering persists for sufficient time or b) if the soil is sufficiently heavy to restrict relatively rapid water movement. If enough water is applied often enough, the roots will likely be suffocated, even in soils with good drainage characteristics.
The difference in rate of percolation between container growth medium and surrounding soil is easily demonstrated using two containers with similar volumes of water. Pour the water from one container directly onto the surface of the container growth medium of a tree or shrub that has been recently planted into the soil. A few feet away pour water from the other container onto the soil surface. The rapid percolation of water into the container growth medium shows why plants grown in containers and planted into soil are **much more** likely to suffer from over watering and root suffocation when watered by hand as opposed to sprinklers or natural rainfall. An exception would be where the surface of the soil slopes to the area of the container or where a depression occurs around the container growth medium such that surface water from irrigation or rainfall drains into the porous mix.

Figure 9.1. The newly planted container-grown tree is wilting but the surrounding clay soil is quite moist. Inspection of the original container growth medium shows it to be very dry. Since tree roots have not yet grown into the surrounding clay the water in the clay is not available to the tree. All water used by the leaves must come from the original container growth medium. In addition, the clay quickly draws water out of the growth medium since the clay is much finer in texture. The opposite complication can also occur. When a rainy period occurs, water will percolate into the container growth medium much more quickly than the surrounding soil creating a bathtub effect.

Irrigating with one-half inch of water will wet the container growth medium to a greater depth than the surrounding soil. This is due to the much lower water holding capacity of the container growth medium per unit volume. The practical consideration is that, if the soil surrounding a newly planted container-grown plant is moist, a relatively small amount of water needs to be applied frequently to keep the container mix moist and support root activity and plant growth. This is because one needs only to wet the container mix. On the other hand, if both the surrounding soil and the container mix are dry, a much larger quantity of water is needed since the water will be quickly drawn away from the container mix by the finer textured dry soil. But once the surrounding soil becomes thoroughly wetted, subsequent quantities of water can be reduced, but not the frequency since the surrounding soil will continue to draw water away from the container mix, although at a somewhat slower rate depending on the texture of the soil, dryness, and other conditions.

Roots of plants grown in containers do not have to extend vast distances in order to establish the plant in the new site. Once roots from the container growth medium extend out into the surrounding soil and can draw water and nutrients from a volume of soil equal to or greater than the volume of mix in the container, the plant can be treated as though it is established. For example, if the volume of growth medium in a #2 (two-gallon or seven-liter) container is approximately 400 cubic inches, plant roots need only to extend about one-inch from the sides and bottom to have contacted 400 cubic inches of soil. Once this point in root growth out from the container growth medium is reached, the moisture level in the container growth medium is no longer of major importance. Since roots absorb water and nutrients almost exclusively at the root tips, and the actively growing root tips are now mostly in the surrounding soil, the roots connecting these root tips and the plant stem serve only as plumbing to transport materials back and forth. The porous container growth medium can become quite dry with little or no adverse effects on the plant or its roots.

Soil Amendments May Create Problems. The principles discussed above emphasize why it is important **not** to amend the soil around the plant **unless** the entire soil area where the plant will develop roots over the next several years is amended. If the soil is amended around the container growth medium, two moisture/water relationship barriers are established as opposed to one (Figure 9.2). When the soil around the plant is amended, the roots are forced to grow out into an amended zone and then later grow from that amended zone into the surrounding soil. The principles of water movement and the capillary attraction of the surrounding soil on the amended soil is the same as the soil has on the container growth medium directly when no soil amendments are used. In short, amending a limited area around a newly transplanted tree or shrub is nearly always detrimental or at best of no benefit.

On the other hand, in some situations, amending a very large area relative to the size of the plant and soil conditions may be beneficial. See the chapter on soil amendments in *Establishment and Maintenance of Landscape Plants* by Carl E. Whitcomb, for a more thorough discussion and specific research results.

Figure 9.2. Roots of this container-grown shrub (six-inch container, see dashed line) grew into the amended soil and stopped at the amended soil/soil interface of the 18-inch diameter planting hole. Roots from the same plants without the soil amendments were not restricted and extended further out into the surrounding soil.

Root Growth Out From Containers. Roots of plants grown in containers do not retain or remember the circular design of most containers. Consequently, following transplanting roots grow into the surrounding soil relative to their position in the container growth medium at planting time. Therefore, the ideal root system in a container would have active root tips oriented in all directions at time of transplanting into the field or landscape. This would anchor the plant most securely and provide the greatest volume of water from the surrounding soil. Unfortunately, most container-grown plants have roots mostly on one side, especially when the plants have been spaced so that the sun hits one side of the container (Figure 9.3).

Only a few hours of direct sun on the side of a container will kill roots, so be especially careful when moving plants onto or around a the nursery before planting in the field.

The key factor to remember is that the more rapidly roots grow from the soil-less container growth medium into the surrounding soil, the more rapid the establishment and the less the stress. Many plants grown by wholesale nurseries in containers are fertilized through the irrigation system and no provision is made for fertilization once the plants leave the nursery. Rapid root growth into the surrounding soil following transplanting is very important due to the rapid water loss from the container growth medium. Costello and Paul (2) concluded that the rapid moisture loss from the container growth medium following transplanting was the result of drainage to the surrounding field soil. They observed that moisture tension increased more rapidly in the growth medium following transplanting than in the surrounding field soil or in the growth medium of the plants that remained in the containers. This is precisely the situation described earlier in this chapter. The soil mix in the container must be porous for aeration and drainage, therefore, the key to success is rapid root growth following planting.

Figure 9.3. Plant roots are quickly killed by excess heat when containers are exposed to direct sun (above). The plant on the left was in a container with one side exposed to the sun, whereas, the two on the right were shaded. This shumard oak was grown in a #3 (10-liter) container that had one side exposed to the sun (below). Following transplanting, living roots existed only on one side of the container, therefore, the plant was unsupported on the other side. Container-grown plants like this are much more subject to drought stress and being blown over than plants with a more or less radial root system which provides equal support in all directions.

Topdress for Better Establishment Success. To determine if topdressing with a slow-release fertilizer during holding prior to planting in the field or landscape would influence the number of roots developed following transplanting, the following study was conducted (1). Mojave pyracantha (*Pyracantha* X 'Mojave') and pfitzer juniper (*Juniperus chinensis* 'Pfitzeriana') in one-gallon containers were obtained from a wholesale nursery that used liquid fertilizer (nitrogen and potassium) injected through the irrigation system. The plants were two years old. The growth medium was 70% pine bark and 30% sand. The plants were received on March 10 and held without further fertilization until April 21, when the plants were treated with either 0, 1/3 or 1/2 ounce of Osmocote 18-6-12 per container as a topdress. After five weeks the plants were shifted from one-gallon to three-gallon containers. However, the medium in the three-gallon containers was a 3-1-1 by volume mix of ground pine bark, peat and sand with no nutrients added. This was done to try to more clearly determine the effects of the topdress fertilizer on the root growth following transplanting. After three weeks in the three-gallon containers the plants were removed and the number of roots that had grown from the original root ball were counted.

The average number of roots growing from the pyracantha root ball were 164, 187 and 189 for the 0, 1/3- and 1/2-ounce Osmocote treatments, respectively. The fertilized pyracantha had 13% more roots compared to the untreated control.

The average number of roots growing from the juniper root ball were 13, 17, and 18 for the 0, 1/3- and 1/2-ounce Osmocote treatment, respectively. The fertilized juniper had 25% more roots compared to the untreated control.

Studies of this type emphasize the importance of nutrition to root development of container-grown plants immediately following transplanting (Figure 9.4). Allowing container-grown plants to remain without fertilizer for even short periods of time reduces the number of roots that develop into the surrounding soil following transplanting. Since newly planted container-grown nursery stock dries very quickly following planting, rapid root growth following planting greatly reduces plant moisture stress and increases survival (Figure 9.5).

*Figure 9.4. These two Japanese honeysuckle (**Lonicera japonica**) came from the same parent. The plant above received a more favorable fertilizer regime in the small container than the one below. They were planted into a landscape situation and dug three weeks later. The condition of the plant, that cannot be seen can have a tremendous effect on root growth. Note that the two labels in the photos are the same size.*

Figure 9.5. Internal energy stress cannot be detected by observing external plant parts. This juniper has received no fertilizer for six months, yet the top looks good. However, when planted, root growth into the surrounding soil will be slower than if proper fertility had been maintained.

Disturb the Roots at Planting? There is considerable disagreement among nurserymen and landscapers with regard to the handling of the root system of container-grown plants at planting time. Many feel that the root system must be cut or in some way disturbed in order to prevent the continued formation of circling roots and to encourage good root development into the soil at the planting site (3). Fulmer and Jones (5) reported that container-grown dwarf burford holly developed a better root system following transplanting when the roots were disturbed.

To study this further, Appleton and Whitcomb (1) selected root-bound plants of Mojave pyracantha, (*Pyracantha* X 'Mojave') and rotunda holly (*Ilex cornuta* 'Rotunda') which were obtained from a commercial nursery and transplanted from one-gallon containers to three-gallon containers using four treatments:

1) repotted, no root disturbance;
2) vertical slits the length of the root ball, 1/2-inch deep, two locations;
3) vertial slits the length of the root ball, 1/2-inch deep, four locations;
4) two vertical slits 1/2-inch deep and the bottom of the root mass pulled apart.

Several large, circling roots were cut on plants of both species. The plants had been grown in a mix of 90% bark and 10% sand. The mix in the three-gallon container was 3-1-1 pine bark, peat, and sand with 14 pounds Osmocote 17-7-12, six pounds dolomite and 1.5 pounds of Micromax per cubic yard. The repotted plants were allowed to grow four weeks, then evaluated for new root growth. The treatments were evaluated by removing the three-gallon containers and counting the root tips extending from the surface of the original container medium.

The rate of root elongation and new root growth was far greater for the pyracantha than for the holly. However, there were no differences in number of roots developed as a result of the root ball treatments. This suggests that if aeration in the back-fill soil is not limiting, the short-term root growth of container-grown plants, even when root bound, is not increased by cutting or disturbing the root ball prior to transplanting. When large roots are cut, the development of secondary branch roots is fairly slow, probably somewhat like the development of roots on a cutting. The root tips lost due to the vertical cuts on the root ball may be similar to the few root tips produced at the ends of the larger cut roots (Figure 9.6). This may explain the absence of treatment effects.

The best advice is to avoid root-bound container-grown nursery stock. If the container is removed and upon close inspection of the root ball few white root tips are observed or if large kinked roots are noted, it is false prosperity to plant it and try to nurse it back to health. Cutting the root ball probably placed additional short-term stress on the plant and provides only modest long-term benefits. This is especially true for shrubs that generally have a more fibrous root system than trees. A root-bound container-grown tree **should not be planted**. Travel at your own risk!

Figure 9.6. If the root system of this oak had been disturbed at planting, fewer roots would have grown into the surrounding soil in the same period of time since many of the root tips that extended to establish this plant would have been damaged. On the other hand, if the tree had been "root-bound" some long-term benefit might result if the tree survived the transplanting stage.

Cuttings Vs. Seedlings. There is a distinct difference in the root systems of shrubs propagated from cuttings and trees grown from seed when placed in containers. Plants propagated from cuttings characteristically have a multitude of roots of similar size and age originating from the base of the cutting. Because there are many roots of similar size and age, there is a limited tendency for one root to become dominant and suppress the activity of others. On the other hand, plants grown from seed have a primary or tap root which results from the radical at germination. Even when this primary root is removed, it may quickly recover and re-establishes dominance over the remaining roots unless proper techniques are used (6). Tree seedlings that are lifted from flats and the primary root cut during the transplanting process into large containers grow at very different rates. The plants

254

that grow rapidly have developed a fibrous root system without redevelopment of a primary root. However, plants that grow slowly have re-established a dominant primary root which suppresses secondary root growth (6).

Two eucalyptus species were subjected to four root treatments prior to transplanting from polyethylene bags. When plants were dug after 2.5 years, it was observed that the combination of vertical slicing and removal of the lower one inch of the root ball increased the number of vertical roots and largely eliminated root curling with both species. Shoot growth was restricted for several months, suggesting a loss of active root tips for a time and the need for careful watering (4, 6).

Disadvantages of Containers. Disadvantages of container-grown plants are:

a) Frequent but light watering is required during establishment due to the soil-growth medium textural difference (Figure 9.7).

b) Root wrapping/distortion occurs due to container design and/or leaving the plants in the container too long. Root-bound container-grown plants should be avoided as there is no practical way to return these plants to vigorous growth. This is a far more serious problem with trees than with most shrubs which develop secondary root branches more readily as a result of root restrictions (Figure 9.8).

c) Root growth may be from only from one side of the container (Figure 9.3). This is a frequent problem with plants in containers that have been exposed to direct sun. Roots of most species are killed in less than an hour in the summer by excess heating of the side wall of the container. Containers that are handled several times from wholesaler to final planting in the field or landscape may, unfortunately, have 50% to 80% of their roots killed before planting.

d) Roots sometimes grow out of the drain holes and into the soil below. Once this occurs, the plant should be rejected as it will perform poorly, if at all, following planting (Figure 9.9)

Figure 9.7. Plants container-grown and recently planted in the field or landscape require frequent watering to aid establishment and growth. Be careful not to suffocate the root system by excess water.

Figure 9.8. The tree above shows one girdling root. However, when it was dug, several circling roots were observed. This tree should not have been grown in a round container when small. There is no practical means to save a tree with such a poor root system.

Figure 9.9.   Roots grew out of the container and into the soil below.   This plant now has few functioning root tips inside the container and will perform poorly or die once planted into the landscape.

Advantages of Containers.   Advantages of container-grown plants are:

a) retention of 100% of the roots, **if** handled properly,
b) lightweight relative to plants dug B & B,
c) ease of handling and transporting,
d) harvest and shipping is more nearly independent of weather conditions.
e) little or no mess in handling; this is especially advantageous for retail customers.
f) if handled properly and carefully, may be planted any time of year in the South and the entire growing season in the North.   However, there are some distinct "best" times for planting which minimize maintenance.   See the chapter on spring vs. fall planting.
g) new container designs minimize or eliminate the root circling and twisting problems associated with conventional round or square containers.

Literature Cited

1. Appleton, Bonnie L. and Carl E. Whitcomb. 1984. Establishment of container-grown ornamentals. SNA Nursery Res. Conf. Proc. 31:106-108.

2. Costello, L. and J.L. Paul. 1975. Moisture relation in transplanted container plants. HortSci. 10:371-372.

3. Deneke, F.J. 1984. Blueprint for spring tree planting. Amer. Forests 90(4):13-15.

4. Ellyard, Roger K. 1984. Effect of root pruning at planting on subsequent root development of two species of eucalyptus. Jour. of Arboriculture 10:214-218.

5. Fulmer, J.P. and E.V. Jones. 1974. The effect of four transplant treatments on root growth of container-grown *Ilex cornuta* 'Burford Nana'. SNA Nursery Res. Conf. Proc. 19:27.

6. Harris, R.W. 1971. Root pruning improves nursery tree quality. Jour. Amer. Soc. Hort. Sci. 96:105-108.

7. Whitcomb, Carl E. 1988. *Plant Production in Containers.* Lacebark Publications, Stillwater, Ok.

CHAPTER 10

ROOT STIMULATORS

ROOT STIMULATORS

Various products are sold as root promoters or root stimulators for nursery and landscape use. These are, no doubt, the outgrowths of research reports showing that auxins applied to the base of bare root nursery stock do stimulate additional root formation.

Supporting Research. As early as 1938, Romberg and Smith (9) used auxin impregnated toothpicks to stimulate the initiation of new roots at transplanting. Since that time the technique has been used successfully many times (1, 3, 4, 7). Recently, Magley and Struve reported that three- to six-inch caliper pin oaks dug either bare root or with a 44-inch tree spade produced more roots from cut root ends when auxin-treated toothpicks were inserted (5). They noted that with the auxin-treated trees, great numbers of new roots developed at the points of toothpick insertion. These roots were longer and of greater diameter than those produced by the untreated roots. The problem with the technique is the time and cumbersome steps involved in inserting the toothpicks in the ends of cut roots of trees dug either bare root or balled-in-burlap (B & B).

A spray or dip application of auxin solutions would be more practical and easier to apply. Lee, Moser and Hess (3) used a 20-second dip of 2000 parts per million (ppm) of IBA (indolebutyric acid) on scarlet and pin oaks and found increased root produced. Cut root ends of northern red oak trees dug with a tree spade were sprayed with 3000 ppm IBA or NAA (naphthelene acetic acid) before planting (5). IBA stimulated more roots than no treatment. Large roots sprayed with IBA produced 45 roots while untended roots of similar size only produced 13.

IBA root dips are somewhat more effective than sprays of the same concentration. While dips may be practical for small plants, sprays are more practical for large trees either bare root, B & B or dug with tree spades (8).

The consistent benefits of either dips or sprays using 3000 ppm of IBA show that chemical stimulation of new roots is possible. However, several products are marketed, primarily through retail stores, that are said to stimulate new root production when added to water during the watering process following planting.

Root stimulators are products which are promoted to hasten both plant root growth and establishment of newly planted trees and shrubs. Commercially available root stimulators are generally low analysis liquid nitrogen-phosphorus-potassium fertilizers with trace amounts of IBA and/or other chemicals. The IBA traces range from four to 30 ppm, however, when the solution is mixed with water at the recommended rate, the concentration is much lower. IBA is a well known root promoting substance widely used in plant propagation, but there is little information regarding the fate of IBA when applied to field soil. The average cost of actual nitrogen per ton in root stimulator is many times more expensive when compared to conventional sources of nitrogen with the same analysis. Does a commercial root stimulator of such extravagant expense justify itself in plant response?

In order to answer that question, asexually produced spreading euonymus (*Euonymus kiautschovica* 'Manhattan') and wateri pyrancantha (*Pyracantha coccinea* 'Wateri') in four-inch containers and bare root pin oak (*Quercus palustris*) seedlings were selected for uniformity and planted in a sandy loam soil (9). Treatments were as follows:

a) control: no root stimulator,
b) root stimulator at the manufacturer's recommended rate,
c) root stimulator four times the recommended rate.

All treatments were replicated 18 times with all three species. The asexually propagated woody shrubs were chosen as test plants to avoid the variability associated with using seedling trees. When there is a great difference in plant response, even without treatments, the response to treatment becomes difficult to identify with certainty. Uniform planting holes were prepared, plants were placed in the holes and the treatment added. After the solution soaked in, more soil was added around each plant. Treatments were applied as directed on the label. Thereafter, sufficient rainfall distribution continued through July 20. After that date, plants were watered with drip irrigation.

No consistent visual benefit could be measured from either of the root stimulator treatments, and most plants treated with the four-fold rate were stunted. On June 15, observations of root development were made by excavating five replications of both test species. Only slight differences in root growth could be detected between the root stimulator treatments and the untreated control with the untreated control slightly superior. Six of the 18 plants of all species receiving the four-fold concentration of root stimulator were dead. Final evaluations of the remaining 12 replications were done on August 2. The root stimulator used in this study did not improve stem caliper, top growth, root weight, nor top weight of euonymus (Figure 10.1), pyracantha (Figure 10.2), or pin oak.

Figure 10.1. Top and root growth of euonymus following treating with a commercial root stimulator. The control plant (C) had more roots and about the same top growth as the recommended rate (R) and much more than the high rate (R4).

Figure 10.2. Effects of a commercial root stimulator on plant growth. Above, pyracantha at recommended rate (left), four-fold recommended rate (center) and control (right). Below, control (left) recommended rate (center) and four-fold recommended rate (right). No benefit to root growth could be detected from the root stimulator.

The commercial root stimulator used in this study was not effective in aiding plant establishment and growth (9). The reason for the lack of response at the recommended rate or detrimental effect of the four-fold rate is not understood, but is probably related to soil absorption of the chemicals. The concentration of IBA (auxin) is far below the rates routinely used to treat cuttings during mist propagation. Even at much higher rates the IBA would probably not be injurious to plant roots. Studies by several researchers has shown that IBA treatments to scarlet oaks and other species are effective in stimulating roots at planting time (1, 2, 3, 4, 5, 6, 8). The fertilizer concentration in the root stimulator solution is very low and unlikely to cause injury or stunting even at much higher rates.

A recent study of a root stimulator compared the commercial product which contained IBA, thiamine and fertilizer with an untreated control and each of the three components separately (11). The product and each of the components were used at three rates. They found that plants treated with IBA alone, or thiamine alone, at any of the three rates had no better top or root growth, number of branches, or leaf color than the untreated controls. Positive effects on leaf color, number of branches, and top and root growth were obtained when fertilizer or fertilizer with IBA or thiamine were applied to the plants. They concluded that the only benefit was from the fertilizer (11). Additional work is needed to determine why the commercial products studied were not effective and what, if anything, can be done to create a safe and effective product for the future.

At this point, the use of commercial root stimulators appears to be a **travel-at-your-own-risk** situation. On the other hand, spraying cut root ends with 3000 ppm IBA is a practical, and in some cases, perhaps, economical treatment.

Literature Cited

1.   Farmer, R.E. 1975. Dormancy and root regeneration of northern red oak. Can. Jour. Forest Res. 5:176-185.

2.   Hartwig, R.C. and M.M. Larson. 1980. Hormone root soak can increase initial growth of planted hardwood stock. Tree Planters Notes 31:29-33.

3.   Lee, C.I., B.C. Moser and C.E. Hess. 1974. Root regeneration of transplanted pin and scarlet oak. New Horizons, Hort. Res. Institute, Washington, D.C. 1:10-13.

4.   Looney, N.E. and D.L. McIntosh. 1968. Stimulation of pear rooting by pre-plant treatment of nursery stock with IBA. Proc. Amer. Soc. Hort. Science 92:150-154.

5.   Lumis, Glen P. 1982. Stimulating root regeneration of landscape-size red oak with auxin root sprays. Jour. of Arboriculture 8:325-328.

6. Magley, S.B. and D.K. Struve. 1983. Effects of three transplant methods on survival, growth and root regeneration of caliper pin oaks. Jour. Environmental Hort. 1:59-62.

7.   Maki, T.E. and H. Marshall. 1945. Effects of soaking with indolebutyric acid on root development and survival of tree seedlings. Bot. Gazette 107:268-276.

8.   Moser, B.C. 1978. Research on root regeneration. New Horizons, Hort. Res. Institute, Washington, D.C. 5:18-24.

9. Reavis, Rick and Carl E. Whitcomb. 1979. Do root stimulators really work? Okla. Agri. Exp. Sta. Res. Rept. P-791:63-65.

10. Romberg, L.D. and C.L. Smith. 1938. Effects of indole-butyric acid in the rooting of transplanted pecan trees. Proc. Amer. Soc. Hort. Sci. 36:161-170.

11.   Williams, Donald B. and T.E. Daly. 1986. Effects of IBA, thiamine and fertilizer on the growth of 'Manhattan' euonymus in containers. Proc. Nurs. Res. Conf. 31:75-77.

CHAPTER 11

TOP PRUNING AT PLANTING

TOP PRUNING AT PLANTING

One of the widely held beliefs regarding bare root nursery stock was the necessity of cutting back the top at, or prior to, time of planting. This was probably based on the idea that since most of the plant's roots have been lost, the top of the plant must be reduced in order to maintain a root-to-top balance. This is **not true** when balled-in-burlap, bare root trees or shrubs are dug, stored and planted properly.

The practice was questioned one spring when a large number of trees of five different species were planted for a weed control study. The plan was to come back after planting and watering and cut back the tops of all species. The entire planting was complete, except for cutting back two species, when Mother Nature decided to water the plants well and water and water. Over four weeks passed before the newly tilled field dried sufficiently to allow access to prune the tops of the remaining trees. However, by that time the trees that had not been pruned were beginning their spring flush of growth. Since all trees of both unpruned species were growing, the decision was made to leave them alone. On the other hand, the three species that had been top-pruned were slower to begin growth, and plant losses were greater than with the unpruned species. Was the difference in survival a difference between the species, or was it related to the pruning treatment? Observations such as this are an excellent basis for further research, but no firm conclusions can be drawn from such experiences without further study.

Experiments and Answers. The first experiment (10) to study the question was set up in the spring of 1978 to evaluate effects of top pruning and fertilizing at planting time on six bare root deciduous species: pin oak (*Quercus palustris*) redbud (*Cercis canadensis*) Bradford pear (*Pyrus calleryana* 'Bradford') Hopa flowering crab (*Malus* spp. 'Hopa') Summit green ash (*Fraxinus pennsylvanica* 'Summit') and Kwanzan cherry (*Prunus serrulata* 'Kwanzan'). All plants were six to eight feet tall, dormant, bare root stock when planted on March 16, 1978. Treatments were removal of 0%, 15%, 30% or 45% of the plant height before the spring flush. Some trees were not fertilized while others were fertilized at time of planting with four pounds of nitrogen per 1000 square feet using a 10-20-0 analysis dry fertilizer (1742 pounds per acre) applied to the soil surface following planting. All treatments were replicated 12 times for greater accuracy since all trees were either seedlings with considerable genetic variation or grafted onto seedling rootstocks. All trees were planted in a sandy loam soil and watered thoroughly following planting. Spring rains were accommodating, but after June 20, no further measurable rain fell during the summer. Drought stress was allowed to progress sufficiently to defoliate some trees before any supplemental irrigating was done.

The second study was started on March 20, 1979 to expand the study to other species and to compare the findings with the previous study. Treatments were 0%, 15%, 30% and 45% removal of the crown of the dormant bare root trees before the spring flush. However, no fertilizer treatments were used. The five tree species were: red delicious apple (*Malus domestica* 'Red Delicious') Kifer pear (*Pyrus communis* 'Kifer') dwarf Alberta peach (*Prunus persica* 'Alberta') Stuart pecan (*Carya illinoensis* 'Stuart') and Arizona ash (*Fraxinus velutina*). All trees were the same size as in the first experiment, were planted in rows adjacent to the first study, and were watered thoroughly following planting. This experiment was also replicated 12 times.

Pruning or fertilizer treatments had no effect on initiation of growth in the spring or survival of any of the tree species planted in 1978. Out of 288 trees of the six species planted, 242 or 84% survived. Numbers of basal suckers on Bradford pear and crabapple increased significantly when tops were pruned back 30% or 45% (Figure 11.1). Pruning in excess of 15% reduced the visual quality (natural form and branch development) of all species.

269

Figure 11.1. Hopa crabapple trees with 0%, 15%, 30% or 45% of the top removed immediately after planting. Note the suckers on the 30% and 45% pruning treatments. Pruning or fertilizer treatments had no effect on initiation of growth or survival of any of the six species tested.

All species planted in 1978 made similar flushes of growth during the spring of 1979 regardless of pruning treatments. This suggests that all trees had recovered from the initial transplant disturbance and assumed normal growth. Except for some unnatural branch development from the severe pruning treatments, all plants were similar in size and vigor at the end of two growing seasons (Figure 11.2).

Figure 11.2.   Apple trees two years after top-pruning treatments. Beginning in the lower left corner of the photo, every group of four trees down the row represent one of each of the four pruning treatments.   Without the aid of the suckers at the base and some unusual branching, it is difficult to tell the pruned from the unpruned trees.

Fertilizing at Planting. Fertilizing at planting time had no effect on tree growth the first growing season and was only detectable as darker foliage color the second season. This was not surprising in this instance since the fertility of the field soil was high. The fact that no detrimental effect of the fertilizer could be detected is important in light of the widespread recommendation that no fertilizer be added at planting time.   In good soils such as those used in this study, adding fertilizer at planting has little impact on top growth the first season since the first flush of growth following transplanting is controlled mostly by conditions experienced by the plant the previous summer and fall when the buds were formed. However, it is important to remember that fertilizing at or shortly after planting is important to the bud development the first summer and

271

fall after transplanting which will be seen with the spring flush of growth one year after planting. To express it another way, the flush of growth of a bare root or balled-in-burlap tree planted in the spring mostly reflects the conditions in the nursery the previous summer and fall, whereas, the flush of growth one year after spring planting reflects the conditions of the new site. Do not make the false assumption that just because plants look good the first growing season following planting that all is well. It is the second spring flush of growth that tells a more accurate story.

In the second study, pruning treatments had no effect on survival of any of the five species planted in 1979. Pecans broke buds slightly earlier when pruned 15% compared to no pruning. Plants pruned 30% or 45% developed slightly more branches as a result of more bud breaks compared to the unpruned trees. Near the end of the growing season, all leaves were stripped from the dwarf Alberta peach and Kifer pear and counted and weighed fresh. Number of leaves and weight of leaves per tree were similar regardless of the pruning treatment. The fact that all treatments had similar quantities of leaves at the end of the first growing season suggests a rapid recovery of the leaf canopy from the severe pruning treatments, mostly from suckers and water sprouts.

There was no advantage to pruning at planting time, and pruning more than 15% of the top was detrimental to the structural development of branches and natural form of the species (Figure 11.3). These studies emphasize that only corrective pruning at planting time should be practiced since excessive pruning reduces visual plant quality, increases suckers on some species, and does not aid in establishment or survival.

Related Research.   Other research has also shown that shoot-pruning decreased root growth (6). Plant dry weight, which is the result of energy from the leaves of young peach trees was reduced by all top-pruning treatments and the more severe the top-pruning, the greater the reduction (9).

In spite of all the data, Flemer (4) notes that, "hundreds of years of experience have shown that trimming at transplanting time increases both survival and subsequent growth." The experimental results do not agree with Flemer's broad statement. Conditions do change and perhaps the improvements in nutrition, weed control, and other factors affecting plant health as well as storage and handling conditions are the difference between the recommendations of nurserymen over the years and the recent research findings. Flemer (4) wrote that "a few small specimens of very easily transplanted species in very favorable conditions" were used in the study by Shoup, Reavis and Whitcomb (10). In fact, a total of 816 trees over three growing seasons using 11 species under Oklahoma's stressful summer conditions were studied. Overall the findings of Evans and Klett (1, 2, 3) on Colorado's arid eastern slope were very similar to the findings of Shoup, Reavis and Whitcomb (10).

Figure 11.3. All Arizona ash pruned at planting time developed double leaders. In contrast, trees unpruned developed a strong central leader and excellent side branches.

273

Top-Root Relationships. A detailed study was conducted of the initiation of new roots in the spring from pin oak, silver maple and honeylocust trees planted bare root in late winter (12). With every specimen of each species, new root growth from the cut ends of old roots **did not** occur until the buds began to swell. Of the 24 trees of each species studied, there were no exceptions. After the first few observations, the extent of new root growth could be predicted by the extent of bud expansion. Very small roots could be observed at the time of the slightest swelling of the buds, but not before bud swell. This shows that new root growth of bare root trees is directly related to bud expansion. Any reduction of the combined growth regulator concentration from **all** expanding buds on the top reduces the strength of the chemical signal received by the roots and subsequent root growth.

What Makes Roots Grow? Initial root development of newly planted bare root trees is supported by energy (carbohydrates) stored within the stem and root tissues. As soon as top growth begins, however, total energy within the plant rapidly decreases (8, 11). When a portion of the top of the plant is removed, the leaf surface area in the spring and the capacity to replace energy used in the initial flush of growth are also reduced. Apparently the moisture stress from leaving the entire plant top intact is offset by the more rapid development of a supporting root system. This is not surprising when one remembers that in most areas, the spring is humid and rainfall is generally frequent enough to minimize moisture stress. On the other hand, by early July in most of the USA east of the Rocky Mountains, high temperatures, dehydrating winds and drought conditions may occur. The greater the root development of the plant before the onset of summer stress conditions, the more likely the survival and good growth the following spring.

These studies support the hypothesis that one of the most important factors in transplanting is the internal condition of the plant when it is dug. All the lavish precautions such as soil amendments, "root stimulators", top-pruning, and other practices are unlikely to help an unthrifty plant, and a thrifty plant does not need it. For further information on pruning at time of transplanting, see the chapter on transplanting large trees.

Research Continued. Recently the research has been carried further (1, 2, 3). Dormant bare root Newport plum (*Prunus cerasifera* 'Newport') and Sargent's crabapple (*Malus sargenti*) were planted in 10-gallon paper mache containers with a medium of clay loam soil, peat and sand (2-1-1 by volume). Selective pruning treatments were approximately 8%, 56% and 68% for the crabapple and 0% and random thinning from 21% to 78% for the plum. The terminal shoot (leader) was left undisturbed in all cases. The experiments were terminated after about three months when all plants had set terminal buds and leaf expansion was complete. With the crabapple they found leaf weights were 31% less when 50% or more of the top had been pruned at planting compared to no top-pruning. Newport plum had similar leaf weights regardless of top-pruning treatments. Pruning at planting time had no effect on root production of either species. Newport plum developed more shoots on top-pruned trees such that total leaf production was not changed.

Hummel and Johnson (7) studied sweetgum trees in Florida. They concluded that removal of 20% to 50% of the tops of the trees by heading back (top pruning) at transplant time did not improve growth or establishment. In addition, severe pruning, (30% and 50% top removal), stunted plant growth.

Summary. Arbitrary top-pruning has no place in modern horticulture. However, top-pruning to aid branch development and structure may be a valid consideration. Branches that are to become the main scaffolds for the tree should be spaced vertically on the trunk as well as around the trunk (Figure 11.4). Wide angles between the major branches and the vertical axis of the tree are stronger and are not likely to need bracing or cabling.

When considering the branch and crown development of a young tree, allow for the natural form. It is unwise to prune a young elm to look like a sweet gum or pin oak or vice versa. Natural branch and crown development of the tree will proceed normally and will be structurally sound with little or no interference by man. Only the occasional crossing branches or branches that are too close for the development of a strong primary stem and crown should be removed. "If you don't want an elm to grow and look like an elm, then don't plant an elm" is a quote from a long-forgotten source that deserves remembering.

275

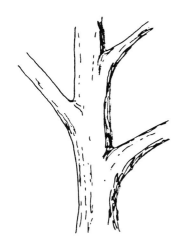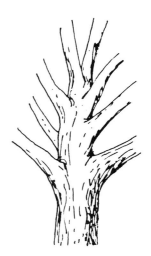

Figure 11.4. Branches should be selected that are spaced vertically on the trunk as well as around the trunk. In most cases, more desirable branch development occurs on unpruned trees (left), whereas, pruned trees tend to form dense clusters of branches (right).

Literature Cited

1. Evans, Philip and James E. Klett. 1984. The effects of dormant pruning on leaf, shoot and root production from bare root *Malus sargenti*. Jour. of Arboriculture 10:298-299.

2. Evans, Philip and James E. Klett. 1985. Pruning at planting may not enhance growth. Amer. Nurseryman 145:53-59.

3. Evans, Philip and James E. Klett. 1985. The effects of dormant branch thinning on total leaf, shoot and root production from bare root *Prunus cerasifera* 'Newport'. Jour. of Arboriculture 11:149-151.

4. Flemer, William III. 1982. Successful transplanting is easy. Jour. of Arboriculture 8:234-240.

5. Fordham, R.   1972. Observations on the growth of roots and shoots of tea (*Camellia sinensis*) in southern Malawi.   Jour. Hort. Science 47:221-229.

6. Head, G.C. 1967. Effects of seasonal changes in shoot growth on the amount of unsuberized roots on apple and plum trees. Jour. Hort. Science 42:169-180.

7. Hummel, Rita L. and C.R. Johnson. 1987. Does pruning at transplanting improve sweetgum growth? Amer. Nurseryman. 165(3):99-105.

8. Kramer, P.J. and T.T. Kozlowski. 1960. *Physiology of trees.* McGraw-Hill Book Co., New York. 642 pages.

9. Rom, Curt R. and David C. Ferree. 1985. Time and severity of summer pruning influences on young peach tree net photosynthesis, transpiration and dry weight distribution. Jour. Amer. Soc. Hort. Sci. 110:455-461.

10. Shoup, Steve, Rick Reavis and Carl E. Whitcomb. 1981. Effects of pruning and fertilizers on establishment of bare root deciduous trees. Jour. of Arboriculture 7:155-157.

11. Siminovitch, D., C.M. Wilson and D.R. Briggs. 1953. Studies of the living bark of the black locust in relation to its frost hardiness.   V. Seasonal transonal transformations and variations in the carbohydrate: starch-sucrose interconversions.   Plant Physiology 28:383-400.

12. Whitcomb, Carl E. 1969. Effects of root competition between trees and turfgrass. Ph.D. dissertation, Iowa State University, Ames, Iowa.

CHAPTER 12

ROOT PRUNING: PROS AND CONS

ROOT PRUNING: PROS AND CONS

Root pruning has been promoted and used either actively (doing it) or passively (talking about doing it) by most of the nursery industry growing woody plants in the field for many years. The point is often put forth that "these trees have been root-pruned" with the implication that they will transplant and grow "better" on the new site. But will they? As with many things, it depends! The following discussion is an attempt to clarify when root pruning is beneficial and when it is harmful.

A Practical Example. Consider trees in a field, growing reasonably well, with good internal energy (carbohydrate) levels and no particular complications with diseases, insects or severe competition from weeds. The nurseryman decides to root-prune for three reasons: 1) improving the root system, 2) making the trees easier to dig and transplant and 3) improving performance (growth and visual appearance) after transplanting. The following sequence of events probably occurs:

a) Healthy plants are grown with good energy levels.

b) Those plants are root-pruned.

c) Abruptly the top of the plant is subjected to stress. First there is moisture stress due to loss of a major portion of the fine roots, then within a few hours or days the top of the plant also suffers stress from the greatly reduced nutrient absorption capacity since nearly all nutrient absorption occurs at the root tips. However, with the closing of the stomates due to moisture stress and blocking of the entrance of carbon dioxide, the leaves can utilize very few nutrients until the moisture stress subsides.

d) Since respiration (the use of energy by all living cells) continues and manufacture of energy by the leaves has been greatly reduced, the plant soon suffers an internal deficiency of readily available energy. There are no doubt substantial quantities of energy in the forms of starches, proteins and other storage forms. However, these cannot be mobilized quickly enough to prevent at least a short-term energy stress in the plant.

e) The cut ends of roots probably undergo a wounding reaction, followed by callus formation at the severed

279

root end and eventually (the length of time depends a great deal on the nature of the species, soil conditions and time of year) new roots form.

f) New roots develop at the ends of severed roots only (Figure 12.1). Only a few species such as *Salix* or *Populus* form secondary roots other than at the very tip of the cut root.

Figure 12.1. Root growth from a cut-root end. New root production occurs only at the cut end. In addition, considerable time is required from cutting until new roots emerge.

g) Slowly, as the new roots extend out into the surrounding soil, the moisture stress of the top subsides. Nutrient absorption resumes with the extension of the new root tips.

h) If the leaves were not lost as a result of the initial moisture stress following root-pruning, they gradually accelerate in the manufacture of energy as water and nutrient supplies increase.

i) Levels of soluble energy within the entire plant begin to build towards previous levels. However, since the transfer of energy from the leaves back to the roots is through living cells, energy levels in the roots are the last to be replenished.

j) At some point in time and subject to influences by an array of soil temperature and other environmental conditions, the plant may reach the total level of soluble energy as before root pruning (2, 3). It is doubtful that the energy level will ever reach the point prior to root pruning. However, this may not be a major complication (4).

Practices to Avoid. Now consider the internal condition of the plant in the following four examples:

1) dug before maximum recovery is reached,
2) dug with a root ball the same dimension (depth and width) as the apparatus used to root-prune,
3) root-pruned too late in the season for maximum recovery of energy before leaf drop or cold weather (for evergreens) or
4) when the soil remains dry following root pruning.

If the tree is dug before maximum recovery (example 1) of soluble energy, the transplant stress may be much greater than if no root pruning had occurred. New roots cannot be produced without energy and if the plant just spent a substantial portion of its supply of readily available energy for new roots as a result of root pruning, and the capacity of the top has not recovered in its capacity to manufacture energy, the plant will be forced to initiate new roots (with minimal reserves) again following transplanting. If the level of soluble energy in the plant and particularly in the roots, has not recovered, development of more new roots into the surrounding soil following transplanting may be very slow, and as a result the plant may experience stress to the point of death.

If the tree is dug with a root ball about the same size as the instrument used for root pruning (example 2), all new roots may be lost. Look at the point of new root development in Figure 12.1 again. Note that new roots develop at the cut ends, not behind the cut ends. Therefore, unless the root ball when transplanting is substantially larger than the root pruning dimensions, the roots produced as a result of the pruning process will be lost (Figure 12.2). This is a common error made.

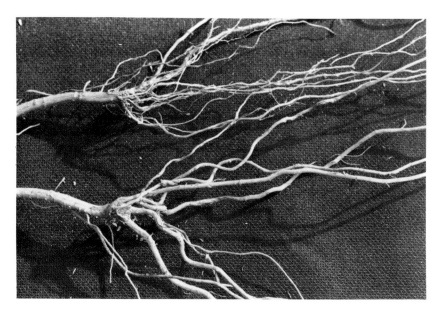

Figure 12.2. New roots grew from the ends of pruned sycamore roots. If the soil ball is dug at the same point as the root-pruning, no benefit will be derived. However, if the soil ball is dug considerably larger than the point of root pruning, many of the new roots will be retained.

If the root ball at transplanting is not sufficiently large to contain most of the roots produced in response to pruning, **and** the tree is dug before the recovery of internal energy levels approaching that before root pruning, the plant will suffer more stress more rapidly than had it never been root-pruned (Figure 12.3).

If the tree is root-pruned late in the season (example 3) and either as a result of time of year, drought or some other complicating factor, the internal energy level never recovers. The plant may suffer more winter injury than if it had not been root-pruned. If these conditions occur and the tree has also been dug and/or transplanted, the stress level and likelihood of winter injury are further increased.

Figure 12.3. This tree was root-pruned on all four sides using a trenching machine (note the straight digging line to the outside of the ball). The tree was watered and maintained for about two months before digging. Because the final root ball was substantially smaller than that cut by the trencher, no benefit was gained from the root-pruning. Probably the tree would have been better off to have been moved when the original trenching was done.

If the soil remains dry following root pruning (example 4), even though new roots develop, their capacity to extend into the surrounding soil and absorb water and nutrients is limited, causing a great deal of stress to the plant. Since the weather is often very unpredictable, and short-term droughts may occur almost anywhere, a drought of only a few weeks may delay recovery and increase the likelihood of injury from cold weather.

On the other hand, if root pruning is practiced at a point well inside the dimension of the final root ball at time of digging, and the energy level inside the plant has recovered to near the level prior to root pruning as a result of favorable moisture, temperature and other conditions, then root pruning may

283

be beneficial (Figure 12.2). If root pruning is to be practiced, it should be done frequently when the plants are young (perhaps as often as every six to eight weeks) in order to stimulate root branching near the stem. Each successive root-pruning should be at least four to six inches beyond the last. Any more than three root-prunings is probably counter-productive, even if all the previous mentioned factors are met (Figure 12.4).

*Figure 12.4. Palms are monocots or enormous "grass" plants. Their root system is very different from dicots or woody hardwood and softwood trees. There is probably no advantage to root-pruning a palm. In this case, a large Canary Island date palm (**Phoenix canariensis**) is being planted at Busch Gardens in Tampa, Florida. Note that lifting is by the root ball as well as the stem. Since there is no cambium just under the bark, the likelihood of stem damage to a palm is less likely, although it can occur.*

A Questionable Practice. Unfortunately, root pruning is probably more often detrimental than beneficial. Like many other time-honored horticultural practices, root-pruning sounds very desirable in print or without a thorough evaluation. It is virtually impossible, at the present time, to evaluate the degree of recovery of energy levels in the plant following root pruning. One can only make an "educated" guess as to the extent of recovery, and educated guesses are just that--guesses. Until a plant makes a flush of growth, internal energy levels cannot be measured. For example, Whitcomb and Appleton (13) treated two species of container-grown nursery stock that had been fertilized using only liquid nitrogen (N), phosphorus (P) and potassium (K) sources, with either none or three levels of slow-release N, P, K fertilizer in late spring, after the first flush. After six weeks, the plants were transplanted and root growth determined three weeks later. The two species had 18% and 25% more root growth as a result of the added slow-release fertilizer. However, since the first flush of growth in the spring was over at the time the slow-release fertilizer was applied, and no new growth had begun, no visual differences could be detected between the plants that received no slow-release fertilizer and the plants which received the moderate level of slow-release fertilizer. The difference in root growth was a result of internal energy that could not be visually detected, yet the root growth response was quite different.

Kramer and Kozlowski (6) contend that each species has a characteristic root:shoot ratio which remains relatively constant but gradually shifts with plant age and size. Root-pruning reduces this ratio or proportion of root vs top growth by additional root growth at the expense of shoot growth. The length of time for the root:shoot balance to be restored depends on the species involved, time of year and a host of moisture, temperature and other environmental and cultural conditions. Rook (11) noted that 80 days were required for Monterey pine seedlings to resume normal root growth while several months were required for white pine (12). Rohrig (10) found that in oak seedlings, growth rates of shoots and roots recovered to be about the same several weeks after root-pruning. However, root-pruned plants were 20% to 30% smaller when the study was concluded indicating stress caused by the root pruning process. Kramer and Kozlowski (6) felt the reduction in plant size was due to water stress. Shoot growth may be inhibited by water stress induced through root pruning (3, 6, 7). Perhaps in conjunction with the water stress, nutrient absorption is also restricted due to root pruning (5, 11). Geisler and Farree (4) observed that shoot growth of young apple trees was reduced as the result of root pruning. This has been reported for other species as well (1, 2, 3, 5, 7, 9). The growth restrictions may generally be explained by a combination of:

a) limited water absorption,

b) reduced nutrient uptake,

c) reduced hormone synthesis, and

d) increased energy translocated to the roots (3).

All this confirms that if root pruning is practiced, and if the proper time is allowed between root pruning and digging, some benefits may occur. However, with the multitude of factors involved, both internally in the plant and environmentally, the likelihood of striking the right combination is remote. Root pruning is probably one of those techniques that is best to talk about rather than practice. In addition, root pruning does not stimulate root branching near the base of the plant, but rather only at the ends of the cut roots (with a few exceptions). The time to stimulate root branching is at the seedling or cutting stage. If this is done properly (see Chapter 3, Container Design and Transplant Success) the need for root pruning in the field will no longer exist. This is the practical way to root-prune and it is one of those few situations where there is everything to gain and nothing to lose.

Literature Cited

1. Alexander, D.M. and D.H. Maggs. 1971. Growth responses of sweet orange seedlings to shoot and root pruning. Ann. Bot. 35:109-115.

2. Fuchigami, L.H. and F.W. Moelle. 1978. Root regeneration in evergreen plants. Proc. Int. Plant Prop. Soc. 28:39-49.

3. Geisler, D. and D.C. Ferree. 1984. Response of plants to root pruning. In Hort. Reviews 6:156-188.

4. Geisler, D. and D.C. Ferree. 1984. The influence of root pruning on water relations, net photosynthesis and growth of young 'Golden Delicious' apple trees. Jour. Amer. Soc. Hort. Sci. 109:827-831.

5. Humphries, E.C. 1958. Effect of removal of a part of the root system on the subsequent growth of the root and shoot. Ann. Bot. 22:251-257.

6. Kramer, Paul J. and T.T. Kozlowski. 1979. Physiology of woody plants. Academic Press. New York.

7. Maggs, D.H. 1965. Growth rates in relation to assimilate supply and demand. I. Leaves and roots as limiting regions. Jour. Exp. Bot. 15:574-583. II. The effect of particular leaves and growing regions in determining dry matter distribution in young apple trees. Jour. Exp. Bot. 16:387-404.

8. Randolph, W.S. and C. Wiest. 1981. Relative importance of tractable factors affecting the establishment of transplanted holly. Jour. Amer. Soc. Hort. Sci. 106:207-210.

9. Richards, D. and R.N. Rowe. 1977. Effects of root restriction root pruning and 6-benzylaminopurine on the growth of peach seedlings. Ann. Bot. 41:729-740.

10. Rohrig, E. 1977. Wurzelschmitt an eichensamlingen. Forest Archives 48:24-28.

11. Rook, D.A. 1971. Effect of undercutting and wrenching on growth of Pinus radiata seedlings. Jour. Applied Ecology 28:477-490.

12. Stephens, G.F. 1964. Stimulation of flowering in eastern white pine. Forest Sci. 10:28-34.

13. Whitcomb, Carl E. and Bonnie Appleton. 1984. Establishment of Container Grown Ornamentals. SNA Nursery Res. Conf. Proc. 29:106-108.

CHAPTER 13

SPACING AND PRUNING

SPACING AND PRUNING

Proper spacing and pruning are essential for good branch development and the accumulation of energy reserves in plants. Plants that are too close together generally have poor branch development, weak stems and root systems and poor energy reserves. Trees should always be spaced to allow for good growth and development relative to the time of harvest (anticipated market demand). For example, if trees with a pyramidal shape when young are expected to be harvested when they have a two-inch stem caliper, the proper spacing is about 30 to 48 inches. If the same species is not expected to be harvested until they have a 3- to 3.5-inch caliper, proper spacing is about 60 to 84 inches. Consider two trees which are pyramidal in form when young. A bald cypress (*Taxodium distichum*) is very intolerant of shade and needs more space than a sweetgum (*Liquidambar styraciflua*) which is quite shade-tolerant. For increased space use efficiency, it is sometimes useful to plant trees on the spacing for the smallest size tree to be harvested, then harvest every other tree, leaving the remaining plants more room for growth. This technique provides for more rapid economic returns from the field with no sacrifice in tree quality at the small or larger size as long as harvest is timely.

Trunk Development. Do not space trees too close together in the nursery. The lower branches may become so heavily shaded that they will be weak and poorly developed or in some cases may not develop at all. The lower limbs on rapidly growing young trees are the major source of energy for growth of the trunk diameter, stem taper and root growth. Consider a young tree with a central leader, a clear stem to a height of five feet, and a moderate to rapid vertical growth. Where there are no lateral branches, the only energy the cambial cells of the trunk receive for growth are from the crown. As a result the upper portion of the clear stem receives the same amount of energy as the lower portion and the stem develops little or no taper. Such trees generally stand satisfactorily in the nursery row due to the protection and support of other trees and limited wind velocities. However, when harvested and planted in the landscape where conditions are generally more open and winds are greater, these trees frequently lean severely unless staked or they break off near the ground.

On the other hand, when the lower limbs are left on the main stem and they have sufficient light to function, the main tree stem develops more stem taper from base to crown. This stem taper allows any wind stresses to be dispersed evenly over the vertical height of the tree (Figure 13.1). The reason for the desirable development of the tapered stem or trunk is the energy contribution from the lower limbs. All of the stem receives some energy from the crown, as noted above, however, when the side branches are present near the soil line, the main stem grows as a result of energy from the main crown plus a contribution of all branches above that point (Figure 13.2). This occurs because the movement of energy within the tree system is downward **only after** the spring flush of growth has begun to mature. This downward flow of energy occurs primarily during mid to late summer and continues until leaf drop in the fall and accounts for most of the increase in trunk diameter and root growth. With this factor in mind, it is also important to provide for the needs of lower (older) leaves. Since a deficiency of nitrogen, phosphorus, potassium or magnesium occurs first and most severely in old leaves and tissues, trunk diameter growth will be greatly affected (Figure 13.3).

Figure 13.1. Good stem taper is favored by the presence of lower branches. The lower branches support not only additional stem growth, but also increase root growth.

Figure 13.2. When the lower limbs are removed before a good trunk taper develops, the strength of the stem and root activity will be sacrificed. This translates into staking and poor root development after transplanting.

Figure 13.3.   When limbs are removed from the tree trunk, the increase in trunk diameter is dependent on energy from the crown. The stem just above the soil line receives no more than just below the crown so no stem taper develops (left).   On the other hand, if the upper portion of the trunk is allowed to retain side branches, the trunk grows in response to energy from the crown plus energy from the side branches (center).   When the limbs are left on the entire trunk, maximum trunk taper develops since energy is provided throughout the vertical axis (right).

Light and Energy.   All leaves of all species have a light saturation point. This is the maximum amount of light that can be used by a leaf under a given set of conditions.   This is not full sun.   A sunflower, which has a very high light saturation point, requires less than 2000 foot candles for maximum leaf energy production. Since full sun is over 10,000 foot candles leaves can be shaded to some degree and still maintain maximum energy output. This is why a tree grows just as well on the more shaded north side as on the more sunny south side.

On the other hand, all leaves also have a compensation point. This is the point where the amount of energy manufactured by the leaf is equal to the amount required for respiration. When the energy output of a leaf of a deciduous plant approaches or reaches the compensation point, an abscission (separation) layer forms at the base of the leaf and it is dropped.

When trees are grown too closely spaced and most of the leaves on the lower limbs are near the compensation point, little trunk taper occurs even though the lower branches are present. There is no general rule or formula for proper tree spacing to insure good energy production by the lower limbs since species differ greatly.

One factor to emphasize is that as nutritional conditions improve, the functional capacity and shade tolerance of leaves also increases. For example, the lower and older leaves of trees that receive less than 1000 foot candles of light might be dropped if overall nutritional conditions are poor. However, if nutritional conditions are good, not only will these leaves be retained but they will make a contribution to the overall energy accumulation as well.

Root growth is first and most affected by any reduction in the total energy level of any plant. As a result, the removal of lower limbs or close spacing such that the lower limbs function poorly, will reduce the rate of root growth and development. When transplanted, new root growth into the surrounding soil is primarily dependent on stored energy reserves. Consequently, not only do improperly pruned and/or spaced trees have poorer root systems, but recovery from transplanting is reduced as well. Add to this the greater need for staking due to poor stem taper and need for staking longer due to poor root growth, and it becomes clear why proper pruning and spacing of trees in the nursery and in the landscape, should receive considerable attention.

Producing Good Quality Trees. If the lower limbs play a key role in stem development and root growth yet market demand for many landscape and street trees calls for a five- to six-foot clear stem, how can this apparent conflict be solved? The answer lies in when and how to prune trees. The following steps are suggested:

a. Space trees sufficiently to allow for good function of all lower limbs. This will provide maximum stem taper and root growth.

b. Leave the lower limbs in place until good trunk taper has occurred or one growing season before harvest. If the lower limbs are removed during the dormant period prior to the last growing season before harvest, the pruning scars will callous over before the trees are marketed.

c. When the lower limbs are pruned, respect the branch-bark collar to insure the rapid growth of callous over the wound and minimize likelihood of decay.

Pruning for the Future. The pruning of young trees for proper crown development is as much an art as it is a science. Branches to remain should be spaced around the stem circumference as well as vertically on the main trunk (Figure 13.4). Two branches that are several inches apart when the tree is in the nursery will soon reach sufficient size to rub one another following transplanting. The key word is anticipate. Pruning young trees for the future requires one to anticipate how the tree will look in three, five, ten or twenty years. Which branches will form the primary structural or scaffold branches of the tree: If the tree is used as a street tree, what branches will remain after allowing vehicle clearance (Figure 13.5)? Consider how branch forks that look satisfactory now will be when a wind or ice load occurs or the limbs are larger (Figure 13.6).

The trees in Figure 13.7 are excellent examples of stem development and pruning for the future. They were allowed to retain the side branches until approximately one year before harvest time. With proper planting and pruning techniques, trees of excellent quality can be produced with a minimum of labor and complications. Remember, it is far better to plant and harvest 1000 good quality trees per acre than to plant 1400 trees but only have 900 that are salable even at a reduced price.

Figure 13.4. Excellent branch development on a young Chinese pistache tree. The branches have wide angles relative to the main stem and are well spaced both vertically and around the circumference of the trunk.

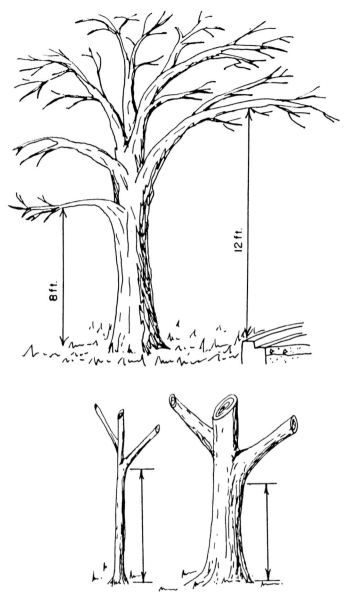

Figure 13.5.   Above, about eight feet of clearance is needed for landscape use, whereas, 12 feet is needed for street clearance. Below, limbs do not move on trees, however, as a limb grows in diameter, the clearance between the base of the limb and the soil surface decreases.

Figure 13.6. Many species of maple tend to develop narrow "V" forks. These are very subject to splitting and often trap bark in the upper portion which prevents the normal intertie of wood. When these weak forks do split, not only is the limb lost, but quite often the trunk is damaged for some distance below.

Figure 13.7. Trees properly spaced and pruned in a field nursery. These trees have 2.5- to 3-inch stem caliper and good branching both vertically and around the trunk. The stem taper was aided by good nutritional practices and the lower limbs which were left in place until one year before harvest.

Pruning Whips. Some nursery stock is grown and sold as "whips" or unbranched seedlings or grafts. When these trees are planted, they are often cut back to stimulate development of lateral branches (Figure 13.8). If the whip is five feet tall and is cut back six inches, most of the lateral branches will develop on the stem 6 to 12 inches below the cut. Likewise, if the whip is cut back 24 inches, the lateral branches will develop much closer to the soil surface. After the side branches begin, if further branching is desired, these branches can be pruned. This is useful in the branch development of fruit trees where low branching is desired, but is usually unnecessary on other species. Often when a whip is planted or has grown the first year, with the beginning of the second spring flush, lateral branches will develop naturally without pruning. The next step is to select among these branches to develop the desired crown of the tree.

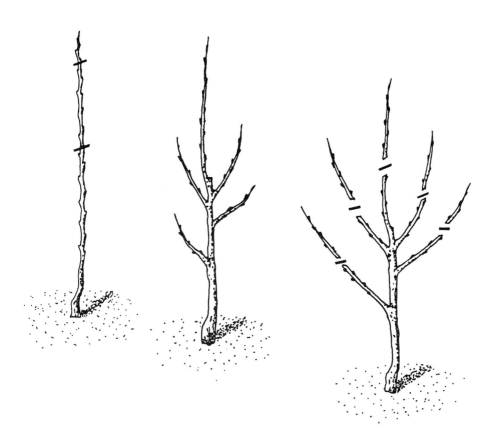

Figure 13.8.   If a young tree is planted as a whip, it may be useful to cut back the top to stimulate lateral branches at the desired height (upper left).   If the top is cut back only a short distance, branch development will be higher or if it is cut back further, branch development will be lower (center).   If further branching is desired, further pruning of the lateral branches may be necessary (lower right).   This technique is especially useful on fruit trees, but may not be necessary on many other species.

Pruning of Young Trees, Pros and Cons.   If soil fertility, weed control, and other cultural factors are approximately correct, most tree species will develop reasonably good branching with little assistance.   Nurserymen sometimes get over-zealous or are misinformed regarding pruning.   The following four drawings provide a basis for this discussion.   In Figure 13.9, a young tree of one or two years has reasonably good lateral branch development. Unfortunately, a very common practice is to remove the top and most of the lower branches (Figure 13.10). **This is wrong.** Even if the young tree has been transplanted, there is no need or advantage to removing the top. Likewise, removal of the lower limbs only reduces the stem and root growth and serves no constructive purpose. The tree in Figure 13.10 shows a typical response to top pruning. There is now a kink in the top, a sizable open wound exists that may or may not become infected with wood decay fungi and the overall appearance of the tree has been compromised. Now consider the plant response if the top of the young tree in Figure 13.9 had been left alone; secondary branches develop, there is no kink in the crown and by removing the lower limbs one season before anticipated sale, the trunk is clean in appearance and with good taper to support the crown.

This topic is also addressed in Chapter 11, Top Pruning at Planting, and again in Chapter 19, Transplanting Large Trees. Note the suckers on the base of the tree in Figure 19.5. Suckers at the base of a tree are the result of reduced chemical control by the terminal buds and shoots. Basal Suckers always indicate stress. Always respect the chemical control of the terminal bud and shoot over the natural branch development of the species.

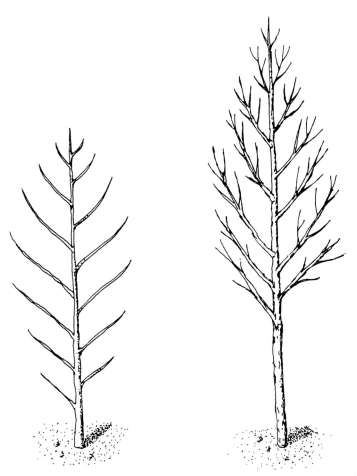

Figure 13.9. When a young tree is growing well, with proper spacing and cultural conditions, natural branch development will generally be good. The young tree on the left may have been a whip or a tree in its first or second growing season. If it is left alone, good branch development generally results (right). If the tree is especially tall and slender with few lateral branches, excess nitrogen, crowding, and inadequate light or especially tall and aggressive weeds are probably the reason. Trees growing rapidly and with proper nutrition, generally develop good branching such that only the selective removal of an occasional branch is needed in order to have an excellent specimen.

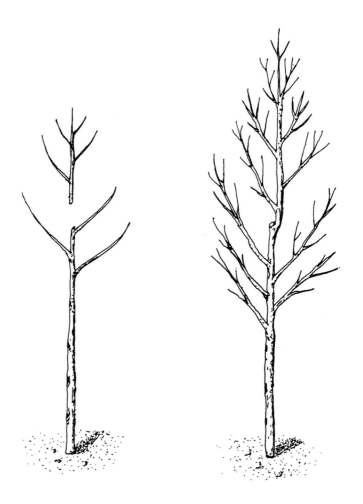

Figure 13.10. Unfortunately, many young trees are pruned excessively or unnecessarily. For example, the young tree on the left in Figure 13.9, is frequently top-pruned (left) when it is planted. The top is removed under the erroneous pretense that top removal will aid in establishment and survival following transplanting. This is not true. The top removal only causes a kink in the top plus an open wound for potential entrance of decay fungi. The removal of the lower limbs is done to aid in stem development which is also incorrect. The presence of the lower limbs aids both stem and root growth. Unless you have a sound reason for pruning, leave the tree alone.

Practical Pruning: Specific Examples. If trees are properly spaced, the branches will just be growing together as the trees reach marketable size (Figure 13.11). On trees with opposite branches such as ligustrum, ash (*Fraxinus*) and maple (*Acer*), the likelihood of undesirable narrow branch angles and double leaders is great. Even if the branches in question are in a position to be removed before harvest, narrow branch angles are sound reasons for pruning (Figure 13.12). Likewise, double leaders are always to be avoided (Figure 13.12).

Other species to watch closely for narrow branch angles and double leaders are pines, oaks, and dogwoods. In the case of pine, the Nantuckett pine tip moth burrows into the terminal bud or just below. When the bud is damaged or killed, several secondary buds are often released to grow. If they get very large, the tree is lopsided and of poor quality following pruning. Because pine wood is quite soft and splits easily, it is very important to prevent "V" forks.

In the case of oaks, the trees sometime go "blind". The terminal bud, although present and may appear to be fully developed, does not grow. With oaks, there are always three to six smaller buds surrounding the terminal. When the terminal does not grow and exert its chemical influence over the secondaries, the result is a disorganized array of branches. It is important to watch for this problem and prune early. The cause of the problem remains unknown.

Narrow branch angles often lead to included (or trapped) bark such that the limb and main stem of the tree cannot form the interlocking growth rings so critical to strong branches (Figure 13.13). Practice, observation and practice can aid the development of the eye and "feel" for when and where to prune a particular species for best results.

304

Figure 13.11.   The green ash (above) have about two-inch stem
diameters and are 9 to 11 feet tall.   If they are not harvested,
overall tree quality will decrease.   If only part of the trees are
sold, harvest every other one in order to allow the others to
increase in value.   On the other hand, if part of the tree rows
are harvested and the other rows are left in tact, the quality of
the remaining trees will suffer.   The multiple-stem crapemyrtle
(below) are ready for harvest.   The lower limbs were removed in
time to allow the pruning wounds to callous over, but were left
long enough to aid good stem taper.

305

Figure 13.12. When the top of a tree with opposite branching is pruned, the likelihood of a double leader is much greater than on trees with alternate branching (above). The top (central leader) of this green ash tree (below) was not removed, but was shaded by a strong branch of an adjacent larger tree in the nursery. As a result, the unshaded branch (on the left) became the dominant "leader" of the tree. Now the choice is either remove the old central leader and perhaps the opposite branch (on the right of the largest stem) or remove the strong limb of the adjacent tree plus cut back the branch on the left. There is no easy answer. This is a good example where prevention would have been best as there is no good cure.

Figure 13.13. When narrow branching occurs, frequently bark is included (or trapped) in the fork (above). Due to the presence of the bark (the dark area), the interlocking growth rings of limb and main stem cannot develop and at some stress point the limb is going to fall. Not all "narrow" branches are weak, however. In the case of this live oak (below) even though the branch angle is relatively narrow, the branch is soundly attached to the trunk. If this was to be a permanent branch of the tree, it perhaps should be removed. On the other hand, if it were part of a young tree below where pruning would be done to obtain the clear stem before sale, it would be acceptable.

When young trees are pruned, respect the branch collar or branch/bark ridge just as when pruning large trees (Figure 13.14). This minimizes the size of the wound while hastening callous growth over the wound to minimize the likelihood of entrance of any decay fungi. In all cases, use sharp pruning shears that cause the least crushing or tearing of tissues (Figure 13.14).

If young trees are "topped" or cut back, always cut just above an existing side branch or strong bud. In this case there is no branch/bark ridge to guide you so look at the side branch or strong bud and cut just above and at a slope. If you cut too far above, you will have a dead stub since there is no active leaf surface beyond that point to support callus development (Figure 13.15). On the other hand, if you cut too close to a strong side bud, the exposed tissues may dry and crack sufficiently as to also kill the bud. Practice and observation of the results will soon reveal the proper cut position.

If young trees require staking, use a stake that is flexible and proportionate to the size of the tree. If the stake is large and rigid relative to the young tree stem, no movement of the stem occurs and stem diameter increase will be minimal (Figure 13.16). Use only flexible/ expandable fasteners for attaching a young tree to a stake. The key is to hold the tree upright and in place while allowing some flexibility. Wrapping a wire around a young tree stem demonstrates two points: a) a young tree stem under good growing conditions can grow very rapidly and b) the downward flow of energy from the leaves does, indeed, take place (Figure 13.16). If a wire or other inflexible material is wrapped around a tree, the stem will grow more **above** the wire than below due to the source of the energy (leaves) and the blockage of the normal downward flow.

Figure 13.14. Limbs on most trees have a branch collar that provides a guide to making the pruning cut (above). Note the two white arrows and the slight collar or shoulder where the branch tissues interlock with those of the main stem. Cut at the face of the branch collar, never inside or outside (below). If the pruning cut is made at the proper point using a pair of sharp hand pruners, the wound will be small and the tissues will not be crushed or torn, thus allowing rapid callus growth to cover the exposed wood. As with larger trees, there is no advantage to painting pruning wounds.

Figure 13.15. These two trees were cut back to force additional side branch development. When pruning back to a strong side bud (above) cut just enough above the bud to prevent the bud from being affected by the drying exposed wood. In this case, the cut was made too far above the bud and it was nearly parallel to the ground. Note the discoloration of the wood back from the cut surface and the weak connection between branch and stem.

When pruning back to a side branch, cut just above the top of the branch/bark ridge (below). In this case, the cut was made too far above the branch and a stub remains. Notice the extent of the new callus tissue below the branch and very little above. This is due to the movement of energy downward from the leaves. Since there is no active tissue and only an inactive stub above the branch/stem connection, little energy is received to promote callus growth.

310

Figure 13.16. When staking young trees, always use a stake that is flexible relative to the size of the stem. The young stem must be allowed to move or flex while being held upright. In this case (above left) the stake is much too large relative to the stem of the young tree. If a wire is used to tie a tree to a stake or is tied around the stem, at some point, the downward flow of energy from the leaves to the stem and roots will be blocked (below). In this case, a wire was wrapped around a young maple tree then around the stake such that the tree stem was completely surrounded. Note the growth of the stem above the wire. This clearly demonstrates the downward movement of energy in the stem as well as the capacity of plant tissues to react to increased levels of energy.

311

Specific Pruning Cases. The following eight examples are all live oaks in two-gallon containers approximately two years old. The first year they were grown in small containers, then shifted into two gallon containers in the fall or winter. The vigorous growth of young trees in containers in conjunction with limited stem taper and trunk development means that light but frequent pruning to direct growth should be the aim of the nurseryman instead of drastic pruning less often. These trees could have been better served by one or two light prunings during the first growing season.

Eight examples were chosen in an attempt to show what should be done during the dormant period to shape the trees for the next growing season. The key word is "anticipate". The person doing the pruning must anticipate the growth and development of the tree in the future. A general knowledge of the growth characteristics of the species and/or cultivar is essential as well as requirements of the market. If a limb is left, the person doing the pruning must anticipate the growth during the following season(s). Likewise, if it is removed, they must anticipate how its removal will influence the growth of the main stem or adjacent branches.

Effective and practical pruning of young trees is as much an art as it is a science. In order to do it well, years of experience must be gained by pruning, watching the resultant growth and learning from the plant response in order to better anticipate pruning effects and plant response in the future.

A key to remember, is that if anything larger than a sharp hand pruner is required to accomplish the pruning, someone has "dropped the ball". Study the before and after photos carefully as well as the text with each figure and an appreciation for what to prune and when to prune can begin. This is a beginning only. In order to grow, the person doing the pruning must also observe carefully what happens as a result of pruning (Figures 13.17 through 13.27). The white markers on the trees on the left in each photo show where the pruning will occur. The photo on the right shows the trees after pruning is complete. In some cases, photos are included to show the actual plant response to the pruning.

312

Example 13.17. This young tree had a very flexible central leader, two side branches that may try to become leaders (top marker), an old central leader that failed to develop (center marker), and several vigorous low branches (bottom marker). The central leader was cut back to a point where the main stem was strong and a good bud was present on the upper side of the stem (right). If the end bud on the upper side of the stem breaks first, it will become the new central leader and make a relatively straight stem. The side branches at the upper marker were cut back to assure they would not rival the central leader. The old central leader that had failed to develop was removed (center marker). This leaves a kink in the stem, however, at this young age, most of it will disappear with (continued top of next page)

further trunk growth. Most of the vigorous lower branches were cut back but not removed. The side branches on a young tree provide the bulk of the energy for stem diameter increase as well as root growth. After one more growing season and a substantial increase in stem diameter, the lower branches may be removed.

Figure 13.18. Note the top of the tree in Figure 13.17 where it was cut back. The pruning cut was made just above a strong bud. With the spring flush of growth following pruning, the bud extended and quickly became the dominant central leader for the tree. Note the difference in size between the top shoot from the second bud to break. This is because of the apical dominance and vigor of the top shoot that became the central leader.

Example 13.19.   This young tree had a good central leader, but several rivals were developing at the base.   If these were not removed, the tree would become a poorly branched "shrub".   The markers show two vigorous lower branches with narrow "V" forks to be removed and one to be cut back.   The central leader has good gradual taper from the base to the tip (right) and was not disturbed.   The two vigorous side shoots were removed at the base along with several weak small branches.   One moderate side shoot (upper marker) was cut back but not removed.   The many side branches were left on the main stem to support trunk diameter growth and taper.   They should be removed after one more growing season.

315

Figure 13.20. The young tree in Figure 13.19 had a cluster of terminal buds at the tip which is typical of oaks. If the center bud expands vigorously, the central leader will remain and the tree form will be good. However, in some cases the central or primary bud goes "blind" and two or more of the surrounding buds vie for the role of central leader. It is important to select the most vigorous shoot of the 2, 3 or 4 that grow in the absence of the central bud so that a new central leader can direct tree form. In this case, the central bud grew and the surrounding buds become supportive lateral branches.

Figure 13.21. This young tree had two leaders of similar height. One is more slender with no side branches near the base while the other had several side branches. The upper markers show two vigorous side branches that must be cut back to maintain a central leader. The central leader has good taper from tip to base and the kink at the base is less noticeable after removal of the competing leader (right). After one growing season there will be little evidence remaining of the kink or the old competing leader. The strong competing side branches were cut back to assure dominance of the central leader, but not removed so as to provide for good stem diameter growth. Note the very tip of the tree.
(continued top of next page)

317

There are two, possibly three, branches poised to become leaders. All three were left because the terminal buds were small and weak. After growth begins in the spring, one should be selected as leader and the others cut back or removed. If one of the three shoots had had a strong terminal bud, the others would have been cut back or removed.

Figure 13.22. The trees in Figures 13.21, 13.22 and 13.23 all had sizable side branches that were removed. In all three cases, with the spring flush of growth following pruning, adventitious or dormant buds began to grow adjacent to the pruning wound. These dormant buds grow because the strength of the chemical signal from the top had been decreased by the pruning. The lower chemical signal allowed these dormant buds to grow. If removal is prompt, it can be done by simply rubbing with a thumb or forefinger. For the procrastinator, it will mean the pruning shears or (gasp!) the loppers. This photo is of the base of the tree in Figure 13.21. Note that there were no branches near the "V" fork at the base before or after pruning. However, there shoots developed very quickly after growth began in the spring.

318

Figure 13.23. This young tree had a central leader that was restricted in growth due to the development of a vigorous side branch (marker). The choice becomes one of leaving the strong side branch with a severe kink at the base or remove the side branch and work with the central leader.

The side branch was removed (right) because if it had been the leader of choice, the kink at the base would have been too severe. By removing the strong side branch, a young tree with good stem taper remains. Two side branches were also cut back after removal of the large side branch to assure that they would not become competing leaders. The resulting young tree has good form and branch development and will make an excellent specimen.

319

Figure 13.24.   This young tree is a good example of branch development on a leaning main stem.   When a main stem leans, branch development is mostly on the upper portion of the stem. This is probably the result of a young container tree seedling either too slender to remain upright or leaning because of improper planting.   Branch development has progressed to the point that the basal branch has more desirable characteristics than the old main stem (note marker at base).

By removing the original stem (right) and heading back a few side branches, the resulting young tree has the potential of becoming a quality specimen.   The kink at the base is not good, but because of the location, will probably have minimal negative effect on the overall tree quality in the future.   The stem taper of the tree following pruning is good as well as good side branch distribution on the stem.

Figure 13.25.   This young tree had four slender stems of about the same diameter and height.   None had good side branch development. The decision was to choose the stem that   provides the best leader after the other three were cut back or removed.   This is an example of pruning that should have been done several months earlier, before the four competing stems   developed this far.   A substantial amount of top growth must be removed in order to obtain a salable tree.   Top growth removed is energy and growth lost.   Like maintaining an automobile, it is better to make minor adjustments frequently than major adjustments less often. The stem selected for the central leader (right) (continued next page)

had the best side branch development, overall stem taper, no kink where it joined the base and a strong terminal bud. The other side branches were only cut back in order to provide branches and leaf surface to support stem growth the following growing season. The remaining central leader is very slender. If it leans severely, the side branch development will occur as shown in Figure 13.24. If the central leader is going to lean, it should be cut back to a point where it does not lean in order to force a new bud to become the leader. If it is planted, tip the root ball to straighten the stem. This is much better than staking.

There are no preferred areas to make a cut when heading back a weak terminal shoot or side branch. However, by cutting back to a strong, healthy bud aimed in the desired direction (review Figure 13.18), new growth can be directed and the time for callous closure of the wound will be minimal. If a branch is cut back to a strong bud and the bud expands quickly with the new flush of growth, the energy manufactured by the leaves on the new growth will hasten the callous cover of the wound. On the other hand, if the bud nearest the pruning cut does not grow or progress slowly and buds further down (back) on the stem grow vigorously, the callous development over the wound will be slow or nonexistent. In some cases a dead stub results. Thus the importance of pruning back to a strong, healthy bud.

The practice of cutting back young trees near the soil line to "get a strong, straight stem" is a questionable practice in much of the U.S.A. In the Pacific Northwest and to a lesser degree elsewhere, young trees are grown for one year, then cut off near the ground during the dormant period. With the spring flush of growth, one shoot is selected to be the new "leader" and the others are removed.

There are several things this author does not like about the practice: 1) every tree grown with this procedure has a crook or "dog leg" at the base, 2) an open wound and/or decay is often associated with this practice, 3) it is labor-intensive to cut off the existing top, prune away the many shoots while selecting one, then stake the one vigorous shoot so it will not separate from the main stem, 4) it is unnatural in that the top that develops the first year is abruptly removed and a vigorous and succulent shoot with few natural side branches regrows the second season. The succulent new growth is very susceptible to aphids and other

322

insects as well as wind damage. The four photos in Figures 13.28 and 13.29 show a field of live oaks. The problems, actions, and plant response are described. If the cut is made too low (near the soil surface), there may not be a dormant shoot bud and the tree will die. If the cut is made too high, it stimulates more "brush" to cut away to get to a good shoot to save.

The best thing to do is to avoid the practice by growing a vigorous tree with a good root system. These trees do not need to be cut back and as a result have no "dog leg" at the base and structurally and visually are superior.

Pruning is a series of judgments. The nature of buds, energy levels, light, competing branches and a myriad of chemical and physical factors make pruning of young trees mostly an art or feel rather than a specific science. These examples should serve only as examples since the trees you will be pruning are different. Good luck.

Figure 13.26. This young tree had a good primary stem with a competing side branch at the top and several undesirable side branches at the base. The removal of the competing side branch at the top assured continuation of a straight central leader. Since there were other supporting side branches, the competing branch was removed. The most vigorous branches at the base were removed in order to avoid interference with development of the central leader and because there were numerous side branches to support main stem growth even after their removal. The kink at the base of the tree is severe and will be noticeable for many years, however, there were no practical alternatives in this case. Use frequent and light pruning to avoid such complications.

Figure 13.27.   This young tree had somewhat the same problem as Figure 13.25, in that there were several stems vying to be leader. The difference is that there is a central leader with good stem taper present among the branches.   The six pruning markers show where the various cuts will be made, but this leaves a curving stem which was noted to be undesirable in Figure 13.24.   The difference is the placement of the root ball and orientation of the stem when the young tree is planted into the field or shifted into a larger container.   By shifting the root ball, the tree has only a graceful curving central leader with good stem taper and good branch development.   This will make an excellent specimen tree in a few years.   There is no harm or complication in placing the root ball slightly tilted in order to have a vertical stem.

325

Figure 13.28. In this field of live oaks a number of trees were poorly branched (above). In order to try to get a straight stem, some of the trees were cut off a few inches above the soil line (below). In a field of trees where only a portion are cut back, these are at a distinct disadvantage for light as a result of shading by the taller trees. The other problem will be that the large trees will be salable before those cut back. This means awkward harvesting and poor space utilization in the field.

Figure 13.29. This tree (above) was cut off a few inches above the soil surface while dormant. With the beginning of spring, many branches develop quickly from dormant shoot buds in the stem. From this "brush", one shoot must be selected as the new stem. In this case, a vigorous shoot was selected near the top of the old stem (below) and all others removed. The problem here is that the new shoot is only weakly attached to the old stem (see Figure 13.15), thus is easily damaged during the clean up pruning process or for most of the following growing season. In addition, the cut was made at an angle about 90 degrees to the right from the ideal. The exposed old stem above the level of the new shoot will not grow and callus growth will not cover the open wound for several growing seasons. If you must cut, do it just above the dormant bud with the cut surface sloping away.

CHAPTER 14

DRIP IRRIGATION

DRIP IRRIGATION

Background and Objectives. Tremendous progress was made in drip irrigation during the 1970s and early 1980s. The crude emitters with no pressure-compensating capacity have been replaced with in-line or lock-on emitters that even-out the water distribution between high and low areas in the field and throughout the row.

The concept of drip irrigation is to slowly wet the soil in the root zone of the plant so that there is no run-off and minimal evaporation loss. With overhead sprinklers considerable run-off may occur and water loss to evaporation can account for up to 50% of the water pumped.

The area to be wetted should be adjusted according to the extent of the root system and need of the crop (Figure 14.1). However, the best technique is to wet the root zone of the plant, then allow the area to dry, then re-water. The dry cycle should not extend to the point of dry soil and wilting, but rather to the point of only slightly damp soil. A wet/dry cycle that does not become excessively dry will allow deeper root development, minimize root rot disease problems and provide for good growth. Do not let the soil become so dry that top growth ceases. At the same time, by encouraging deeper root development, the extent of soil drying that can occur before top growth ceases is extended and plant blow-over is greatly reduced or eliminated. This is in contrast to some who recommend applying a consistent quantity of water at a regular interval such that the soil is kept wet at all times. The disadvantage of the constant wet approach is the shallow root system and greater root disease problems. When the soil is constantly wet, the depth of oxygen penetration is shallow, thus the shallow root system. In addition, serious root rot organisms such as *Phytophthora* are favored by high moisture, low oxygen conditions.

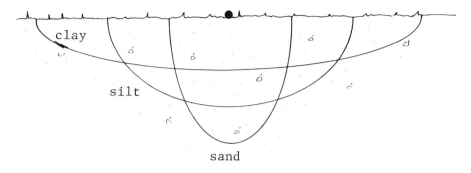

clay

silt

sand

Figure 14.1.   The extent of horizontal vs. vertical distribution of water is directly related to the soil texture (above).   Water will spread more horizontally in a clay soil and more vertically in a sandy soil in the same period of time.   By leaving the system on for a longer time, the wetted zone will be wider (below).   With very sandy soils a spray-stake may give better water distribution than a drip emitter.

330

Types of Drip Systems. Basically there are three types of drip or spot irrigation systems: 1) spot-wetting from a short-life drip line, 2) spot-wetting with a long-life line and 3) area wetting with a low volume, specific area small spray head.

1. For annual or other short-term crops, the spot-wetting, short-life drip lines offer acceptable water distribution at a fairly low cost per acre. Materials such as Dura tape (T-tape), Chapins Bi-wall and Roberts Ro-Drip are prime examples. Of these, Roberts irrigation Ro-Drip, appears to have the longest life and durability and the best water distribution.

For small plants on close spacings, use emitters on 8- to 12-inch centers. This gives a uniform wetted band down the row with limited lateral spread when the plants are small. As the plants grow larger, by leaving water on for a longer time, the wetted area will widen (Figure 14.1).

The cost of this procedure is relatively low, since the tubing and emitters used are less expensive than with the longer life drip system. Cost of a longer life drip system is not so much in the tubing but in the more expensive and durable emitters. The short-life lines are generally good for one growing season, however, the Roberts irrigation product may last for two seasons or more. The life of these lines is in some cases due to the durability and resistance to plugging of the line and emitters, while in other cases the effective life is a result of rodent damage. Rabbits, rats, land turtles, armadillos, raccoons and other pests often damage the thin tubing in search of water or just to be mischievous.

Another problem, especially with the light tubing is movement of the lines by wind or rain. When the lines are empty they are easily moved, and remember that they are filled with water for only a few hours every few days. Line movement can be reduced by weaving the line among the plants if the plants are large enough. Placing the line on the uphill or windy side relative to the crop plants will also help (Figure 14.2). The use of white Dutch clover as the groundcover crop has provided a very effective means of holding the lines in place. If the clover is present when the lines are placed in the field, the leaves hold the lines fairly well. However, after a few weeks or months, the stolons (horizontal, above-ground stems) of the white Dutch clover will grow over the lines and effectively tie them in place (Figure 14.3). The shading of the drip line by the clover greatly reduces the expansion and contraction of the plastic line, thus aiding in the water distribution.

Figure 14.2.   Place the short-life drip line on the uphill side to minimize erosion or wind movement (above) or use white Dutch clover as a ground cover to hold the lines in place and provide other benefits (below).   After four to six weeks the clover will grow over the lines and securely hold them in place.

Figure 14.3. In this case, the white Dutch clover was planted, then narrow strips were rototilled prior to planting the 2- to 3-inch crapemyrtle seedlings. Immediately following planting, the short-life drip line was placed. The clover grew back over the disturbed soil surface, including the drip line. Note the movement of the lines by wind, rain or simply the expansion/contraction from heating and cooling. It is difficult to keep the light weight tubing in place when the crop is small.

2. Long-life drip lines are generally the best choice for trees and shrubs in the field that require more than one growing season before harvest. Nearly all long-life drip lines use 0.5-inch polyethylene lines. This line is thicker and large enough so rodents rarely cause damage and it is less subject to wind and water movement. The cost of the line is relatively low, however, the drip emitters are expensive. As a result, the most used procedure is to provide one emitter at or near the base of each tree or shrub in the row. If the trees are on four-foot centers in the row, the drip emitters are also spaced every four feet on or in the line. This sounds good in print, however, in practice, the expansion/contraction of the plastic line as a result of heating and cooling, moves the emitters a few inches to several feet from the desired spot (Figure 14.4). If the lines are laid

out on a cloudy, cool day, the lines will expand, buckle or kink on a sunny day, such that the lines may be pushed away from some of the plants. On the other hand, if the lines are laid out on a sunny day and cut the length of the row, the next morning the lines will be a few inches to several feet short, depending on the length of the row. One tempting technique is to tie the ends of the lines to stakes to hold the lines in place. However, if the lines are staked out when hot, they will pull apart or pull out the stake when they get cold. Staking out a cool line will provide no benefit, since the expansion continues to occur. Some nurserymen have resorted to springs on the ends of the lines to keep them in place. The most practical approach is to use lines with emitters on 18- to 24-inch centers. On most soils, emitters on 24-inch centers will wet the entire row, thus the relative location of the emitter and the plant is not critical. In addition, all lines can be used on any age plants. The use of white Dutch clover or other ground cover vegetation is equally beneficial in holding long-life drip lines in place as was covered regarding short-life drip lines.

Figure 14.4. These drip irrigation lines with emitters every four feet were placed to coincide with the tree spacing. Note the location of the emitters relative to the tree (arrow) after a few weeks. A better system is to space the drip emitters so that the entire row is wetted as in Figure 14.1.

Turbulent flow, pressure-compensating emitters are far superior to emitters with no restriction to water flow (Figure 14.5). Since the entire drip irrigation system is operated on five to 15 pounds per square inch (psi) of pressure, the effect of gravity on the movement of water in the lines is great. In addition, as water moves through the lines, there is friction, thus the smaller and/or longer the line, the greater the friction. The in-line emitters work best as they are not disrupted by handling (Figure 14.5). The add-on button-type emitters, although pressure-compensating, are easily damaged by equipment, foot traffic or when the lines are rolled or unrolled (Figure 14.6).

Figure 14.5. Turbulent flow, pressure-compensating emitters are far superior to emitters with no restriction to water flow. This in-line emitter is one of the best available. The line can be rolled up and moved without damaging the emitter and it works in any position in terms of line rotation or twisting. When the line is unrolled, simply separate the line at an emitter and start another row. There is no need to cut the line. When the line is removed from the field, it can again be joined together to form a continuous roll. This allows the line to be used for rows of different length without special connectors.

Figure 14.6. The add-on, button-type emitters require considerable time to install and are very vulnerable to damage when the line is moved. Simply walking on the line may knock off an emitter, but it may not be noticed for sometime.

An early lesson was learned by the author when trying to set up a very precise watering study for container nursery stock. The soil surface appeared to be near level, so the drip lines with emitters, with no pressure-compensating capacity, were placed down the rows of containers (Figure 14.7). Prior to beginning the study, small containers were placed beneath each drip emitter to test the uniformity of water distribution. The lines in the system were only 80 feet long and the water pressure was eight psi. Water from the emitters varied from 8 to 20 ounces for a 10-minute-on time. The first attempt to solve the problem of uneven water distribution was to add another water inlet line to the opposite end from the initial water inlet. This was prompted by the fact that the low volumes of water were all at the opposite end from the water inlet. A second test showed little change. Finally, through the use of a level, boards and bricks, a level base was created for all containers and the water distribution was uniform. It is important to note that the differences in elevation in the 80 feet that created the large difference in water discharge from the emitters was only three inches and a good lesson was learned. Pressure-compensating emitters have reduced the variation in water discharge due to elevation or friction in the line a great deal, however, this must still be considered.

The practical approach is to adjust the rows in the field so that they run at right angles to the slope and as much as is practical at the same elevation from end to end. If the rows must slope, whenever possible have the water inlet at the high end of the row. This reduces the friction effect in the line up to a point since water flow is aided by gravity.

3. Area wetting with a low-volume, specific-area, small spray head is especially useful on sandy soils and with large plants (Figure 14.8). On sandy soils where water from drip emitters moves downward with little horizontal spread, area wetting works well. This technique has been used extensively in Florida where the "soil" may be 98% sand. In addition, with established trees with extensive root systems, area wetting distributes the water over a greater portion of the root zone while reducing evaporation losses and large-volume pumping associated with overhead irrigation.

Figure 14.7. These emitters have no pressure-compensation capacity. The on-line emitter (above) simply inserts into a hole in the line. Even on near-level ground it gives uneven distribution since more water exits near the source vs. further down the line. The lead weight on the small tubing works well in a greenhouse with level benches, but does not work outside (below). In addition, the small tubing in the field is a picnic for rodents.

339

Figure 14.8. A low-volume, specific-area, spray head works best on the very sandy soils in Florida. This distributes the water over an area of several square feet (depending on the particular head and water pressure). If a conventional drip emitter is used on a very sandy soil, the water moves downward with limited horizontal distribution.

A typical system may be installed on or below the soil surface. With young trees on three- to six-foot centers in the row, the line may be left on the soil surface. Spray heads may be attached directly to the line or connected by a small diameter tube. The small diameter tube provides some pressure compensation but has the undesirable features of more labor during installation and increased rodent damage. On the other hand, attaching the spray heads directly to the lines often leads to poor water distribution since the lines tend to twist or roll with heating and cooling or as a result of other cultural practices.

The Water Supply. All three drip irrigation systems need clean water for most efficient operation and minimal plugging problems. Most city water has been filtered sufficiently so that no further filtering is needed. In general, some well waters require little or no filtration...with some definite exceptions where sand or other particulate matter is carried or suspended in the water. Nearly all surface waters require considerable filtration due to the likelihood of silt and debris.

A simple screen-type filter with 150- to 180-mesh screen may be satisfactory where a limited volume of water is required from a city water supply or well. Where more filtration is needed, screen-type filters can be a major headache. Not only are screens quick to plug, but they are also difficult to clean. Disc-type filters with built-in back-flushing capacity can filter moderate quantities of water with minimal complications (Figure 14.9).

Figure 14.9. A water filter with disc-type screen. When removed from the case, the discs separate for easy removal of debris. The size of the grooves in the discs determine the screen size.

By installing a pressure gauge on both the inlet and outlet sides of the filter, the need for cleaning can quickly be determined when the gauge on the discharge side shows a lower pressure than the inlet and without taking it apart. In addition, disc-type filters are more easily cleaned than screens since the discs can be loosened and separated, thus trapped particles are removed.

For large volumes and/or particularly dirty water, sand filters like those used on swimming pools work best. These filter by trapping particles on the surface or within a layer of sand. If greater filtration is needed, a finer sand can be used. Changing the direction of water flow will backwash and clean the filter in a few minutes. Since the sand is agitated somewhat by the reverse flow of the water, cleaning is thorough and fast.

As the filtering capacity and efficiency goes up, so does the cost. The decision frequently must be made between a low-cost water source and an expensive filtration system (such as water out of a pond, lake or stream) vs. a higher cost water source (a well or city water) and minimal filtration. In addition to the volume of water and direct cost of the water, the quality of the water must be considered.

Water Quality, Quantity and Wells. Water that contains substantial quantities of calcium, sodium, bicarbonates, chlorine or boron should be avoided if possible. The accumulation of sodium over time can damage soil structure and reduce water infiltration and aeration. Calcium and bicarbonates increase soil pH and reduce the availability of micronutrients. In general, surface water supplies contain fewer dissolved minerals than well water but require greater filtration. In addition, surface water supplies can provide the least water when it is needed most (late summer). **Because waters vary greatly, each source must be considered individually and few generalizations can be made.**

Because the various chemical elements are dissolved in the water and therefore cannot be seen, it is difficult to maintain an awareness of their importance (Figure 14.10). An additional water analysis should be done with any change in water source, such as adding a new well or a catch pond to re-cycle run-off water from the nursery. In the latter case, water samples should be taken of the run-off water, the primary source, and a typical mixture.

342

Figure 14.10. Water quality cannot be seen. Therefore an analysis of water by a reputable laboratory is a must before the land is purchased or the water is used on any crops. In this case, water is added to a holding pond to maintain a uniform water quantity while diluting any salts from the run-off from recycled water from the container nursery and greenhouses.

It is difficult to define the "ideal" irrigation water. A rather wide range of water quality may be used to produce good quality crops as long as the water quality is known and fitted into the overall production and management program. For example: As the total amount of soluble salts in the irrigation water increases, the frequency of watering must increase so as to prevent drying of the soil which has the effect of concentrating the salts and increasing the likelihood of salt injury to roots or tops.

Some general ranges of water quality characteristics are listed below:

a) The pH of irrigation water reveals very little about its quality. The pH may range from very acid (pH 4.0) to moderately alkaline (pH 9.0). Acids or acid-generating salts and dissolved carbon dioxide in the water may cause a very low pH reading. Carbonates, bicarbonates, and hydroxide, particularly of sodium, calcium, or magnesium, cause the pH of the water to increase. Water with a pH of 7.5 to 8.0 may produce excellent crops and require no specific treatments if the bicarbonates are not excessive. For example, the pH of the city water in Stillwater, Oklahoma is about 7.9 but contains only 40 ppm (parts per million) of calcium and 20 ppm magnesium with a bicarbonate level of only 160 ppm. This water causes no precipitate on the leaves and requires no specific treatment. By contrast, some wells in east Texas have water that has pH of about 10.0, yet has very low levels of calcium, magnesium, and bicarbonates and can be used without special treatment.

When irrigation water is very alkaline and contains high levels of bicarbonates, acid injection may be required. Sulfuric acid may be used. The rate will depend on the specific requirements of the water and, in general, no two water needs are the same. Acid injection is expensive and corrosive and it poses a distinct hazard. Safeguards should be carefully considered to minimize the chance of injecting excesses and to avoid contact with eyes, skin and clothing of personnel.

b) Soluble salts are any soluble salt-forming chemical in the water. They generally come from water slowly dissolving rocks and minerals as well as from fertilizers. Intrusion of salt water may occur either directly from the ocean or from trapped deposits of salt water in the earth seeping into fresh water deposits as the level of fresh water is lowered.

In general, the lower the level of soluble salts, the easier the water needs of the plant are to manage (Table 14.1). Water with less that 500 parts per million soluble salts is ideal. However, water with salt levels of 1200 to 1600 parts per million have been used successfully when adequate precautions are taken.

Table 14-1.   General Interpretation of Water Quality.
- -

Solu-bridge Reading	Parts Per Million Soluble Salts	Water Quality
0-0.25	0-150	Very good
0.25-0.75	150-500	Good
0.75-1.50	500-1200	Fair (caution)
1.50-2.0	1200-1600	Questionable
2.0 or above	above 1600	Unacceptable

----

c) High levels of sodium can be injurious to some plants. Sodium alone is more likely to be injurious than sodium in conjunction with calcium and/or magnesium. The sodium adsorption ratio (SAR) gives a general indication of the possible damage from sodium and is calculated as follows:

$$SAR = \frac{\text{Sodium level in ppm}}{\dfrac{\text{Calcium level} + \text{magnesium level}}{2}}$$

Water with 40 ppm (parts per million) calcium, 20 ppm magnesium, and 40 ppm sodium would have a SAR of 7.3. (40 + 20 = 60) divided by 2 = 30. The square root of 30 is 5.5. The level of sodium, which is 40, divided by 5.5 = 7.3. Sodium adsorption ratios below 10 generally do not pose a problem to container plant production; 10-15 is marginal and over 15 is generally unacceptable.

   d) Chlorine is commonly found in irrigation water as part of a dissolved salt, sodium chloride. Chlorine levels above 40 to 60 ppm (parts per million) may be injurious to some sensitive crops.

   In some areas, boron may pose a problem. In general, boron levels below 0.5 ppm are safe; levels of 0.5-1.2 may cause injury to sensitive crops or crops grown in the same container for a long period. Levels of 1.5 to 3 are suspect and should be avoided if possible.

   There is no quick or easy answer regarding water source. It depends on the alternatives, soils, crops and other factors. Thus, all alternatives must be considered prior to beginning to minimize problems and accent performance.

Building the Irrigation System. Plastic pipe, particularly pvc (polyvinylchloride) is used almost exclusively for irrigation systems due to the ease of assembly and cost. Schedule 40 pvc has a working pressure of 160 psi (pounds per square inch) and is satisfactory for all but a very few high pressure situations.

   A major consideration in laying out an irrigation system is the friction loss associated with the flow of water through the pipe. The greater the distance, the greater the friction loss, especially in small pipes. Friction is the reason there is good water pressure at a hose outlet on your house but if you connect five or six water hoses together, only a trickle comes out the end.

345

Table 14.2 provides a range of pipe sizes from 1/2 inch to 4 inches across the top and flow in gallons per minute (gpm) down the side. Keep in mind that the velocity of the water in feet per second (fps) should not exceed approximately 3 to 3.5 for most efficient operation, and a pressure drop of more than 1 to 2 (psi) per 100 feet of pipe will reduce irrigation efficiency, especially if large areas are considered.

One factor that can sometimes be very helpful in designing and operating a drip irrigation system is a simple bypass. Consider a well that will pump about 15 gallons per minute. The desire is to obtain maximum output from the well without pumping it dry or wasting part of the water-supplying potential of the well. Use a pump sufficiently large so as to pump the well dry, then place a bypass line such that some of the water pumped is returned to the well. Adjust a valve in the bypass line so that the maximum water is supplied by the well without the pump sucking air (Figure 14.11).

In this example, the pump can supply 15 gpm (gallons per minute) throughout the year. This means 15 x 60 = 900 gallons per hour. If emitters that discharge one gallon per hour (a good general purpose rate) are used, then about 800 emitters can be used at one time. If the emitters are on two-foot centers, this means 1600 feet of row can be watered at one time. The reason 800 is used as a figure instead of 900 is to allow for friction loss in the lines and a degree of safety or buffer. If the thin wall tube short-life line is used with 0.25 gallons per hour outlets on 12-inch centers, 3200 feet of line can be supplied at one time, however, the length of time required to wet the desired area will be twice as long.

Table 14.2. Water flow relative to velocity and pressure in various pipe sizes.

Flow G.P.M.	1/2" Velocity F.P.S.	1/2" Pressure Drop P.S.I.	3/4" Velocity F.P.S.	3/4" Pressure Drop P.S.I.	1" Velocity F.P.S.	1" Pressure Drop P.S.I.	1 1/4" Velocity F.P.S.	1 1/4" Pressure Drop P.S.I.	1 1/2" Velocity F.P.S.	1 1/2" Pressure Drop P.S.I.	2" Velocity F.P.S.	2" Pressure Drop P.S.I.	2 1/2" Velocity F.P.S.	2 1/2" Pressure Drop P.S.I.	3" Velocity F.P.S.	3" Pressure Drop P.S.I.	4" Velocity F.P.S.	4" Pressure Drop P.S.I.
5	3.95	4.14	2.36	1.19	1.43	.35	.87	.10	.67	.05								
6	4.73	5.80	2.83	1.67	1.72	.49	1.04	.14	.80	.08								
8			3.78	2.84	2.29	.84	1.39	.24	1.06	.13	.68	.04						
10			4.72	4.29	2.86	1.27	1.74	.37	1.33	.20	.85	.07	.58	.03				
15					4.29	2.68	2.61	.78	2.00	.41	1.27	.14	.87	.05				
20							3.49	1.33	2.66	.70	1.70	.24	1.16	.09	.78	.04		
25							4.35	2.01	3.33	1.06	2.12	.36	1.45	.14	.97	.05		
30									4.00	1.49	2.55	.50	1.74	.20	1.17	.08		
35									4.66	1.98	2.98	.67	2.03	.27	1.35	.10		
40											3.40	.86	2.32	.34	1.56	.13	.94	.04
45											3.84	1.06	2.61	.42	1.75	.16	1.06	.05
50											4.25	1.29	2.90	.51	1.95	.19	1.18	.06
60													3.48	.72	2.33	.27	1.41	.08
70													4.06	.96	2.72	.36	1.65	.11
80													4.64	1.23	3.11	.46	1.88	.14
90															3.50	.58	2.12	.17
100															3.89	.70	2.35	.20
125															4.86	1.06	2.94	.31
150																	3.53	.43
175																	4.11	.58
200																	4.70	.76

347

Figure 14.11. In this case a 1/2-horsepower submergible pump was installed in the shallow well. The capacity of the pump is about 20 gpm with a 40-foot deep well, but the capacity of the water bearing sand is about 15 gpm. The bypass valve is opened at first, then slowly the valve is closed until the pump begins to surge from sucking air, then opened up slightly to provide a degree of safety.

By dividing the field into sections or circuits such that one circuit uses the capacity of the pump at the desired pressure (approximately 10 to 15 psi for most conditions), the maximum water is supplied to the plants using the pump to its fullest capacity and thus the greatest efficiency. In the example, one circuit only needs to be watered for 12 hours every four to five days under the most severe conditions, thus eight circuits can be watered from the pump that produced 15 gpm. If the 0.25 gallons per hour emitters are on 12-inch centers in the short-term, thin-wall drip lines, then 8 X 3200 linear feet of row can be watered by this well, or about 25,600 feet. If the rows are on four-foot centers, then 2.3 acres can be watered from a very small and inexpensive shallow well system (25,600 feet X 4 feet = 102,400 square feet/43560 square feet per acre). These same principles and techniques can be applied to larger systems as well.

The length of a drip irrigation line depends on the size of the line, the rate of water discharge from the emitters, the spacing of the emitters and the slope of the land. It is far better to be cautious than to have stressed or dead plants at the end of the row. Most manufacturers of drip irrigation equipment provide charts to show the maximum recommended length for each drip line size and configuration. By spacing one gallon per hour emitters on two-foot centers instead of four, in order to get complete row wetting as was discussed earlier, only half as many linear feet of line can be operated at a time assuming a fixed capacity water source. On the other hand, the on time of the system would be reduced by about 50%, so the overall efficiency of the system is about the same.

A larger example: irrigating 40 acres with drip. Assume trees are planted on 10-foot rows and four feet in the row = 1089 trees per acre (10' X 4' = 40 sq. ft. per tree. Divide 40 into 43560 = 1089 trees per acre). This requires 1089 X 4 feet per tree in the row = 4356 linear feet of drip line. A drip emitter should be every two feet and one gallon per hour emitters used which equals 2178 gallons per hour per acre. Thus to water a five acre block at one time requires 10890 gallons per hour---in reality, consider 12,000 gallon per hour = 200 gallons per minute pump output.

The aspect of running a pump at full capacity with little or no restriction as long as your aquifer will supply that volume has merit. This means limited back pressure and the greatest efficiency of the motor (lightest load).

The water management system whereby the drip lines are run for eight to 12 hours, which soaks the row well, then not watered for four to seven days, is preferred and is simpler to operate than light, more frequent waterings. The first year, when the trees are small and the root spread limited, six hours every four days may be better than a longer period less frequent. However, in the second year, when the trees are larger and actively growing and the temperatures are high in mid summer, a 12-hour watering every four to six days would be desirable on many soils.

Design the system for the maximum water need by the crop. If you have more capacity and do not need it, you can shorten the on-time. This is better than to need capacity that is not there.

Create a circuit system using the 200 gpm pump, such that it runs 24 hours per day and does eight five-acre blocks then shuts off. Thus 12 hours, block A; 12 hours, block B;...12 hours, block H, off. This sequence would require the pump to run continuously for four days. Under the extreme of heat and drought, it might be necessary to start the sequence over immediately or wait one day, two days, or longer. Only with very sandy soil and extremes of summer is there need to water more frequently than four days. A simple controller and a series of 24-volt solenoids could make the system quite automatic.

An important point here is to think of the equipment as "automatic", but when to turn on and how long to stay on a circuit should remain manual. Irrigation is beneficial as long as it is needed, but excess irrigation leads to pathogen problems.

Look at Table 14.2, a five-inch main line is necessary to handle 200+ gpm. Depending on where the well is located relative to the field, you may be able to have a five-inch line down the center with connecting lines at intervals to make the five-acre blocks. Come off the five-inch line, then into a five-inch "T", then reduce down to a three-inch line going in either direction you still have the volume needed at much less pipe expense. Then come off the three-inch line with further reductions to finally get to an above-ground manifold system of 1.5- or 1-inch black poly pipe and the drip lines.

At the point of attachment of the above-ground manifold to a buried PVC line, a pressure regulator/reducer to about 15-20 PSI is needed. Many drip lines can go about 400 feet + or - on level ground and have good water distribution end-to-end. A rectangle 400 feet by 550 feet = five acres. If it is possible to lay out the fields in such a manner, then run the main line down the long axis and go 400 feet to the right for one five-acre block and 400 feet to the left for another five-acre block, one ends up with the maximum run of the lines and row length while still getting good water distribution.

Use one-inch poly pipe for headers and one-inch by one-inch by one-half inch reducing nylon "T"s. Run 10 lines (five on either side of the "T") per connection, thus it would require 5.5 connections per acre. (This is based on the 10-foot rows and two-foot centers of the emitters so that 3.0 gpm is needed per each 400-foot row).

Once the system is up and running, a simple bypass as described earlier will reduce the load on the pump if it can be used to adjust the output volume/pressure as needed from a submergible pump. With a centrifugal pump this is generally not necessary or desirable.

This should serve only as an extremely limited example of how an irrigation system might begin to be designed. Irrigation is such a critical factor to container plant production that it deserves much attention, checking, and re-checking of details before the commitment is made.

Fertilizer Injection. Any water soluble or liquid fertilizer can be injected into the drip irrigation system, although nitrogen is the primary nutrient added in most cases. As is covered elsewhere in this book, all other nutrients should be incorporated into the soil at the proper rate **before** planting.

A simple siphon system is very easy and inexpensive to construct when a centrifugal pump is used. Simply add a small secondary inlet line into the suction side of the pump (Figure 14.12). By opening the valve while the pump is in operation, any liquid can be injected and is thoroughly mixed with the water as it passes through the pump's impellor. (Be careful or the pump will loose its prime).

With a submerged pump or city water, a siphon apparatus can be added to accomplish a similar function. Caution: When city water or well water is used, an anti-backflush apparatus must also be used to ensure that the fertilizer does not enter the drinking water system by accident.

There are many types and brands of commercial fertilizer injectors available, however, in many cases a simple siphon system is equally effective at a fraction of the cost. The main advantage of a commercial injector is that it can be attached to a large tank of nitrogen solution and automated with a time clock or other device. A siphon system requires someone to add the nitrogen solution to a specific container from which it is taken into the system. There are obvious advantages and disadvantages to both techniques.

351

Figure 14.12.   By using the suction on the inlet side of a centrifugal pump, liquid fertilizers can be distributed throughout the area being watered with good uniformity.

The key factors to remember when injecting fertilizers into a drip irrigation system are to use a reasonable rate and flush the lines thoroughly after the nitrogen injection is complete. For example, if the drip system is to run for eight hours, inject the nitrogen during the first hour and allow the remaining seven hours for flushing the lines and completing the wetting of the plant root zone. The reason for this is algae which will grow inside the drip lines, even though they are black, if nitrogen remains in the lines when the system is turned off. Algae is a major cause of plugging of drip emitters, especially when surface water is used. By using drip lines with close spacing of emitters, there is less chance of any water remaining in the lines between irrigation cycles.

Nitrogen can be injected at rates of from 20 to 50 pounds of nitrogen per acre. For rapidly growing plants on sandy loam soils, a rate of 25 to 30 pounds per acre every two weeks, depending on rainfall, may be ideal. On the other hand, with heavier soils that have higher nutrient retention and less leaching, a rate of 50 pounds per acre every four to six weeks may be best, whereas, on a very sandy soil a low rate with each watering is ideal.

Ammonium nitrate is very water-soluble, provides both nitrate and ammoniacal nitrogen and is economical. Potassium nitrate is more expensive, but provides potassium if needed, and is very soluble in water. Liquid fertilizer containing nitrogen, potassium or both, may or may not be economical, depending on the geographic area and supplier.

Summary. Most irrigation waters contain various dissolved minerals which accumulate in the soil over time. The rate of accumulation depends on the level of minerals in the water, the amount of irrigation water applied and the nature of the soil.

Bicarbonates, calcium and sodium create the greatest problems. All these raise the soil pH and interact with the micronutrients, especially iron and manganese, making them less available for plant growth.

In order to minimize the effects of irrigation water, the following steps should be practiced:

1. Minimize irrigation. Excess water, above the needs of the crop not only deposit more minerals in the soil, but may cause other complications such as root rot diseases and increase overall cost of pumping and equipment maintenance.

2. Between each crop, plow the fields deep and subsoil as described elsewhere. Minerals from irrigation water accumulate more rapidly in a heavy soil with slow water percolation than on lighter soils with good aeration and better internal drainage. Plowing mixes and loosens the soil and subsoiling further enhances this process.

3. Grow a soil-building crop on the land between crop cycles. Hybrid sudan or sudex develops a tremendous root system and can add several tons of organic matter per acre in a single growing season. As the roots of the sudex grow through the soil, they loosen and aerate as well as absorb a substantial quantity of nutrients due to their very rapid growth rate. Each time the sudex is mowed during the growing season, a substantial portion of the root system dies and new roots grow through new pathways in the soil, and a further absorption of minerals and buffering of the soil occurs. This process is described in detail elsewhere.

4. In extreme cases, elemental sulfur can be applied to the soil to lower the pH, release calcium and sodium from the soil

complex so it will leach downward and out of the root zone, and help break the bicarbonate complex. Sulfur applications may also assist on some fields simply by supplying needed sulfate for plant growth. Plants absorb substantial quantities of sulfate, and as soils become more alkaline sulfate levels generally go down. Rates of sulfur vary from one to three tons per acre. No two soils are the same, thus the rate and frequency of application should be adjusted according to the changes in the soil chemistry that have occurred as a result of irrigation and the nature of individual soil. Good soil tests and records are a must.

5. In extreme cases, where the bicarbonate level in the water is above 200 ppm, it may be practical and economically feasible to inject industrial grade sulfuric acid into the water supply. The quantity of acid to be added depends on the individual water and the current status of the soil. The acid will reduce the level of bicarbonates in the water, but it will not reduce the level of calcium, sodium, or other dissolved elements. However, if the water is high enough in bicarbonates, certain plants may not grow unless acid water treatment is done. It is important to note that no two waters or soils are the same, thus nothing more than broad, general recommendations can be made. Each site and water source must be considered on an individual basis.

CHAPTER 15

WEED CONTROL

WEED CONTROL

The Basics. Weed control in field nursery stock is very important. Since most weeds are very aggressive, they compete for the water and nutrients that would otherwise be used by the nursery crop. Weeds have been defined in many ways, but perhaps the most functional definition of a weed is "a thoroughly successful plant". In that sense, weeds are capable of utilizing and responding to the cultural conditions more than most nursery stock. Grassy weeds have a far more fibrous root system and thus are more severe competitors than broadleaf weeds (Figure 15.1). Wilburn and Rauch (34) found that growth of pyracantha and juniper plants in containers were restricted by 24% in the presence of bittercress (*Cardamine* spp.), pigweed (*Amaranthus retroflexus*), and curled dock (*Rumex crispus*). Later Fretz (8) found that one redroot pigweed could reduce the growth of a Japanese holly by as much as 44%. These findings emphasize the importance of weed control if maximum growth and quality are to be obtained.

When most nurserymen are asked their principle method of weed control, they generally reply, "herbicides". However, herbicides **should not** be the principle emphasis of a weed control program. In the nursery, sanitation and general cleanliness of the entire operation, including all aisles, roadways, ditch banks or other areas of the nursery should be the number one defense in the weed control process. Weeds are thoroughly successful plants and can tolerate growing conditions that would be unsuitable for most of the nursery crops being produced (Figure 15.2). Because of their success in adverse conditions, they become very aggressive in an array of locations in and around a nursery. These locations often serve as the principle sources of weed seed to be blown by the wind, carried by birds, rain or irrigation water or if those weed seeds fall into surface water systems, some nurseries unknowingly provide additional spread of weeds through their irrigation systems and drainage ditches.

*Figure 15.1.   Grassy weeds develop aggressive root systems, even when small.   A young goosegrass (**Eleusine indica**) seedling has become established in a container and looks relatively innocent (above), however, even before the top of the plant reaches a menacing size, the root system is very extensive and is a very aggressive competitor for water, nutrients and oxygen (below).*

357

Figure 15.2. A tear in the polyethylene cover of a nursery holding area provides an entry for weeds. Soon these plants will produce seeds to spread throughout the nursery.

In addition to their competitive nature, weeds become a source of weed seeds for adjacent areas. Many weed species are also harborers of disease and insect pests. For example, if a nursery has wood sorrel (*Oxalis* spp.) by checking the oxalis, one can generally monitor the spider mite population. Likewise, aphids in the spring season can be found on bittercress, dog fenal or marestail long before they are found on pyracantha, holly and other nursery plants (Figure 15.3). Checking these weeds for insects can sometimes provide an easy clue to know when spraying needs to be done, however, it would be much better to not have the weeds and simply eliminate a favorite habitat of that insect population and thus reduce the need for spraying.

*Figure 15.3. Weeds adjacent to container nursery stock provides a home for insects and diseases. In this case, bittercress or flickweed (**Cardamine pennsylvanica**) is a host for aphids. In most cases, the aphid population increases on the weeds before becoming a problem on the crop plants.*

Within the arsenal of weed control methods, pre-emergent herbicides (those applied prior to weed seed germination), post-emergent herbicides (those that kill existing plants) and soil sterilants (those chemicals that eliminate all vegetation from a particular site) should be considered in combination with other sanitation management practices in and around the nursery. Certainly the safest and most effective of these three herbicide approaches is the use of pre-emergent herbicides. There are, however, some herbicides such as Ronstar (oxadiazon) and Goal (oxyfluorfen), that are principally pre-emergent in nature but also have some post-emergent properties in that they will also kill very small weeds of some species, even after the seed has germinated (21) (Figure 15.4). This can be particularly advantageous since one can wait until small weeds are noticed

359

before making the next application of herbicides without having to go to the additional labor and expense of hand pulling the weeds from the containers or cultivating in the field. There is, however, the additional risk of foliar crop damage when using herbicides with post-emergent property. In addition, timing is critical. A matter of waiting a few days may make the difference between successful weed control and a lot of hoeing or spraying. Damage is rare with most pre-emergent herbicides with no post-emergent activity (1, 2, 7, 24).

*Figure 15.4.   Weeds, mostly prostrate spurge (**Euphorbia supina**), were 1/4-inch to 1/2-inch tall when Ronstar was applied.   Treated with Ronstar (left), and untreated (right) five weeks later.*

Currently, the pre-emergent herbicides most used on nursery stock are: Treflan (trifluralin), Ronstar (oxadiazon), Goal (oxyfluorfen), Surflan (oryzalin), Princep (simizine), Devrinol (napropamide), and Casoron (dichlobenil). These are not registered for use on all plant materials, only certain species.   Always check the label to be certain the herbicide is registered and

360

cleared for use on the particular crop plant in question. This may not always be possible in that a particular block of nursery stock may contain 20 species, four of which are not labeled. Under these practical circumstances, the nurseryman proceeds at his own risk, since no liability can be implied or assumed by the manufacturer when the herbicide is used on species not listed on the label. It is important to conduct trials of the herbicide(s) considered, on all species of plants being grown or held.

Herbicides vary in their phytotoxicity or potential to damage plants depending on air temperature, watering practices, nature of the field soil, perhaps nutrient levels, stage of growth of the species, and other factors. Therefore, there are probably plants with an adequate tolerance to an herbicide that because of some question under some particular circumstance, have been left off the registration label. Under your circumstances, the tolerance of the crop to a specific herbicide may be sufficiently different that you may wish to assume the liability for using that herbicide. Regardless of the rules, procedures, and regulations dealing with the applications of herbicides and nursery stock, discretion of the nurseryman must prevail in practical situations. It is illogical to assume that because a nurseryman has a few species that are not on the label that he should not use the herbicide on his entire nursery crop. Somewhere the judgement and responsibility must lie with the individual nurseryman as to whether or not the potential of injury from the herbicide outweighs the difficulty of otherwise using less efficient herbicides or other methods of controlling weeds.

Pre-Emergent Herbicides. Pre-emergent herbicides are generally available and most safely applied as either wettable powders (WP), emulsifiable concentrates (EC), or as granular formulations (G). Whether a particular herbicide is available as a WP or EC generally depends on the chemistry of the compound involved and the necessary processes in manufacturing. Be cautious when using herbicides marked E.C. or emulsifiable concentrate. In some cases it has been found that the pre-emergent herbicide does not cause injury to the crop plant, however, the benzine or other organic chemical carriers and solvents that comprise part of the liquid may cause foliage injury. On the other hand, if the same herbicide is applied as a wettable powder, which does not contain the organic solvent, injury is less likely to occur.

Because of the difficulty of uniformly applying a very precise rate of herbicide around or among plants with spray equipment, several herbicides are available in the granular form. The granular formulations are more expensive since additional manufacturing effort is required, as opposed to the EC or WP form, but in many cases are worth the expense.

Granular herbicides are on some type of carrier or granule such as calcined clay, sand, ground corn cobs, vermiculite or other materials. The granule is simply a mechanism for carrying the herbicide onto the surface of the soil in a convenient manner. Granular herbicides are typically 2%, 4% or 5% active chemical on the carrier granule. Ronstar, for example, is commonly available as a 2% granule, thus for every 100 pounds of herbicide granules, there are two pounds of actual Ronstar herbicide. **The importance of getting the right rate of herbicide applied at the right time cannot be over-emphasized and is essential for successful pre-emergent weed control.** Be cautious of herbicides where the granule consists of 6%, 8% or 10% concentration. In those cases, there will be an insufficient number of granules to allow even dispersal of the herbicide over the soil surface.

In research studies, it has been shown that high concentration granules frequently miss spots allowing weeds to escape (24). The function of the herbicide granule is to carry one herbicide in a convenient mechanism onto the soil surface, then with one or more irrigation(s) or rainfall, release the herbicide on the surface of the soil. When the herbicide concentration is low and the granules are many, each granule releases a small amount of herbicide onto a specific area, however, when the concentration increases and the herbicide granules are fewer, voids or skips are more likely to occur. It is true that the major cost of granular herbicides is the shipping and handling, however, the relative cost of the chemical and the granular formulation proportionate to the value of the weed control and labor requirement of cultivating, pulling weeds by hand, or applying post-emergent chemicals, more than justifies this slight increase in expense.

Numerous devices have been developed to aid in the dispersal of granular herbicides. Probably the most widely used procedure is the cyclone or whirlybird-type spreader. This may be an apparatus carried around the neck and shoulders of the applicator that holds a few pounds of the herbicide (Figure 15.5). It may be

362

carried by the back of a tractor. The operation of the two types is the same. A small gate or opening in the bottom of the hopper can be adjusted to allow a flow of the dry granules onto a spinning propeller-type apparatus either hand- or motor-powered which spins. The herbicide granules contact ribs or branches on the propeller apparatus and are thrown either to the left or to the right, depending on the design of the equipment. Three key factors are important in calibrating an apparatus of this type:

1) the size of the opening releasing the herbicide onto the spinning plate,
2) the speed at which the plate is being turned, particularly if it is being cranked by hand and
3) the forward speed of the individual or machine applying the herbicide.

An additional technique that helps in uniform dispersal of the herbicide is to split applications. Once the horizontal spread of the herbicide granule is determined with a particular speed of the apparatus, calculate the rate of application of 1/2 of the desired rate. The approach is to apply 1/2 of the rate of the herbicide in one direction and apply the other 1/2 over the same field row or block of plants in containers in the other direction. Cyclone or whirlybird herbicide applicators are not uniform in distribution of granules from near the operator to the farthest point of horizontal spread. Therefore, when an area is covered on the left side for example, the plants nearest the operator will receive a lower rate, however, when this is reversed and a second 1/2 rate application is made over the same block of plants, the plants that previously got the light rate, now get the heavy rate and vice versa. This helps compensate for the unevenness of distribution from the spreader and also compensates for some deflection of the granules by the top of the plants. Deflection of granules by plants that are relatively tall or bushy, must be considered.

Figure 15.5. When a cyclone or whirlybird-type spreader is used to spread granular herbicides, over small plants in containers or in narrow rows, 1/2 the application rate should be applied from one side of a row or block of plants and 1/2 from the other side. This provides a more uniform distribution and prevents blank spots caused by the plant canopy. In other nursery and landscape situations, this split application procedure is not necessary.

In calibrating the granular herbicide spreader, it is important to train a very conscientious employee, since the rate of herbicide applied and the accuracy of the distribution is very important. It is helpful in calibrating, and likewise in the routine distribution of granular herbicides, using a hand spreader to sing or think of a favorite marching song. Unimportant as this may seem at the moment, it allows the person to establish a particular rhythm in turning the hand crank which propels the horizontal distribution of the granules and provides a repeatable pace or walking speed. Lullabies work poorly, whereas marches are especially effective. With a small tractor, use the same gear and engine speed each time to assure a consistent forward and pto (power take off) speed.

364

One effective procedure for calibrating a granular herbicide spreader, either hand- or machine-powered is as follows:

a) Weigh a known amount of herbicide, for example, 1/2 pound in a hand spreader, more in a tractor unit.

b) Place this in the hopper of the spreader.

c) Guess as to what may be an appropriate opening or setting of the discharge gate at the bottom of the applicator.

d) Proceed with the normal walk and hand crank speed of the applicator or appropriate tractor speed with the gate open over a parking lot, driveway, or other open area where distribution of the herbicide granules can be observed.

e) Measure the length and width of the herbicide coverage.

f) Determine the rate of herbicide per unit area of surface.

g) If the herbicide rate is too high, reduce the opening of the gate at the bottom of the hopper, put in another 1/2 pound (any known amount) of herbicide and repeat the procedure. On the other hand, if the rate is too low, increase the opening of the hopper and proceed to a second trial. Several tries may be required before the proper rate of herbicide distribution is reached. Remember that if you choose the split application procedure, 1/2 would be applied on one side of a planting and 1/2 on the other, the discharge rate would also be 1/2.

The same technique can be used for calibrating other spray applicators. Additional information on sprayer calibration is readily available from county agents and sprayer manfacturers.

Granular herbicides should be applied only when the foliage of the crop is dry (Figure 15.6). If moisture droplets, either from irrigation, rainfall, dew, or gutation are present on the leaves at the time the herbicide granules are applied, some release of the herbicide may begin. The most desired procedure is to apply granular herbicides when the foliage is dry and just prior to a normal irrigation or rainfall. With rainfall or the normal quantity of overhead watering, the granule may be dislodged or the herbicide will be leached from the granule and thus carried onto the soil, preventing plant injury. This is especially true with granular herbicides applied to crops such as yucca, liriope, or other plant species that have foliage in rosettes or dense whirls that may catch and trap granules (Figure 15.7). In some cases, it may be necessary to avoid using granular herbicides on these species and use a spray instead.

Figure 15.6. When leaf surfaces are dry, the herbicide granules may stick but are quickly washed off by irrigation water. On the other hand, if water is present on the leaf, the granules may release a portion of the herbicide and cause plant damage.

Figure 15.7. Entrapment of granules of Ronstar, Goal, Rout or Ornamental Herbicide I or II by the whirl of yucca leaves will cause injury. Use the EC or flowable formulation over plants that may trap or hold granules or an herbicide that does not cause leaf burn such as Treflan 5G.

Pre-emergent compounds such as Treflan can be applied to some woody landscape plants two or three times during the growing season (Figure 15.8) if necessary, with little, if any, detrimental effect. Probst (17) reported no buildup of Treflan in the soil occurs with time. Treflan treatments of five pounds active ingredient per acre (aia) gave increases in top weights of 150%, 50%, 50% and 120% over no herbicide controls and increases in root weights of 130%, 40%, 40% and 100% over controls for variegated pittosporum, green pittosporum, ligustrum, and juniper, respectively, grown in containers. In no case did the highest rate of Treflan suppress top or root growth of test shrubs below that of the hand-weeded control, nor was visual damage noted on any test plant. The rate of Treflan per acre would be 1.5 to 2.5 pounds for field soils. Treflan is a safe and effective herbicide for weed control in containers and most field nursery and landscape situations when applied properly (15, 25, 29). **The key is to apply the herbicide before any weed seeds germinate so do not procrastinate.**

367

Figure 15.8. Fine, fibrous roots are more susceptible to herbicide injury than larger roots, yet the fine, fibrous roots play the major role in water and nutrient absorption. If root injury from pre-emergent herbicides is suspected, check the fine roots.

Unfortunately, the weed population in any given area is constantly shifting and with the use of herbicides, the shift is accelerated (7). For example, if an herbicide controls all weeds except prostrate spurge, in a short time prostrate spurge goes from a very minor weed to a major problem. With the elimination of competition from other weeds, the weed(s) missed by the herbicide produce more seeds and become more aggressive (Figure 15.9).

The activity of pre-emergent herbicides is affected by container growth media and field soil type (6, 14). Moles and Whitcomb (16) showed that as long as ground pine bark was a component in a container growth medium, Ronstar did not leach even after repeated heavy waterings. However, if only peat and sand were used, Ronstar continued to leach downward with successive waterings.

Figure 15.9. Above, the pre-emergent herbicide controlled all weeds except two pigweeds. If these are allowed to go to seed, next year there will be more pigweed to contend with, assuming the same herbicide is used. Below, this plot was treated with an herbicide that controlled nearly all weeds except prostrate spurge. After two seasons, a minor weed became a major problem.

369

The Ronstar was "tied up" on the bark in some manner which provides a "slow-release" mechanism. This slow-release mechanism increases the safety factor for the crop plant by retarding downward leaching of the herbicide, plus, it appears to prolong effectiveness of the herbicide, thus extending the weed control. This observation of long-term weed control has been reported by Weatherspoon and Curry (22, 23) and others (16, 20, 27). This mechanism works equally well with mulches in plant beds.

A similar relationship exists with field soils. As organic matter and/or clay content of a field soil increases, the rate of pre-emergent herbicide must increase in order to obtain weed control similar to a sandy loam soil. This is related to the greater surface area and chemical attachment sites as a result of the organic matter or clay. It is impossible for someone to predict precisely how an herbicide will perform under the conditions of a specific nursery.

Look at Figures 15.10 and 15.11. In general, as the water solubility of a pre-emergent herbicide increases, so does its downward movement by water. When dealing with an array of species, such as in a nursery, use only pre-emergent herbicides very insoluble in water (generally less than 1 ppm). Plants are compatible with herbicides either by being tolerant to the herbicide, or by avoiding herbicide/root contact. A good example of plant tolerance of an herbicide exists in the case of junipers, taxus and most species of pine and the pre-emergent herbicide, Princep (simizine). With these species, Princep can be used at a rate that would stunt or kill sensitive woody species such as crapemyrtle, hibiscus, flowering quince, lilac, forsythia and many others, yet these conifers are not adversely affected and weed control is likely to be good. The bad news is that if the conifers are harvested and a susceptible species is planted in the field, there may be plant damage as a result of residual Princep. This has happened many times, thus it is best to avoid herbicides with carryover problems.

*Figure 15.10. Effects of Karmex (K), Lasso (L) and Devrinol (D) at four pounds aia (4.5 kg./ha.) on **Viburnum suspensum**. Note the stunting by the Karmex and Lasso compared to the Devrinol treatment. In this case, weed control was similar for all three herbicides. The injury from the Karmex and Lasso is probably due to their greater water solubility.*

The other option is to use an herbicide that is very insoluble such as Treflan, Ronstar or Goal, whereby the herbicide stays at or near the soil surface and **away** from the roots (Table 15.1). In addition, these herbicides are generally more quickly broken down by microorganisms, thus little, if any, residue remains in the soil after one season.

To demonstrate the importance of this, the author has used Goal and Treflan among crapemyrtle which are very sensitive to herbicides. When the Goal or Treflan was rototilled or cultivated into the soil, plant stunting occurred. However, when the herbicides were left on the soil surface, the plants grew just as well as the untreated control plots where weeds were controlled by frequent sprays of the contact herbicide, cocodylic acid. Keep in mind that on 20 acres of field nursery stock, there may be 50 or more species of plants, whereas, if the entire field was planted to cotton, corn or peanuts, only one species is involved and an herbicide specific for that crop could be used.

Table 15.1. Water solubility of several common herbicides labeled for use on nursery stock.

Goal	0.1 ppm	Simazine	3.5 ppm
Ronstar	0.7 ppm	Karmex	42.0 ppm
Treflan	0.3 ppm	Devrinol	75.0 ppm
Prowl	0.5 ppm	Lasso	242.0 ppm
Galaxy	1.0 ppm	Dual or	
Surflan	2.5 ppm	Pennant	530.0 ppm

Figure 15.11. Effects of Surflan (S) and Ronstar (R) at four pounds aia (4.5 kg./ha.) on the growth of sandanqua viburnum (**Viburnum suspensum**)*, compared to the untreated control (C). In all cases the plants treated with Ronstar were larger and of superior quality compared to the control. The injury from Surflan was probably due to its greater water solubility.*

When the cultural practices stimulate vigorous plant growth which quickly shades the surface of the soil, herbicide may not have to be used a second time during the growing season or only twice instead of three times, depending on the species and circumstances. Any cultural practice that can increase plant vigor and reduce total herbicide usage and labor required to distribute herbicides or spray or pull weeds, is money in the bank.

In general, avoid incorporating pre-emergent herbicides. When pre-emergent herbicides are incorporated, two distinct complications occur: 1) the herbicides is introduced deeper into the soil, thus increasing the root/herbicide contact and 2) the rate of herbicide at the soil surface is decreased or diluted. Since most weed seed require light to germinate, it stands to reason that the greatest herbicide concentration should be at the soil surface. Likewise, since virtually all herbicides are likely to have some adverse affect on the roots of crop plants if direct contact is made, keep the herbicide and root system separated as much as possible.

The desire to incorporate pre-emergent herbicides is probably related to several factors: 1) the age-old tradition/desire to cultivate the soil, 2) the general incorrect belief that weeds germinate deep in the soil and, 3) the recommendations by some chemical companies that their herbicide should be incorporated. Consider each of these factors individually.

Cultivation was for many years the only method of weed control prior to development of herbicides. Freshly tilled soil is attractive and the various means of cultivation are often used to control the weeds that escape the pre-emergent herbicide. On the other hand, consider that cultivation generally causes root pruning and in many cases, well established weeds survive the cultivation either by deflecting the cultivator or re-establishing themselves. On many occasions, the soil is cultivated to kill weeds only to have it rain that night or the next day, enabling many of the weeds to survive. In addition to the time, labor, machinery expense and root pruning of cultivation, the other major problem is that it is not possible to cultivate close to the plant where the weeds will cause the greatest restriction on the crop (Figure 15.12).

By maintaining a field soil in good tilth by using cover crops at regular intervals, the "need" for cultivation will be greatly reduced or eliminated. The soil surface will remain friable and loose instead of hard and crusty. With good soil management, a lack of oxygen or buildup of carbon dioxide in the soil is very unlikely to restrict crop growth, even when the soil surface appears crusty or hard. Cultivation is more of a tradition than a requirement.

Figure 15.12. This nursery failed to to get the pre-emergent herbicide down before the grassy weeds germinated in the spring (above). Cultivation between the rows has no effect on the grass competition in the row. When a pre-emergent herbicide is used, it may be desirable to cultivate between the rows before applying (below). However, it is very important to get this done and the herbicide applied before the weeds germinate in the row.

374

Most weed seeds require light to germinate. The major exceptions are cocklebur, field bindweed and morning glory. This can be demonstrated easily by simply disturbing an area otherwise free of weeds due to post-emergent sprays or shallow hoeing. When soil from below the surface is exposed to light, many new weed seeds are exposed and quickly germinate unless there is some restricting factor.

Why do some companies suggest that their herbicides be incorporated? In the case of a product like Treflan, it is because the chemical is subject to decomposition by light and is also volatile when sprayed on warm surfaces. On the other hand, since Treflan is very insoluble in water, by applying it to the soil either in early spring or in the fall when the soils are cool and just before a rain which does a good job of shallow incorporation, light decomposition and volatilization can be minimized, while leaving the herbicide at or near the soil surface and away from the root zone (Figure 15.13). In short, incorporation is used as a crutch and should be avoided.

<u>Herbicides **must** <u>**be**</u> **applied** at precise rates at all times. Too little will provide poor weed control, too much may cause slight to severe damage or stunting. Do not take chances, always test a new herbicide on a small plot of all plants grown before treating large numbers of plants.</u>

Some Practical Examples. Weed control in field nursery stock is a major problem. The presence of weeds, especially grasses, can restrict the growth of some trees and shrubs up to 50% or more. On the other hand, soil erosion can be a major problem on sloping land when all ground cover vegetation is eliminated.

Figure 15.13. Trees on a clay loam soil where Treflan was applied promptly after planting in the spring and again in early fall (above). Crapemyrtle are very sensitive to herbicides, yet the plants are growing well here with a high rate of Treflan on a sandy loam soil (below). In both cases the Treflan was applied in the spring when soil was cool and a rain followed soon after. This left the herbicide on the soil surface to best control weeds and away from the crop roots.

The herbicide or combination and sequence of events depends on the size of the crop and the weed(s) to be controlled, time of year and soil conditions. Here are three examples in practical situations.

Example 1. In April, Goal liquid was applied to a block of trees at a rate of 2.5 pounds of aia. The spray was applied using a boom approximately 20 inches above the soil surface and 15 gallons of water per acre. The trees were five to six feet tall and the lower branches had been removed approximately two feet above the soil. The field was free of weeds at the time of herbicide application. Goal is toxic to any green vegetation even though it is primarily a pre-emergent herbicide, therefore, if lower leaves had been present they would have been damaged.

Control of broadleaf weeds was excellent (Figure 15.14) but a few grassy weeds began to appear in June, especially around the trees which were drip-irrigated. The drip irrigation increases the rate of decomposition of the herbicide, in addition, since the soil surface is moist, the grassy weeds can survive in a very shallow layer of soil above the herbicide zone. In this case, nearly all of the grassy weeds could be easily pulled by hand revealing a shallow, horizontal root system no more than 1/4-inch thick. Although unsightly, these weeds had little influence on the growth of the trees and may have provided a small benefit by creating a mulching effect over the soil surface.

By late September, the herbicide had decomposed to a level allowing more weed growth in the tree rows and action was necessary. The centers between the rows were still relatively weed-free. The few weeds in this area could have been easily removed by cultivation; however, the larger, more competitive weeds among the tree rows were beyond the reach of any equipment. For comparative costs (1985) and approximate rates of various herbicides, see the appendix.

Figure 15.14. When a pre-emergent herbicide is applied to the soil prior to weed seed germination, excellent weed control can be obtained. In this case, the herbicide was applied to the trees on the right as well as an area on the left. Note the weed population on the untreated strip.

A tank mix of the pre-emergent herbicide, Surflan, and post-emergent, Roundup, was applied in order to kill the existing weeds, (Roundup) and to prevent further weeds from germinating (Surflan). Roundup was used at the rate of three quarts (three pounds of actual chemical) and Surflan at 2.5 pounds of actual chemical per acre. The Surflan was **not** incorporated. (This treatment would be a practical solution to the weed problem in Figure 15.12).

Roundup was chosen in this case because there were several tough perennial weeds such as Johnsongrass and bermudagrass present. In an adjacent field where only annual grassy and broadleaf weeds were present, cacodylic acid sold under the trade names of Dilic or Phytar 560 was used in a similar tank mix at the rate of 1.5 gallons per acre with equal success. Cacodylic acid is very effective in killing annual weeds but only kills the tops of perennial weeds, which soon re-grow. Roundup, on the other hand, will kill perennial weeds as well as annual weeds, but is more expensive. Roundup should be used at a rate of about three quarts per acre to control tough perennial weeds. However, if only annual weeds are present, Roundup can be used at a much lower rate, about two quarts per acre or less, with good results.

This procedure provided total weed control in the field from the spray applied in late September until the following May. However, it could not have been used if the trees had been smaller or if the lower branches were present. Roundup is quickly absorbed by any green vegetation and if any of the lower limbs of the trees had been sprayed, some damage would have occurred. There appears to be little absorption of Roundup into the stem of the tree unless it is green. Be cautious when spraying trunks of young ash, honeylocust, bald cypress, sycamore or crabapples that have not yet developed a bark resistant to herbicide absorption.

Products such as Surflan and Treflan work best on grassy weeds, especially during the spring, fall and winter. Treflan could have been substituted for Surflan with no loss in weed control but at a savings of several dollars per acre. Likewise, Treflan would have been a better choice if the soil was very sandy since it is less water-soluble compared to Surflan. See the summary Table 15.2 for approximate costs of various spray combinations.

Example 2. Crapemyrtle seedlings in 2 1/2-inch containers were planted into a well tilled field of sandy loam soil in May and watered in. Because the plants were actively growing, Goal and Surflan could not be used without severe foliage damage. Goal is absorbed by the leaves and has some post-emergent properties as well as pre-emergent properties for controlling germinating weed seed. Surflan wettable powder has no post-emergent properties on most weeds, however, it will damage the leaves and buds on many woody species, when they are young and actively growing.

The field had not been used for nursery stock previously and a wide assortment of weeds had been observed the previous growing season. The herbicide of choice in this case was Ronstar 2% granules applied at the rate of two pounds of actual chemical per acre (100 pounds of actual granules). Treflan 5% granules could also be used safely in this situation. The granules were broadcast when the foliage of the young plants was dry and no damage occurred. Several spring rains the following week activated and shallowly incorporated the herbicide. Weed control was excellent until mid August when another application of herbicide was needed. Because the plants were small and actively growing, **no** post-emergent chemicals such as Roundup or cacodylic acid could be used. The existing weeds were removed by a hoe (Figure 15.15).

*Figure 15.15. If the weed population is allowed to get out of hand, before a second application of a pre-emergent herbicide is made, the only control procedure is the hoe. In this case the space between the young plants could be cultivated, but because of the succulent growth on the young plants there is no chemical to take out the weeds without damaging the nursery stock. The error here was one of timing and/or procrastination. **Anytime you procrastinate, the weeds win**!*

A second application of Ronstar at the same rate was applied. Had the time been mid to late September, or later, the herbicide of choice would have been Treflan granules at the rate of about 2.5 to 3 pounds aia. Several reasons exist for choosing Treflan over Ronstar later in the season and when there is a good likelihood of rain:

a) Treflan is much less expensive than Ronstar.

b) Treflan does an excellent job of controlling fall grassy weeds and winter annuals and biannuals, equal to, or better than, Ronstar.

c) Treflan granules are not toxic to green vegetation even if there is moisture on the leaves or following application, a heavy dew begins to release the herbicide from the granule.

d) If used during the cooler months and left unincorporated, except for the shallow incorporation of rain, Treflan is one of the safest, most economical and effective herbicides (see Figure 15.13). Treflan as a spray (the liquid, emulsifiable concentrate formulation) should be used carefully over the tops of valuable crops. The Treflan is not toxic to the existing foliage, however, the solvent used to dissolve the Treflan and keep it in solution is toxic to some species.

Example 3. A recent situation arose where winter weeds were thick in among a large block of small crapemyrtle. The crapemyrtle were planted in July and were treated with granular Treflan which did a good job. However, the winter weeds germinated and established in the fall while the crapemyrtle were still growing. The choice seemed to hoe or have a mess next spring and then hoe. After looking over the plants and weeds for several months, in mid February drastic action was taken. A tank mix of two quarts Roundup and five quarts Goal was sprayed over the tops of the dormant crapemyrtle as well as a few elm and tree lilac when the air temperature was about 50 degrees F.

The winter annuals remained green for three to four weeks before dying. When growth began in the spring, no injury from the Roundup could be detected on any of the three species at any time. **Note, this has been done only once. Travel at your own risk.** If you try it, treat only a few plants. Be sure the plants are fully dormant. Plants with large buds may be more susceptible to injury. These factors aside, it appears to be a possible way of cleaning out the winter annuals and biannuals that always seem to get started early in the fall. It deserves further study.

This discussion of practical situations represents only two of many different situations that could be encountered in a field nursery. Use this information only as a guide or starting point. Rates, times and methods of herbicide application and control achieved will depend on many factors, some of which are particularly difficult to evaluate:

a) soil type,

b) weather conditions, especially temperature and rainfall and,

c) the specific weed population present. A consistent and effective weed control program is made more difficult by the ever-changing weed population.

Example 4. A pre-emergent herbicide was applied in the spring and all but a few weed species (or perhaps just one) were controlled. What does one do about those? One practical solution is a "weed wedge" cultivator. This device was built using scrap steel and an old blade from a road grader (Figure 15.16). The wide V-shaped blade is sharpened on the front edge and adjusted so that it is pulled about 3/4 to one inch below the soil surface. The advantages are many if it is used timely:

a) Since the cultivator goes just under the soil surface, little energy is required and the tractor can be operated at considerable speed.

b) Any weeds that escape the pre-emergent herbicide are cut off just under the soil surface and with the lifting, crumbling action, the few roots are generally loosened from the soil so that the weed dies.

c) The chemical herbicide barrier on the soil surface is disturbed very little, if at all, since any incorporating that occurs is very shallow.

d) Virtually no root-pruning occurs to the nursery stock.

e) With a light tractor and proper soil moisture, very little soil compaction occurs.

f) No weeds escape as often occurs between shovels or tines.

The disadvantages are:

a) A commercial cultivator of this nature is not currently available.

b) The fields need to be relatively level for best results.

c) It is not a tool for the procrastinator, since a large population of weeds, or weeds three or four inches tall, cause plugging and poor performance of the cultivator.

Of the various tools evaluated over the years, this was number one if it was used timely. A disc was most undesirable followed by a shovel-type cultivator and rototiller. The "weed wedge" would cover an acre of nursery stock in less than one-fourth the time and one-fourth the fuel, when compared to the disc, cultivator or rototiller.

382

Figure 15.16. The "weed wedge" consists of a wide V-bar sharpened on the front edge (above). It operates about one inch deep or less, thus cutting off any weeds that escape the pre-emergent herbicide while causing very little incorporation or disruption of the chemical field barrier on the soil surface (below). It is offset to allow close cultivation to the trees and minimize escapes.

Figure 15.16 (cont'd). Because little soil is disturbed, little energy is required and it can be operated at much faster speeds than conventional cultivating equipment. In this case it is being operated on a clay loam soil at about six miles per hour at a very low engine rpm.

Herbicides for Use in Closed Structures. The control of weeds on the floors of overwintering or holding structures that have either soil or gravel floors is a serious problem. Container-grown nursery stock being held for planting in the field is much more vulnerable to cold than plants established in the field. One of the advantages of establishing a field nursery from container stock is that the plants can be tall enough to make spraying and other weed control procedures easier. Weeds like Pennsylvania bittercress or flickweed (*Cardamine pennsylvanica*) and yellow wood sorrel (*Oxalis stricta*) have mechanisms for propelling the seed at maturity and thrive in these conditions (Figure 15.17).

384

Figure 15.17. Above, bittercress is a particularly troublesome weed in containers and on the floor of holding structures or greenhouses. Bittercress produces large quantities of seed following a lush bloom of white flowers. The seed pods are very slender, spine-like sections at the tips of these mature plants. As the seed pod matures and drys, it opens with a snap, throwing seeds 8 to 10 feet or more. Below, oxalis also spreads by seeds which are propelled through the air when the seed pod matures and it also develops a vigorous rhizome. The oxalis in this container was probably the result of one seed, the rest are from the rhizomes just under the surface of the growth medium. The presence of this underground stem makes removal by hand difficult and if any portion is left, the weed control gain is short-lived.

385

Weeds may harbor disease organisms, insects, mites, and also give the nursery an unsightly appearance. Many herbicides cannot be used inside structures because of volatility or residual which may cause injury to nursery stock, especially at high temperatures. There has been little research to show what herbicides may be used for weed control in holding structures. Karmex (diuron) and Princep (simazine) have been mentioned in some greenhouse-related publications but with no supporting evidence. Burt (3) and Kearney et al. (13) have shown that triazine herbicides (atrazine, simizine, bromacil) will volatilize under laboratory conditions, however, whether they volatilize from a soil surface had not been established. The objective of a study by Whitcomb and Santelmann (33) was to determine if certain herbicides could be safely used at soil sterilant rates on the soil floor of a closed chamber as evaluated with sensitive species.

Unvented chambers of 27 cu. ft. were constructed and covered with 4 mil polyethylene plastic and placed on the floor of a greenhouse equipped with fan-pad cooling (Figure 15.18). Three 12 inches by 2 inches by 2.2 inches (30.5 cm. by 56 cm. by 5.7 cm.) plastic flats filled with unsterilized sandy loam soil were placed inside each chamber. The soil in the flats was kept moist throughout the study.

The herbicides and rates were applied to the soil in flats:

Hyvar X (bromacil) wettable powder (WP) and Princep (simazine) WP at 0, 15, 30 and 60 pounds aia (0, 17, 34 and 68 kg./ha. active ingredient),

Pramitol (prometon) 5 (PS) pellets and wettable powder (WP) and Karmex (diuron) (WP) were used at 0, 10, 20 and 40 pounds active ingredient per acre (aia) (0, 11.25, 22.5, and 45 kg./ha. active ingredient). A pot containing a test plant was placed on top of an inverted empty pot on top of the treated soil, to simulate a bench-like arrangement and to avoid direct root/soil contact with test plants about 3 in. (8 cm.) above the treated soil, but not in direct contact (Figure 15.18). The 4 treatments were replicated 3 times with 3 subsamples per replication for each test species. Three plants 4 to 6 in. (10 to 15 cm.) tall of each of the following species in 3 sq.in. (7.5 sq. cm.) containers were placed in each chamber:

aluminum plant (*Pilea cadierei*),
Jacob's coat (*Alternanthera amoena*),

386

English ivy (*Hedera helix*),
tomato (*Lycopersicon esculentum* 'Rutgers').
In addition, kalanchoe (*Kalanchoe* spp.), and grape ivy (*Cissus rhombifolia*), were used with Hyvar X and Pramitol.

Only one herbicide was studied at a time due to space requirements of the chambers. During each study the test plants were evaluated with a 0 to 10 rating scale where 0 = no injury; 1 to 3 = slight injury; 4 to 7 = moderate injury from which plants sometimes recovered; 8 and 9 = severe injury; and 10 = dead plants. Plants rated 5 or above were considered unsalable.

After 26 days in the chambers with Hyvar X at the 60 pounds aia (68 kg./ha.) rate, English ivy plants developed marginal chlorosis. The chlorosis became severe after 36 days. At the 15 and 30 pounds aia (17 and 34 kg./ha.) rate, slight injury was observed.

Damage was evident on the leaf margins of tomatoes from Pramitol (prometon) 5 PS at the 40-pound aia (45 kg. ai/ha.) rate after 7 days. This injury was different from "typical triazine" herbicide injury (that is, interveinal chlorosis). Tomato plants became limp as though frozen or cooked and later the tissue turned brown, but chlorosis was not detected at any time. After 10 days similar damage was visible at the 20-pound aia (22.5 kg. ai/ha.), and after 15 days, damage to tomatoes could be detected at the 10 pound aia (11.25 kg. ai/ha.) rate. All tomatoes were killed at the 20 and 40 pounds aia (22.5 and 45 kg. ai/ha.) rates.

Figure 15.18. Above, experimental greenhouse simulation chamber. Below, position of plants in relation to treated soil: (top) test plant pot; (center) inverted pot to provide bench-like condition; (bottom) herbicide treated soil.

Some damage could be detected on grape ivy, English ivy and Jacob's coat at the 20 and 40 pounds aia (22.5 and 45 kg. ai/ha rate after 20 days (Figure 15.19). Damage continued to develop at the 20 and 40 pounds aia (22.5 and 45 kg. ai/ha.) rates on grape ivy after 25 days. English ivy and Jacob's coat (particularly at the 40 pounds aia (45 kg. ai/ha.) rate looked like they had been cooked or frozen on the leaf margins. Aluminum plants showed no leaf discoloration after 25 days, but at all rates the plants appeared wilted. The stems drooped, although the color of all stems and leaves both old and new, still appeared normal. The plants appeared to be suffering from lack of soil moisture although the soil moisture was adequate. Roots of these plants continued to appear normal until the tops died. Tips of kalanchoe plants at the 40 pounds aia (45 kg. ai/ha.) rate began to show a scorched effect on the leaf margins after 25 days. A slight yellowing could be detected at the 20 pounds aia (22.5 kg. ai/ha.) rate and a few leaves began to drop. Leaf and stem injury to the kalanchoe at both 20 and 40 pounds aia (22.5 and 45 kg. ai/ha.) was much more dramatic after 28 days.

When the study was terminated after 4 weeks, the tomato plants were dead in the chambers receiving the 20 and 40 pounds aia (22.5 and 45 kg. ai/ha.) rates of Pramitol 5 PS, and severely damaged at the 10-pound aia (11.25 kg. ai/ha.) rate (Table 15.2). Tomatoes in chambers with untreated soil, although spindly from the high temperature [frequently exceeding 100 degrees F (38 degrees C)] remained healthy. Grape ivy was the most resistant plant to Pramitol. Only six grape ivy plants out of the 36 in the treated chambers were moderately to severely injured. All English ivy plants were dead at the 40 pounds aia (45 kg. ai/ha.) rate. They appeared to be severely injured at the 20 pounds aia (22.5 kg. ai/ha.) rate but only slightly injured at the 10 pounds aia (11.25 kg. ai/ha.) rate. Jacob's coat plants were dead at the 40 and 20 pounds aia (45 and 22.5 kg. ai/ha.) rates and severely injured at the 10 pounds aia (11.25 kg. ai/ha.) rate with no likelihood of recovery. Kalanchoe plants were dead or nearly dead at the 40-pound aia (45 kg. ai/ha.) rate and severely injured at the 20-pound aia (22.5 kg. ai/ha.) rate. However, injury was only slight at the 10 pounds aia (11.25 kg. ai/ha.) rate. Maximum soil temperature was 80 degrees F (27 degrees C).

389

Figure 15.19. Effects of Pramitol (prometon) 5 PS at (0, 10, 20 and 40 pounds aia (0, 11.25, 22.5 and 45 kg. ai/ha. on Joseph's coat after 14 days (above) and tomatoes after 21 days (below).

Pramitol (prometon) WP. Within two weeks after plants were placed in the chambers with Pramitol WP, all plants were dead or severely damaged. This suggests that the WP formulation began volatilizing more rapidly than the pellets. Extent and appearance of damage was similar to the pelletized formulation.

390

Table 15.1. Effects of prometon 5 PS treated soil in enclosed chambers on six herbaceous species, evaluated after four weeks exposure.

- -

Species	0	Pramitol lbs./aia (kg./ha.)		
		10 (11.25)	20 (22.5)	40 (45)

- -

Injury rating*

- -

Species	0	10 (11.25)	20 (22.5)	40 (45)
Tomato	0	7.0	9.8	10.0
Aluminum plant	0	6.3	5.8	8.3
Grape ivy	0	3.3	3.8	4.0
English ivy	0	1.8	5.8	10.0
Jacob's coat	0	6.8	9.6	10.0
Kalanchoe	0	2.0	5.0	9.0

- -

*Scale 0-10, with 0 being no injury and 10 being dead. Values represent the average rating of 9 plants.

- -

Karmex (diuron) WP. The first study with Karmex was begun January 27 and was terminated after six weeks. Maximum soil temperature was 73 degrees F (24 C) and air temperatures in the chambers never exceeded 90 degrees F (32 C). A second study was begun April 29 and was terminated after 6 weeks. Air temperatures in the chamber reached 115 degrees F (46 C) and soil temperatures reached 94 degrees F (34 C). No injury could be detected on any plant during or at termination of the experiments. All rates of Karmex (diuron) controlled all weeds in the treated soil suggesting that 10 pounds aia (11.25 kg. ai/ha.) is sufficient to give weed control. Only the sensitive species, aluminum plant, Jacob's coat, English ivy and tomato were used in this study.

Princep (simazine) WP. All plants showed some marginal necrosis in chambers treated with the 30 and 60 pounds aia (34 and 68 kg. ai/ha.) rate after six weeks. However, no further damage occurred during the study. Maximum soil temperature recorded was 86 degrees F (30 C). Based on the initial injury observed, although not severe, Princep (simazine) should not be used in any enclosed structure.

Of the five herbicides studied, Karmex (diuron) WP at the 10, 20 or 40 pounds aia (11.25, 22.5, or 45 kg. ai/ha.) rate did not damage any test plant. Neither did Hyvar X (bromacil) at the 15-pound aia (17 kg. ai/ha.) rate but higher rates caused injury. Pramitol (prometon) 5 PS or WP or Princep (simazine) should not be used in any enclosed structure. None of the herbicides used in these studies are labeled for use in closed structures. **Remember, however, that once the floor of a greenhouse or structure is treated, if roots of any container-grown or balled-in-burlap plant grow into the treated soil, plant injury will result since all five of these products are root absorbed.** A very effective procedure is to apply the herbicide, then cover the soil with groundcover cloth or gravel to keep the roots away from the chemical. As long as soil and/or organic matter is not allowed to build up on the surface, repeat applications of herbicides can be made and watered into the soil and off of the gravel without complication (Figure 15.20).

If injury from herbicides applied to the floor of a closed structure is suspected, mixing activated charcoal into the soil at rates up to 8 pounds per 100 square feet or more (3 kg./10 sq.m.) may inactivate the herbicide (5, 11, 19). Activated charcoal is available under the trade name of Gro-Safe, manufactured by ICI United States Inc. Specialty Chemicals Division, Wilmington, Delaware and Darco charcoal. Other sources may also be available.

Karmex (diuron) appears to be safe for use in enclosed structures such as greenhouses or holding overwintering houses for nursery stock at rates up to 40 pounds aia (45 kg. ai/ha. Under conditions of higher than normal temperatures and no ventilation, no injury from volatilization of the herbicide could be detected. Hyvar X (bromacil) at 15 pounds aia (17 kg. ai/ha) also appeared safe. Pramitol (prometon) killed many of the test plants even at 10 pounds aia (11.25 kg. ai/ha) while Princep (simazine) at 60 pounds aia (68 kg. ai/ha) caused slight injury. However, none of these herbicides are registered for use in closed structures.

Figure 15.20. Gravel was applied to this holding/loading area and then it was treated with Karmex for weed control. As long as the plants do not remain on the gravel for more than a few weeks, no crop injury occurs. Areas such as this should be cleaned and re-treated each year.

Post-Emergent Herbicides. In general, post-emergent herbicides kill the growing plant (generally anything green), as opposed to pre-emergent herbicides that kill the germinating seed or seedling. Post-emergent herbicides are most effective when used to control weeds not controlled by pre-emergent herbicides and perennial weeds.

Several post-emergent herbicides are available:

a. Cacodylic acid (sold as Dilic, Phytar 560, Ansar and other names) is an arsenic base herbicide that kills any green plant vegetation. It is useful for controlling annual weeds when the air temperature is above 55 degrees F, however, it is not effective in controlling perennial weeds since even though the top of the weed will be killed, it will quickly re-grow from the crown, rhizome or root system. The toxicity or LD-50 is 830 mg./kg. or moderately toxic (the lower the number, the greater the toxicity) (see the listing of toxicities of several herbicides and other chemicals commonly used around a nursery in the appendix).

393

b. Paraquat is one of the most toxic herbicides available and has an LD-50 of 150. Paraquat kills any green vegetation very quickly and at any air temperature, whereas, some other post-emergent herbicides are less effective during cool weather. However, because the toxicity is high and Paraquat is suspected of accumulating in the body, it is not recommended for use.

c. Roundup (glyphosate) is a very effective post-emergent herbicide effective on most annual and perennial weeds. It has an LD-50 of about 5,000. Roundup is non-selective, with a few exceptions and is readily absorbed by any green plant part, especially on sunny days. Unlike cacodylic acid, which leaves a residue of arsenic in the soil, Roundup breaks down to carbon dioxide and water.

In order to obtain the most effective results from Roundup, remember the following steps (9, 26):

1. Good coverage of the weed with the spray is essential.
Good coverage and rate of Roundup are related. Good weed control will result from poor coverage and a high rate or good coverage and a low rate.

2. Roundup must be translocated to the roots of perennial weeds in order to be effective. If the weed is rapidly growing, little downward translocation is occurring and control may be poor. However, when most plants are maturing or flowering (no longer making rapid vegetative growth), translocation of carbohydrates from the leaves downward is occurring and Roundup will be most effective. Likewise, if the weed is under drought stress, control will probably be poor.

3. Spray dry foliage on a sunny day to be most effective. However, the plant may not show any symptoms of injury for 3 to 6 days or longer. By contrast, Paraquat generally causes browning in 24 to 48 hours.

4. The lower the volume of water carrier with the Roundup, in general, the more effective it will be. It's the concentrated chemical that does the job, not the water and if so much water is used that some of the spray runs off the foliage of the weed and carries the Roundup with it, money is wasted.

5. Roundup is an acid and will react with galvanized and mild steel and release hydrogen gas which is explosive. In addition, the Roundup is modified to ferrous glyphosate which has no effect on weeds. Use only spray tanks of plastic, fiberglass, aluminum or stainless steel.

6. Fall applications are much more effective than spring applications on problem perennial weeds such as Johnsongrass, bermudagrass, nutsedge and field bind weed, because of the strong downward translocation.

7. Some species of the rose family: pyracantha, rose, peach, pear, flowering quince, etc.; also bald cypress and forsythia are very sensitive to Roundup at very low rates.

8. Rodeo is Roundup without the surfactant and is labeled for aquatic weeds. It is very effective on cattails and other weeds around the edges of water reservoirs and in moist or seepy areas.

9. As soon as an area is sprayed with Roundup to kill perennial weeds or a mix of annual and perennial weeds, provision should be made for the re-growth of weeds from seeds that are present on the site. As soon as the existing vegetation is killed and exposes the soil surface, more weed seeds will germinate (Figure 15.21). In some areas, a pre-emergent herbicide may be mixed with the Roundup or applied later to control the germinating weed seeds. Check with a Monsanto representative for pre-emergent herbicides that are compatible with Roundup.

d. Poast and Fusilade 2000 are post-emergent herbicides that are specific for young annual and perennial grasses. In general, the grassy weeds should be less than three to four inches tall when sprayed. Thus these products are useful during a limited time in the growth of the weed. The good news is that they have been sprayed over the tops of many species of trees and shrubs with little, if any, injury. Both work best when a good surfactant is added to the spray solution.

These compounds appear to be quite safe on a wide assortment of plants. They control young grasses only, thus their application and use in the nursery is quite specific. Remember, grassy weeds are very competitive with nursery stock and must be controlled if optimum growth is to be attained.

Figure 15.21. The grassy weeds in the rows were sprayed with Roundup. With the death of the grassy weeds and exposure of the soil surface, other weed seed will germinate. In order to be most effective, a good pre-emergent herbicide should be mixed with the Roundup. Where vegetation exists on the soil surface, a Roundup/Treflan mix works well since the dead weeds reduce the light decomposition and volatility of the Treflan.

Root-absorbed Roundup. A block of seedling shumard oak were grown in a field with areas heavily infested with nutsedge (nutgrass). The trees were planted in April and the soil surface treated with Treflan for pre-emergent weed control. Drip irrigation was used and fertilizer was banded along the rows. By late summer the nutsedge in some parts of the rows was a solid sod. Roundup at the rate of 5 tablespoons per gallon of water (4 quarts per acre) was applied to the nutsedge in late September using a hand sprayer and nozzle shield made from a plastic bottle. None of the chemical contacted the foliage or stems of the trees. The nutsedge tops were killed within a week, but no injury could be detected on the oak trees prior to normal leaf drop in late October. The following spring, trees in areas that had been heavily infested with nutsedge and sprayed with Roundup had distorted leaves and made little growth the entire season even though fertility was good and drip irrigation continued. The trees did not leaf out in the spring.

During early October, a dense area of honeyvine milkweed surrounded a group of two- to three-inch caliper pin oak trees on 12-foot centers in two locations. Previous treatments of this weed with Roundup at two to three tablespoons per gallon of water (two to three quarts per acre) caused moderate top dieback, but recovery the following season showed little, if any control. The honeyvine milkweed was sprayed on October 10, using Roundup at five tablespoons per gallon (four quarts per acre) using a boom sprayer on a tractor. Since the leaf surface is very glossy, a surfactant (Rhom & Haas Ag 98) was added to improve leaf wetting. Trees in all areas sprayed were seven to eight feet tall and lower branches had been removed to about three feet. The trees had been planted from five-gallon containers, two years earlier and drip-irrigated to aid establishment. No spray contacted the stems or leaves of the trees.

Leaf emergence of the trees in April was normal. By early June, considerable leaf injury (yellowing and death of leaf margins and some leaf distortion) was readily visible (Figure 15.22). By mid July trees in the areas where the honeyvine milkweed had been sprayed with Roundup were completely defoliated and twig dieback was visible. Trees the same age and under similar growing conditions where annual grasses and some common bermudagrass had been sprayed with the same Roundup surfactant combination at the same time did not show any injury. This is consistent with results of repeated use of Roundup to control bermudagrass in both field nurseries and landscape situations.

Figure 15.22. Injury of pin oak leaves where Roundup had been sprayed on the soil surface the previous fall to control honeyvine milkweed. This is similar to injury observed where high rates of Roundup have been used to control nutsedge adjacent to trees in nursery or landscape situations.

Nutsedge has a sizable storage organ beneath the soil surface. Honeyvine milkweed has a very extensive root system. Since roots of all plants are growing in the aerated soil near the surface, perhaps the Roundup could have been translocated from the foliage of both weed species into the soil whereupon death and decomposition of the weeds, the chemical was absorbed by roots of the trees. Bermudagrass, on the other hand, has a strong rhizome near the soil surface in addition to the stolons aboveground and may not carry the Roundup into the soil in the same way or to the same depth as the other two weeds.

The likelihood of this happening seems remote, yet the trees were dead only in the areas where nutsedge and milkweed were treated with Roundup. At this point **additional caution** appears justified when using Roundup on perennial weeds with extensive roots or storage organs near woody landscape plants.

Wick Applications of Roundup. When the pre-emergent herbicide fails to give 100% weed control, which is most of the time, the backup is often Roundup. Sprays of Roundup are effective, however, when the weed population is light, most of the Roundup goes on the soil, not on weeds. In addition to the expense and wasted chemical, there is the potential of foliar contact and crop damage.

One very effective alternative is to build a Roundup wick applicator. The process is to apply a small quantity of concentrated Roundup to the top of the weed. Since Roundup is translocated downward in the plant system, the effect is similar to a spray which covers most or all of the foliage, except that with the wick applicator, unless a weed is present, no Roundup is lost. This is not quite true, since in order to maintain free liquid on the wick, a few drops are lost if no weeds are contacted for some distance. On the other hand, the effectiveness per acreage covered per gallon of Roundup is far greater than with sprays. It should be noted, however, that where there are both tall and short weeds and a moderate to high weed population evenly distributed, a spray is superior.

When weeds escape pre-emergent herbicides, they are the next problems in the nursery. If they are allowed to go to seed, the population of that species will be greater next year and far greater the next. Weed population shifts are hastened by pre-emergent herbicides in that normally competing plants are removed and the opportunity to grow larger and produce more seed is greatly accelerated.

The apparatus consists of a reservoir of concentrated Roundup solution (2:1 or 3:1, water to Roundup) and a wick applicator assembly. This can be either homemade or purchased. A reasonably effective homemade apparatus can be made using two-inch PVC pipe and wool felt. The PVC pipe must be split lengthwise using a saber saw. Mark a straight line down the side of the pipe using a piece of angle iron. After cutting with a jig saw (a circular saw will not work), the split will close tightly. Insert two pieces of wool felt about 10 inches wide and folded once into the slit by prying it open. (Two edges of fabric will be inserted into the pipe leaving a loop exposed about three inches.) The wool felt must be inserted about two inches into the pipe. Position the pipe so that the slit with the fabric faces forward at a relative position of about 4 o'clock. When the end caps are secured using silicone seal or acrylic caulking compound, a trough is created that will hold the Roundup solution and maintain a free source of liquid to feed the wick (Figure 15.23).

Commercial wick applicators are available that utilize saddle/glue connectors for two-inch PVC pipe and special nylon over cotton rope wicks. The rope wick units are positioned such that they are about 18 inches long and overlap each other. To be certain of good chemical transfer to the weed, it may be best to double the number of rope wick units so that every weed gets touched by two ropes instead of one.

The wick applicator can be used either as a rigid unit or on a pivot. The pivot works well among trees large enough to sustain some pressure from the end of the unit. The apparatus in Figure 15.23 was built using a 3/4-inch rod, two-bearing assemblies and a piece of two-inch pipe for the PVC receiver bracket. The PVC pipe was attached to the metal bracket using water hose clamps. By attaching a long spring near one end of the pipe to a stationery arm, the end of the wick applicator can contact the stem of the tree and pivot around it, contacting any weeds near the stem. The end cap should be beveled or rounded to decrease any likelihood of stem damage. Other modifications may be useful with specific nursery/cultural practices.

Figure 15.23. A Roundup wick applicator on the three-point hitch of a small tractor (above). The wick-pipe apparatus pivots on central bearings, so weeds are contacted within a few inches of the tree stem. Weeds in the rows that otherwise could not be removed by mowing or cultivating were killed. Two passes per row are required, but few weeds escape. Adjust the three-point so that the wick apparatus is level or nearly so, then adjust the height to contact the weeds to be controlled. Do not allow the fabric to touch the soil as Roundup activity is greatly reduced upon soil contact. Rinse out the fabric after each use by running clean water through the system and thoroughly hosing down the exposed fabric. Below, results of using the apparatus with Roundup (two parts water to one part Roundup) in a field nursery. Note the weeds in the row that were killed by Roundup.

Soil Sterilization. Some nurseries choose to hold plants on gravel, sea shells, or similar materials treated with herbicides. Unfortunately, most of the herbicides that are registered for soil sterilization (Karmex, simazine, Hyvar, and Pramitol) are readily absorbed by roots. When plants are set on a gravel surface for a long period of time, some roots may grow out of the drain holes of containers or from the B & B soil mass (Figure 15.24). Since these herbicides are moderately water soluble, over a period of time with irrigation and rainfall, the herbicide leaches down and roots of weeds can survive in a shallow zone at the soil surface (Figure 15.25).

As with most herbicides, soil sterilants rarely control every weed species. As with weeds controlled by pre-emergent herbicides, the weed population on any soil area treated with soil sterilants is constantly shifting. Any weed that can tolerate the herbicide is freed from competition with other weeds and produces more seed than before and the species spreads. The spread may be slow at first but as the population builds, it can present a major weed control problem (Figure 15.26). It generally requires a shift to another herbicide or some other cultural practice that makes growing conditions less favorable to that particular weed species. In some cases where soil sterilant herbicides are used on holding beds, the problem may be such that plastic or ground cover cloth will be required for several growing seasons in order to eliminate the problem weed. If plastic is used, do not forget about the importance of surface drainage.

Figure 15.24. Above, a leaf of rose-of-sharon or althea (**Hibiscus syriacus**) injured by Karmex absorbed when roots grew out of a B & B root ball and into the soil below. Below, Persian lilac (**Syringa persica**) injured by simazine in the ground bed beneath the container.

Figure 15.25. As the herbicides slowly decomposes or leaches downward, roots can survive outside of the container if left in place too long. This means greater work when lifting for shipping and more stress to the plant.

*Figure 15.26.   A severe infestation of bittercress or flickweed (**Cardamine pennsylvanica**), among container nursery stock.   The weed neither competes with, nor shades the crop plants, however, it does harbor insects, particularly aphids and mites and perhaps disease organisms and becomes a visual eyesore as well as providing a constant barrage of seed onto the surface of the growth medium since at maturity this species throws its seeds.   In this case, simazine was used on the ground bed surface for many years.   Slowly this species, which is tolerant to the herbicide, increased and became a major problem.   It was controlled by shifting to Goal as a soil treatment at a high rate.*

In some cases, plants may be killed when the soil sterilant herbicides are applied adjacent to containers or B & B plants and rainfall or irrigation moves a sufficient quantity of the herbicide into the bottom of the container growth medium or root ball (Figure 15.27).

405

Figure 15.27. Mugo pine in three-gallon (11-liter) containers adjacent to a roadway treated with a soil sterilization rate of Hyvar X (bromacil). In this case, the containers were setting on ground cover cloth (polypropylene knit fabric) yet enough of the herbicide leached from the gravel into the base of the containers to kill most of the plants along the edge.

Roots of trees generally extend far beyond the outer branches. In some cases, if there are few other competing plants, roots of a tree may extend several times the distance from the trunk to the tip of the outermost branches. Because soil sterilant herbicides are generally absorbed readily by roots, especially roots of woody plants, desirable trees may be damaged (Figure 15.28).

If used carefully and with full knowledge of the destructive qualities they possess, soil sterilant-type herbicides can be safe and useful in some areas. Weeds of many species are spread by wind, therefore, weeds on ditch banks, around storage buildings and various other out-of-the-way locations can be a major source of weed seeds in the nursery or landscape. Proceed with caution!

406

Figure 15.28.   Herbicide damage to a tree that was part of the landscape around a nursery office building. In this case, the soil sterilant, Pramitol (prometon) was applied to the soil surface before a parking lot was paved with asphalt (mecadum or bitumin), the next growing season the herbicide injury became severe and killed the tree.

Literature Cited

1. Ahrens, J.F. 1966. Trials with dichlobenil and diphenimid for controlling weeds in container nursery stock. Proc. N.E. Weed Control Conf. 20:232-236.

2. Bingham, S.W. 1968. Influence of herbicides on Japanese holly and hand labor for weed control. Weeds 16:478-481.

3. Burt, Gordon W. 1974. Volatility of Atrazine from plant, soil and glass surfaces. Jour. Environmental Quality 3:114-117.

4. Butler, Joel F. and Carl E. Whitcomb. 1972. Effects of method of application of trifluralin in containers. HortSci. 7:341.

5.   Carpenter, Philip L. 1973. Chemical weed control in container-grown nursery stock. HortSci. 8:385-386.

6.   Dean, S.G., Carl E. Whitcomb and C.A. Conover. 1970. Effects of media and container type on herbicidal activity in container-grown woody ornamentals. Proc. Fla. Sta. Hort. Soc. 83:502-507.

7.   Fretz, Thomas A. 1972. Control of annual weeds in container-grown nursery stock. Jour. Amer. Soc. Hort. Sci. 97:667-669.

8.   Fretz, Thomas A. 1972. Weed competition in container-grown *Ilex crenata* 'Convexa'. HortSci. 7:341.

9.   Goodale, Toby, Robert D. Hathaway, James D. Ward and Carl E. Whitcomb. 1977. Controlling common bermudagrass with hand applications of Roundup. Fla. Nurseryman 22(4):71-72.

10.   Harowitz, M. 1964. Evaluation of herbicide persistence in soil. Weed Res. 9:314-321.

11.   Hasseltine, B.B. and W.H. Mitchell. 1976. Activated charcoal for turfgrass establishment. Proc. N.E. Weed Sci. Soc. 30:313-319.

12.   Jagschitz, J.A. 1979. Charcoals neutralizing powers. Gold Course Mgmt. 47(10):21-25.

13.   Kearney, P.C., T.J. Sheets and J.W. Smith. 1964. Volatility of seven S-triazines. Weeds 12:83-86.

14.   Mason, D.D. and R.P. Upchurch. 1962. The influence of soil organic matter on the phytotoxicity of herbicides. Weeds 10:14-18.

15.   Milbocker, Daniel C. and Henry Wilson. 1975. Dinitroanalines as nursery herbicides. Proc. SNA Nursery Res. Conf. 20:131-132.

16.   Moles, Ann and Carl E. Whitcomb. 1976. Movement of Ronstar in containers as influenced by the growing media. Proc. SNA Nursery Res. Conf. 21:137.

17.   Probst, G.W. 1967. Fate of trifluralin in soil and plants. Jour. Agri. and Food Chem. 15:592-599.

18.   Ryan, G.F. 1977. Multiple herbicide applications for bittercress control in nursery containers. HortSci. 12:158-160.

19.   Thompson, J.T. and W.S. Hardcastle. 1956. Influence of incorporated trifluralin on cotton in Georgia. Proc. S. Weed Conf. 18:79-84.

20.   Wadsworth, Grady L. 1975. Evaluation of eight herbicides in container nursery stock. Proc. Int. Plant Prop. Soc. 25:471-476.

21.   Ward, James D., Toby Goodale and Carl E. Whitcomb. 1976. Control of prostrate spurge and other weeds in containers with a post-emergence applications of Ronstar. Okla. Agri. Exp. Sta. Nursery Res. Rept. P-741:61-62.

22.   Weatherspoon, D.M. and W.L. Curry. 1975. Evaluation of Treflan, Lasso and Ronstar herbicides for use in woody ornamental nurseries. Proc. Fla. Sta. Hort. Soc. 88:535-540.

23.   Weatherspoon, D.M. and W.L. Curry. 1976. Repeat applications of Treflan, Lasso and Ronstar applied separately and in combination on container ornamentals. Proc. SNA Nursery Res. Conf. 21:125-128.

24.   Whitcomb, Carl E. 1976. Effects of herbicides on growth of container nursery stock. Nursery Res. Jour. 3(2):1-12.

25. Whitcomb, Carl E. 1977. A comparison of Ronstar, Lasso and Treflan for weed control in containers. Okla. Agri. Exp. Sta. Res. Rept. P-760:79-84.

26.   Whitcomb, Carl E. 1978. Roundup--Effective for controlling perennial weeds. Amer. Nurseryman 147(7):11, 67-68.

27.   Whitcomb, Carl E. and Carol Boyer. 1980. Activity of Ronstar (oxidiazon) in containers as affected by the growth media. Nursery Res. Jour. 6:14-18.

28.   Whitcomb, Carl E. and Carol Boyer. 1981. Growth media composition influences herbicide performance. Amer. Nurseryman 153:11, 122-124.

29.   Whitcomb, Carl E. and Joel F. Butler. 1975. Performance of trifluralin, nitralin and oxyzalin in nursery containers. Jour. Amer. Soc. Hort. Sci. 100:225-229.

30.   Whitcomb, Carl E. and Toby Goodale. 1977. Effects of Tolban, Ronstar and Devrinol on plant growth and weed control in containers. Nursery Res. Jour. 4(1):20-27.

31.   Whitcomb, Carl E. and Philip E. Perryman. 1975. Effects of irrigation on the movement of Treflan and Lasso in containers. Nursery Res. Jour. 2(1):1-9.

32.   Whitcomb, Carl E. and Jon G. Rackley. 1974. Effects of multiple applications of Treflan on weed control and growth response of four woody ornamentals in containers. Nursery Res. Jour. 1(2):1-9.

33.   Whitcomb, Carl E. and Paul W. Santelmann. 1983. Evaluation of herbicides for use in closed structures. Jour. Environmental Hort. 1:93-95.

34.   Wilburn, T.A. and F.D. Rauch. 1972. Weed competition in container-grown nursery stock. HortSci. 7:341.

35. Wright, W.L. and G.W. Warren. 1965. Photochemcial decomposition of trifluralin. Weed Sci. 13:329-331.

CHAPTER 16

TREE-INTERCROP RELATIONSHIPS IN THE FIELD

TREE-INTERCROP RELATIONSHIPS IN THE FIELD

An Alternative to Herbicides. Clean cultivation or bare soil maintained by the use of pre- and post-emergent herbicides may be the practice of choice in some field nurseries (Figure 16.1). However, other alternatives should be considered since bare field soils are subject to:

  a) wind and water erosion
  b) compaction by pounding raindrops and equipment,
  c) destruction of soil structure,
  d) depletion of soil organic matter,
  e) potential of herbicide buildup over repeated uses,
  f) a buildup of any weed species not controlled by the herbicide program will occur and
  g) the cost in labor, equipment and chemicals may be higher with chemicals than with an alternative program.

Figure 16.1. Where the land is relatively level and erosion is not a problem, clean cultivation in conjunction with herbicides works well. However, this is not always the best practice. Note the erosion in the foreground and center of the photo, even though this is a relatively level field.

Grasses are severe competitors with woody plants. In studies with several species of trees and shrubs, grasses can restrict growth of most woody plants by up to 70%. Not all plants are competitive or antagonistic with each other as some can be symbiotic or compatible. Kentucky 31 fescue is used in some field nurseries between rows for erosion control and to aid access when soils are wet. Fescue provides a good roadway surface among fields, however, it is very competitive when used between rows (Figure 16.2).

Figure 16.2. Roadways around this nursery are of K-31 fescue and work well when only light traffic is involved. The fescue roadways or waterways also aid in erosion control. Since fescue does not creep, it does not become a weed in the nursery as long as it is mowed occasionally to avoid seed production.

In an intercrop study conducted for two growing seasons in central Oklahoma, all four tree species were larger when grown with bare soil or crimson clover (*Trifolium pratense*) than K-31 fescue (Figure 16.3, Table 16.1). Differences in tree height between clover and bare soil were slight, suggesting that the clover provided little growth restriction or provided sufficient

413

mulching, soil cooling, moisture retention benefits to compensate for any competitive effects. Other clovers may also hold promise in this area, however, if they grow taller they may tend to shade lower branches of young trees.

*Figure 16.3.   Trees grown intercropped with Kentucky 31 fescue (right) and crimson clover (left).   Due to the angle of the photo and distance, plant size and quality is difficult to see, however, all four species of trees adjacent to the clover were taller and of superior quality compared to those adjacent to fescue.   The species visible in the photo are lacebark elm (**Ulmus parvifolia**) (E), shumard oak (**Quercus shumardi**) (O), and loblolly pine (**Pinus taeda**) (P).*

414

Table 16.1. Effects of intercrops on growth of trees in the field. Tree growth (height in inches) after two growing seasons in central Oklahoma with no irrigation.

	K 31 fescue	crimson clover	clean cultivation
Loblolly pine	53 inches*	65 inches	66 inches
Chinese pistache	55 inches	80 inches	81 inches
Shumard oak	33 inches	49 inches	45 inches
Lacebark elm	39 inches	69 inches	67 inches

*Values are averages of 12 to 18 observations.

Factors to Consider with Crimson Clover:
   a) Crimson clover can be planted from seed in the fall or very early spring. Drilling in three- to five-foot bands between rows is preferred but seed can also be distributed by broadcast or drop-type seeders and lightly incorporated.
   b) Plant height is no more than 12 to 16 inches tall, which does not shade lower limbs of young trees as can occur with taller vegetation.
   c) A thick stand left unmowed will eliminate nearly all weeds.
   d) Since this is a cool season annual, growth is during the fall and spring. After the production of seed in late spring, the plant dies and is not competitive with the woody nursery stock for water during the summer.
   e) If the vegetation is left, it provides an effective mulch and further resistance to weed growth throughout the summer and re-establishes from seed in the fall.
   f) Soil is protected against wind and water erosion, soil compaction and the destruction of soil structure all year.
   g) While aiding soil management and the current nursery crop, plants also build soil organic matter and supply some nitrogen fixation.
   h) If the intercrop strips are maintained properly, crop production can be alternated between strips with excellent

415

plant performance. When the current rows of nursery stock are harvested, rototill the clover as deep as is practical and replant in these strips. Following lining out trees or shrubs, replant clover between rows to re-build the soil from the previous crop.

Two- to three-foot-wide strips containing the newly planted nursery stock should be treated with Treflan or other effective, safe pre-emergent herbicide to control weeds in the rows. Care should be used to select only those herbicides that do not buildup in the soil or maintain a long-term residual that would prevent germination of the alternating cycles of nursery stock and clover.

White Dutch Clover. More recent studies suggest that an intercrop for nursery stock may be white Dutch clover, (*Trifolium repens*). Maximum height growth is 8 to 10 inches, it is a perennial with moderate stolon development for spreading into disturbed areas and it can be readily established from seed planted either in fall or spring. The seed is very small, but can be dispersed using a rotary seeder/fertilizer spreader. About 6 to 10 pounds of seed per acre are required for good coverage and it must be accompanied by the proper innoculum. Note that the innoculum for white Dutch clover is *Rhizobium trifolium* and is not the same as for white sweet clover (*Melilotus alba*) which requires *Rhizobium medicago* and grows five to six feet tall. Ladino white clover is a taller growing variety of white Dutch clover and may be an acceptable substitute, where trees are grown. However, its height of 16 to 20 inches makes it impractical for shrubs or small trees. White Dutch clover can provide an effective weed barrier/mulch/ erosion control cover over the soil surface while providing little or no restriction to the growth of most trees and shrubs. Where drip irrigation is used, the stolons will grow over the drip lines and develop roots on either side, thus effectively holding it in place and providing shade, which also reduces the expansion and or contraction movement problem of the lines.

The following is presented as a practical example. The sloping sandy loam field was subsoiled, fertilized according to the soil test and rototilled during late winter. White Dutch clover seed with innoculum mixed in was placed in a rotary seeder/fertilizer spreader on the three point hitch of a small tractor. With the discharge gate closed, about seven pounds of seed per acre were dispersed (from leakage past the gate by the fine seed) over the entire field about one month before the frost-free date. Seedling crapemyrtle were planted into the field well after the frost-free date when rapid establishment of this crop would occur. When planting time came, strips 12 to 14 inches wide were rototilled on three-foot centers throughout the field to aid the establishment of the crapemyrtle seedlings that were only two to three inches tall in small containers.

Following planting, drip irrigation lines were installed on the up side of the row and the young plants were thoroughly watered. About six weeks after planting, the clover provided a complete cover over the soil surface. Because of the small size of the seedlings, the clover was mowed several times until the young plants reached a height comparable to the clover. The drip irrigation system used was the thin biwall type with openings on 8-inch centers and subject to movement by wind or water. However, as soon as the soil surface was again covered by the clover, the drip lines were firmly held in place by the stolons and shaded so that expansion/contraction movement of the lines was minimal.

By the end of the growing season, the crapemyrtle were 18 to 24 inches tall and the clover continued to function. Weeds were effectively controlled without the use of herbicides by the shading of the soil surface since nearly all annual weeds require light to germinate. On one occasion, seven inches of rain fell in a 24-hour period, yet no erosion occurred and no drip irrigation lines were moved (Figure 16.4).

With larger nursery stock, the white Dutch cover may be seeded as soon as planting is complete. In the case of lining out bare root or container-grown trees or shrubs, the field should be prepared as in the example. As soon as planting is complete, seed the clover to obtain a vegetative cover over the soil surface before the weed seeds germinate. Do not procrastinate!

Another alternative would be to seed the white Dutch clover whenever conditions are favorable, then till only the strips for the rows of trees or shrubs. If fabric rootbag containers are to be installed, seed the entire area with clover, then auger holes for the containers in the clover. When planting is complete, the clover will spread into the area of the fabric container and provide an effective weed barrier without growth restriction to the crop. If the clover is not wanted at harvest time, a very low rate of Roundup herbicide will kill it with minimal risk to the trees or shrubs.

417

Figure 16.4. In this case the white Dutch clover was seeded in early spring, then when cover of the soil surface was complete and the seedling crapemyrtle were ready in June, strips about 14 inches wide were rototilled in the clover. After four to six weeks, the clover again covered the entire soil surface (top photo) yet growth of the crapemyrtle seedlings was excellent. The field was a sandy loam and sloped enough so that soil erosion was a major concern on the site. During a period in late September and early October, over 15 inches of rain fell, yet little or no erosion occurred. Some areas of the field sloped as much as 18 inches in a span of about 50 feet (bottom photo from left to right) yet little erosion occurred, drip irrigation lines remained in place, and plant growth was excellent.

418

Intercrops such as white Dutch or crimson clover provide a safe and effective alternative to herbicides while preventing erosion, looking attractive, fixing about 50 pounds of nitrogen per acre and providing little or no growth restriction to the crop. In addition, no cultivation is required, yet the soil surface remains uncompacted and open for water and air entrance. The savings in herbicide and cultivation expense are substantial while removing the likelihood of injury from herbicides or growth restricting root pruning from cultivation. Low-growing clovers provide all of the soil protecting advantages of grasses without the growth restrictions to the crop. The only disadvantage observed to date, is that the drip irrigation lines are difficult to get up prior to harvest. One possible solution might be to spray the clover with a low rate of Roundup sufficiently in advance so the stems would be partially decomposed by the time the drip lines are to be removed.

Alfalfa has also been tested as an intercrop and generally was unsatisfactory. Weeds grew among the alfalfa, during the spring fruquent mowing was required, and it continued to grow during dry periods which appeared to restrict the growth of the adjacent nursery stock.

The most recent legume ground cover to be added to the list of test species is Korel lespedeza (*Lespedeza stipulacea*). It is fine-textured both in leaf size and stem diameter, grows 12 to 20 inches tall and flowers in late summer. It does not require innoculation. One drawback may be that it does not compete well with weeds. However, mowing can be done and flowers are produced even on four- to six-inch tall plants. **This is also new and relatively untested, so proceed with caution.**

Few studies have been conducted in this area, probably due to the time and space required in conducting such research. Further studies should be conducted as superior nursery stock/intercrop combinations may be found. An intercrop not competitive with the nursery stock, but low growing and sufficiently dense to eliminate weeds might be suitable for broadcast planting over the entire field instead of just strips between rows. Or perhaps the crop could first be planted throughout the field and nursery stock planted later. The greatest restriction to new ideas is tradition and the lack of imagination.

CHAPTER 17

HOLDING FIELD STOCK AFTER HARVEST

HOLDING FIELD STOCK AFTER HARVEST

An additional technique that deserves more attention is the placing of B & B, bareroot, or fabric container-grown trees and shrubs in large containers following harvest. The initial reaction is generally one of, "additional expense that can't be justified". However, consider the following sequence of events:

1) Trees or shrubs are dug in the field. At this point the plants are at their prime relative to transplant success.
2) The plants are held at the field production site for several days or weeks, and the drying out and quality deterioriation begins.
3) During shipping and handling, further drying and deterioration continues.
4) The plants are often placed in a holding area either by the wholesale or retail nurseryman, garden center or landscape contractor. The plants may remain here from a few days to several months before being installed in the field or landscape.

From the time the plants are harvested in the field, there is no opportunity for recovery to begin until planting. If the root ball dries out at any point during this process, roots are damaged thus delaying root development. If the root ball is maintained overly wet, root suffocation may occur or the soil may slump during shipping, breaking some of the fine roots in the ball. If roots grow out into the mulch material while in a holding area, when the plants are finally moved, many of these roots are lost or damaged. The plant spent precious energy to grow those roots, yet in a matter of minutes they are often lost. Unfortunately, many of the roots that develop in a loose mulch are very course, poorly branched and easily broken. These large coarse roots are the result of excessive aeration, are brittle and watery and as a result, dehydrate quickly or if broken, are easy entrances for disease organisms.

The end result of this scenerio is a plant that was of excellent quality when dug in the field may be stressed and of mediocre quality at best when it goes into the landscape. If the plant is to survive, it must produce additional roots in the landscape site. Because the energy level in the plant is lower and the most active root buds are already spent, establishment is often slow which, in turn predisposes the plant to a host of other, secondary, disease, insect, and stress problems.

On the other hand, consider the events if the plants are placed in containers with a root trapping configuration such that root branching is stimulated and as a result of nutrients added, recovery can begin:

1) Trees and shrubs are dug in the field either bareroot, balledin burlap, or in fabric containers.

2) They are placed in containers with vertical sides (no taper) (Figure 17.1). Any twine around the stem (Figure 17.2) removed and in the case of the fabric container, the fabric is removed.

3) The space around the soil ball is filled with a soilless container mix suitable for the depth of the container. Remember that drainage from a container (and aeration) is controlled by the depth of the container and the porosity of the mix. If the mix is correct, water will drain around the root ball of soil such that existing roots in the soil and new roots produced can function well.

4) By either incorporating nutrients into the mix or topdressing immediately after arrival at the holding site, the few roots in the soil ball and any new roots produced, can begin absorbing nutrients and supporting the top, even if the top is dormant (except for bare root).

5) As new roots grow out into the mix and contact the sides of the container they are guided by recesses in the wall. When a root tip extends into the opening and is air-root pruned, it loses its apical dominance and root branching occurs, which in turn, improves nutrient absorption.

6) Since these containers have vertical sides, the plants are less subject to blowing over than if they were in either tapered round containers or mulched-in in the classical fashion used on B & B nursery stock.

7) When the container is removed at planting time, the plant has recovered substantially from the harvest shock, has produced new roots which are supporting the top and the roots are positioned to grow laterally in all directions with no wrapping or spiraling.

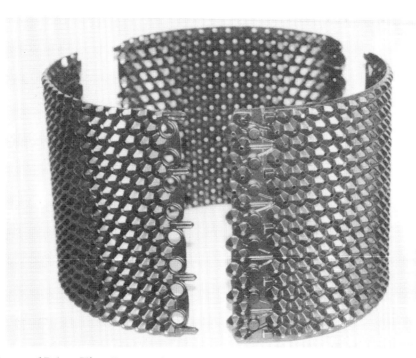

Rigure 17.1. The RootBuilder modular container can be made to fit any size tree or shrub. Each section is 19 inches long and 14 inches tall. Each added section increases the diameter of the container by six inches.

Trees and shrubs handled in this way will establish quickly in the landscape and shrinkage (losses) in the holding area will be vastly reduced. In addition, the plants have increased in value and health during the holding procedure instead of decline. This procedure does require capital ($) but in the long run will pay substantive dividends. See Figures 3.22, 3.24 and 3.25 in Chapter 3 for further details.

Figure 17.2. Plastic twine or string that is not removed during the planting process will restrict plant growth. In most cases, the stem grows above the twine, further obscuring it from view. The restriction seen here is from one growing season.

Overwintering Nursery Stock. Roots of plants growing in field nurseries or in the landscape are insulated by the soil mass and to some extent, heated by warmer temperatures deeper in the earth. Even when the soil freezes, the actual temperature of the soil rarely drops more than a few degrees below the freezing point except very near the surface. If the soil is insulated by vegetation, leaves, or snow cover, the soil may not freeze at all even when air temperatures are far below freezing.

For the temperate and sub-temperate zone species, it is not the freezing process that injures roots in containers, or balled-in-burlap (B & B) plants above ground, but rather the specific temperature. The tops of most temperate zone species have the capacity to harden (increase cold tolerance) with the decreasing day length and cooler temperatures in the fall. By contrast, roots have little, if any, capacity to increase their tolerance to cold. For example, the top of a Chinese holly (*Ilex cornuta*) can survive air temperatures of -10 degrees F (-26 C), whereas the roots of the same plant in a container will be killed when temperatures drop to 15 degrees F (-8 C). The small roots are more vulnerable to injury than larger roots and the injury may go unnoticed if the plant survives. This is often observed in the spring in the form of stunting or very slow growth as new small roots must be produced in order for the plant to resume normal growth. If enough of the small roots are killed, the plant is essentially bare-rooted if it is sold and planted into the landscape before some root recovery occurs. **Any plant held above ground with the roots exposed to unnatural low temperatures is subject to root injury or death. Plants balled-in-burlap have somewhat more buffer because of the soil density and water in the soil, than plants in containers, the same type of cold injury or death can occur.**

Plants grown in containers are especially vulnerable to cold injury because with conventional round containers, the bulk of the roots are in the outer sheath of growth medium against the inner wall of the container (Figure 17.2). Therefore, the only insulation is the thickness of the sidewall of the container. When temperatures drop below the lethal point for a few hours, the roots contacting the inner surface of the container may be killed. In such cases, the roots may re-grow from the surviving roots in the center of the growth medium and at the base of the plant. However, if the temperature stays at or below the lethal point long enough, the temperature of the entire mass of growth medium will eventually reach the lethal temperature, killing the entire root system. Unfortunately, there is no easy way to determine the extent of the root injury until the following spring. This is because the top of the plant is alive and only when desiccation occurs is the complete effect of the root injury realized. One technique that does work is to place plants suspected of suffering moderate to severe root injury in a heated greenhouse well in advance of spring planting. If the tops of the plants quickly die, little doubt remains. However, if the top survives and begins slow to moderate growth, the survival and performance of the plant in the landscape is still somewhat in question. This is because the stress level in the field or landscape is generally greater than that experienced in the greenhouse.

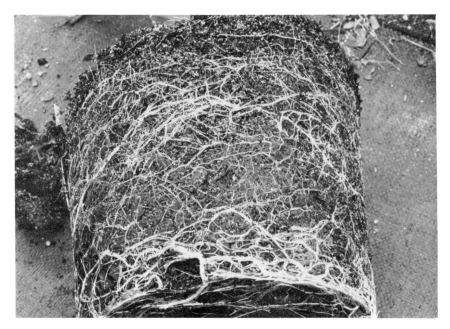

Figure 17.2. With conventional round container, the bulk of the roots are in the outer sheath of growth medium against the inner wall of the container making them extremely vulnerable to both low and high temperatures.

One of the major factors limiting the use of containers by the nursery industry in the northern states is root damage when ornamentals are held above ground in containers (2). Until recently, most winter injury has been attributed to desiccation of the top when the root mass is frozen. To prevent desiccation, relatively inexpensive, unheated, plastic-covered greenhouses are often constructed to protect the plants from drying winds, scorching sun, and rapidly fluctuating temperatures (Figure 17.3). To reduce heat buildup during warm winter days and in the early spring, the greenhouses are either covered with opaque white plastic or sprayed with white latex paint. However, even in the protection of these greenhouses, roots of many species of ornamentals may be damaged during severe winters and the injury may go unnoticed until late spring or early summer.

Figure 17.3. Above, quonset polyethylene-covered structures provide good overwintering protection. If additional protection is needed, a layer of polyethylene or microfoam laid over the tops of the plants inside the houses will greatly increase protection against cold. Below, plants closely spaced in a polyethylene-covered quonset-style structure. The center support posts provide greater snow loads with wider houses. It is much easier to use center supports and sleep well than to leave them out and wonder.

427

The difference in winter hardiness of plants growing in soil and of the same species growing in containers or planters has been a difficult-to-resolve problem. Winter injury is seldom a problem in these species when the plants are grown in the nursery field or landscape. Several studies have demonstrated that winter injury of many species of plants growing in containers can be attributed to lack of root hardiness.

The age and maturity of roots influence their cold hardiness. Mityga and Lanphear (7) found that young white roots of *Taxus* X *media* 'Hatfieldi' were killed at 27 degrees F (-3 C), secondary roots, red to brown in color were killed at 20 degrees F (-7 C) and the mature roots near the base of the stem were not killed until 12 degrees F (-11 C).

Studer et al. (8) published lists of several species and the killing temperature of immature roots (Table 17.1). Havis (6) and Studer et al. (8) have also listed the killing temperatures of mature roots of several species. Their findings have been combined in Table 17.2.

The average air temperature in an overwintering structure or holding facility for container-grown or B & B plants is generally less critical than the extreme temperature experienced by the root. Plants along the outer edge of a block of plants are more likely to be injured than those in the center (Figure 17.4). It may be practical, in some cases, to place plants with more cold-tolerant roots around those with less cold-tolerant roots for insulation.

428

Table 17.1. Root killing temperatures of immature roots.

Species	Killing temperature	
	degrees F	degrees C
Buxus sempervirens	26.6	- 3
Cotoneaster microphylla	24.8	- 4
Cotoneaster dammeri	23	- 5
Cornus florida	21.2	- 6
Euonymus alatus 'Compacta'	19.4	- 7
Euonymus kiautschovica	21.1	- 6
Ilex cornuta 'Dazzler'	24.8	- 4
Ilex crenata 'Helleri'	23	- 5
Ilex 'Nellie Stevens'	23	- 5
Ilex opaca	23	- 5
Juniperus conferta	12.2	-11
Juniperus horizontalis 'Plumosa'	12.2	-11
Juniperus squamata 'Meyeri'	12.2	-11
Kalmia latifolia	15.8	- 9
Koelreuteria paniculata	15.8	- 9
Leucothoe fontanesiana	19.4	- 7
Mahonia bealei	24.8	- 4
Magnolia stellata	21.2	- 6
Pieris japonica	15.8	- 6
Pyracantha coccinea 'Lalandi'	24.8	- 4
Rhododendron 'Purple Gem'	15.8	- 9
Rhododendron schlippenbachii	15.8	- 9
Taxus X media 'Hicksii'	17.6	- 8
Viburnum plicatum tomentosum	19.4	- 7

Table 17.2. Root killing temperatures of mature roots.

Species	Killing temperature	
	degrees F	degrees C
Acer palmatum 'Atropurpureum'	14	-10
Cornus florida	19.9	- 7
Cornus florida	10.4	-12
Cotoneaster horizontalis	15	- 9
Cotoneaster microphylla	8.6	-13
Cryptomeria japonica	16	- 9
Euonymus alatus 'Compacta'	6.8	-14
Ilex cornuta 'Dazzler'	17.6	- 8
Ilex crenata 'Convexa'	19.9	- 7
Ilex crenata 'Hetzi'	19.9	- 7
Ilex 'Nellie Stevens'	14	-10
Ilex opaca	19.9	- 7
Ilex opaca	8.6	-13
Juniperus conferta	- 9.4	-23
Juniperus horizontalis 'Plumosa'	- 4	-20
Juniperus horizontalis 'Plumosa'	0	-18
Juniperus squamata 'Meyeri'	- 0.4	-18
Koelreuteria paniculata	- 4	-20
Leucothoe fontanesiana	5	-15
Magnolia X soulangeana	23	- 5
Magnolia stellata	23	- 5
Magnolia stellata	8.6	-13
Mahonia bealei	10	-12
Pieris japonica 'Compacta'	15	- 9
Pyracantha coccinea	17.9	- 8
Pyracantha coccinea	17.6	- 8
Rhododendron carolinianum	0	-18
Rhododendron catawbiense	0	-18
Rhododendron 'Hinodegiri'	10	-12
Rhododendron 'P.J.M. Hybrids'	-10	-23
Taxus X media 'Hicksii'	- 4	-20
Viburnum carlesii	15	- 9

*Figure 17.4. Aluminum plants (**Pilea** spp.) are killed at temperatures about 32 degrees F (0 C). In this case, the heater in the greenhouse went out and the plants around the edge were killed or severely injured, whereas, the plants in the center were not injured. This emphasizes the cooling effect of the edge. Also note that more plants on the left hand side of the photo (north) were damaged than on the right hand side (south). This was probably due to a very small difference in temperature in the container and surrounding surfaces on the side exposed to the low angle of winter sun.*

Methods of Protection. Gouin (4) has worked extensively with microfoam insulating blankets over container nursery stock as a means of insulating roots from lethal temperatures. This technique can also be used with plants dug B & B or in fabric containers. In one study, plants were over-wintered in polyethylene covered structures as compared to covering with microfoam. Both groups of plants showed no visible injury to the tops, however, the roots of the plants from the polyethylene-covered structure were damaged. By early summer the plants could be easily distinguished by the size of the current season's growth which was nearly double with the microfoam insulation as compared to the polyethylene-covered structure.

Microfoam is a white, pliable, styrofoam-like packaging material available in rolls of various thicknesses. It is light in weight, has considerable insulating value and reduces light intensity by about 50%. Gouin (3) suggests the following steps when using microfoam for protecting nursery stock. First water the plants thoroughly. Then in a well-drained area, lay upright plants on their sides and leave spreading plants standing. Pack the plants tightly together, but expose as much of the foliage to light as possible. Cover the plants with a layer of microfoam so that the edges touch the ground. Several sheets may be taped together to form a wide blanket. Cover the microfoam with white polyethylene plastic and seal its edges to the ground. In late winter or early spring, uncover the plants and stand upright those that were laid on their sides. **Do not wait too long to uncover** in late winter or early spring. If the buds break (begin growth) beneath the microfoam, the tissues will be weak and quickly damaged when uncovering occurs. This technique can be used for a few days or a month or more as long as the weather is cold. The key factor to remember is **it only takes one cold period below the lethal point to cause death of the roots of the species** (Figure 17.5). It is equally important to remember that with a few sunny days the temperature beneath the microfoam can reach 90 degrees F or more and plant growth begins. The microfoam technique probably has much more application in areas with severe winters than in the South where sunny skys and 70 degrees F can occur during any month. Replacing containers or B & B nursery stock that have dead roots due to cold is very embarassing as well as expensive.

In some areas, and especially with trees and large plants that have more cold-tolerant roots, simply spacing the containers or root balls very close together and surrounding with straw or similar materials will provide sufficient protection for the winter or for brief periods until the material can be sold or planted (Figure 17.5). If straw is to be used, remember:

a) rodents love it,

b) there will always be some grain that will pose a weed problem if herbicide protection is not provided and the plants have not been sold or planted when spring arrives. Treflan (trifluralin) works very well if applied to the surface of the containers or soil root balls before the straw,

c) a layer of straw that looks more than adequate will settle and provide little protection after a rain or heavy snow (Figure 17.6). Straw must be 4 to 6 inches thick to provide appreciable protection (Figure 17.7).

Figure 17.5. In this case, orders of container nursery stock were taken from their protected environments and assembled ready for shipping. It only takes one night with sufficiently low temperatures to kill part or all of the roots of plants above ground either in containers or B & B. It sometimes occurs in a holding/staging area such as this or at the unloading point before protection is provided. The key point to remember is that the roots of container-grown and B & B plants must be protected from cold below the lethal point at all times.

Figure 17.6.   Above, barberry plants closely spaced and surrounded
by a heavy layer of straw.   In Oklahoma, this will provide
adequate protection for the roots of this species.   Below, using
Treflan or a similar herbicide before spreading straw, controls
weeds.   In this case, the straw compacted after a heavy snow
leaving some containers with little or no protection.

Figure 17.7. Roots of two plants of the same species in the spring. Roots of the plant on the left (P) were protected by styrofoam insulation, whereas, the plant on the right (M) was mulched with an insufficient amount of straw. Both plants lived, however, the extent of the early flush of growth was about four times greater where the roots were not injured by the cold.

In summary, several factors are especially important in overwintering nursery stock:

a) Allow plants to harden normally in the fall. Do not apply excessive fertilizer in the fall and extend the plant growth too late into the season. At the same time, plants under nutrient stress are more likely to suffer injury. Moderation is the best advice.

b) Water plants thoroughly before the first prolonged freezing weather. The specific heat of water is quite high; therefore, the more water in the container or root ball, the longer the cold period must be before freezing occurs.

c) Don't place plants in polyethylene-covered structures or under microfoam too early as this may encourage late fall growth due to increased air temperatures. Likewise, don't wait too long. Early December is about right in U.S.D.A. zones 6 and 7.

435

d) A double layer of polyethylene over the structure with air inflation provides greater insulation than a single layer and will tolerate more wind stress.

e) Ventilate polyethylene-covered structures on sunny days to prevent excessive heat buildup. This is more critical in areas with considerable winter sunshine. Remember to water from time to time when the containers are not frozen, to replace water lost during the ventilation process.

f) In more severe climates, cover plants inside polyethylene-covered structures with a second layer of poly or microfoam over the tops of the plants provides additional protection.

g) In more northern areas, milky polyethylene is generally recommended, whereas, in milder climates, milky or clear poly has been used satisfactorily.

h) With the first break in the consistent cold in late winter, emphasis must be placed on ventilation of polyethylene structures to prevent heat buildup. Once the buds of most plants have received sufficient chilling, growth will begin abnormally early if the polyethylene-covered structure is not kept cool. This is one of the major drawbacks to overwintering in polyethylene-covered structures or under microfoam (Figure 17.8).

i) Exposure to wind will increase both the desiccation of the tops plus cause the container or root ball to cool down more quickly to the lethal point. Wind protection of containers can sometimes mean life or death to the plant (Figure 17.9).

j) Plants of the same species and cultivar grown in containers will be more subject to cold injury than plants in fabric containers or B & B above ground. This is because most of the roots of container-grown plants are against the inner wall of the container (Figure 17.2). However, if the temperature drops to the lethal point for the species and stays there long enough for the entire root mass of both the container and B & B root ball to reach the lethal point, both plants will be killed.

Figure 17.8.   A dormant bud of photinia (above) will tolerate temperatures below 0 degrees F (-18 C).   However, once bud break occurs (below), the new growth will be killed or damaged at temperatures at or just below freezing.   The very early bud break in polyethylene-covered structures generally means that the plants cannot be planted out-of-doors until the frost-free date is reached.

Figure 17.9.   Above, container-grown plants left unprotected.   All plants on the northern edge were killed while many plants which enjoyed the protection of the other containers survived.   Below, in some cases a layer of heavy paper to prevent wind movement among the container can reduce or root injury.   However, this does not work when temperatures are severe.

438

Literature Cited

1.   Foster, Stanley. 1977. Winter plant protection at Greenleaf Nursery Co. Oklahoma Division. Proc. Int. Plant Prop. Soc. 27:298-299.

2.   Gouin, Francis R. 1973. Winter protection of container plants. Proc. Int. Plant Prop. Soc. 23:255-258.

3. Gouin, Francis R. 1974. A new concept in over-wintering container-grown ornamentals. The Amer. Nurseryman 140(11):7, 8, 45, 48.

4.   Gouin, Francis R. 1976. Soil temperatures of container plants overwintered under microfoam. The Amer. Nurseryman 44(8):9, 82.

5.   Havis, J.R. 1972. Winter injury. In Nursery Container Production. U. of Mass. Coop. Ext. Serv. Pub. 73:35-37.

6.   Havis, J.R. 1976. Root hardiness of woody ornamentals. HortSci. 11:385-386.

7.   Mityga, H.G. and F.O. Lanphear. 1971. Factors affecting the cold hardiness of *Taxus cuspidata* roots. Jour. Amer. Soc. Hort. Sci. 96:83-87.

8.   Studer, E.J., P.L. Steponkus, G.L. Good and S.C. Wiest. 1978. Root hardiness of container-grown ornamentals. HortSci. 13:172-174.

9. Tinga, J.H. 1977. Factors affecting physiology of roots in winter. Proc. Int. Plant Prop. Soc. 27:291-293.

CHAPTER 18

TRANSPLANTING WITH TREE SPADES

TRANSPLANTING WITH TREE SPADES

Advantages and Disadvantages. Digging and planting landscape trees with tree spades is likely to increase in the future due to demand for an immediate landscape effect at a reasonable installation cost. Despite disadvantages such as the need for a special equipment operator, the inability to use tree spades in unfavorable weather or where underground utilities exist, or where buildings, paving or vegetation reduce mobility (1), some advantages and the immediate landscape effect encourage their use. Tree spade-dug and -planted trees have been promoted for year-round planting (1) and can reduce manpower and save time under some conditions (6). Cool (1) conducted a 10-year study in Michigan of bare root vs. tree spade-dug and transplanted trees. Mortality of bare root trees was 28% while mortality of trees dug and transplanted with a tree spade was only about 1%. Even though the expense of operating a tree spade is much greater than planting bare root trees, he concluded that 1.5 tree spade trees could be planted for the same cost as one bare root tree when survival was considered. In other instances, tree spades allow use of larger trees that can better withstand mechanical abuse and vandalism along streets (8) and may be less expensive in the long run (1, 6).

When tree transplanting fails, profits decrease for the grower and the landscape contractor (3). All production and preplanting efficiencies then are in vain. In tree digging and planting, many factors must be considered (6, 8): time of year, climate, exposure, production site, landscape site, soil types, digging-to-planting time span, post-planting care, and tree species.

Watson and Himelick (9) found that up to 98% of the root system can be lost when a tree is dug with a tree spade. Such injury also permits pathogen entry. Therefore, efforts to minimize the loss of roots and reducing shock and recovery period should be made (5). Although more roots may be retained by a properly dug bare root tree than with balled-in-burlap or tree spade-dug trees (3, 7) they sustain more damage to the important small shallow fine roots and with large trees, show less growth one year after transplanting than with tree spade-dug trees (8).

When roots are cut during digging, new roots develop from the point where the older roots were severed (Figure 18.6). These new roots grow and branch (4). One of the key soil characteristics important for new root development is soil aeration (9).

A frequent criticism of the tree spade is that holes dug to receive the tree are not quite the same shape or size as the ball dug with the tree spade, thus, various gaps or voids exist between the two soil masses following transplanting. These air spaces are thought to restrict root development since roots seldom extend through large air spaces. An additional concern lies with the glazing of the sides of the tree spade-dug hole and the face of the soil ball dug with the tree spade. Soil glazing may be sufficient to retard root penetration and development into the surrounding soil in some instances and restrict normal moisture movement in the soil following planting and watering. The relative shape and size of the tree spade-dug ball is also frequently a concern among landscape contractors. Balls of earth from tree spades are narrower and deeper than conventional hand-dug balls and may contain a smaller proportion of the fine roots.

Pulling Trees. An additional technique which contrasts with both the tree spade and hand digging is the procedure of pulling the tree from the ground using a pin and clevis through the trunk. At first, this technique seems very undesirable, however, with close inspection, it has merit. Root tips which survive the harvesting procedure and those which develop quickly following transplanting probably play the greatest role in insuring survival of the tree. With either the tree spade or hand digging, a sizable portion of the root tips are lost and the number and extent of larger roots which are most responsible for developing new root tips are greatly reduced. If the soil is moist when the tree is pulled, many of the small roots as well as a higher proportion of the larger roots will be retained. It is important to prevent drying of the root mass once it is removed from the soil, and replanting should be done as soon as possible. With a pulled tree, the quantity of functioning roots and the potential for development of new roots at the new site appears greater than with the tree spade or conventional B & B.

Comparing Transplanting Techniques. In order to determine the merits of the various transplanting methods for trees, the following digging/planting treatments were made (7):

442

1) tree spade-dug tree planted into tree spade-dug hole,
2) tree spade-dug tree planted into hole dug by a backhoe,
3) hand-dug balled-in-burlap (B & B) tree planted into hole dug by a backhoe,
4) trees pulled from moist soil by pin and clevis and planted into hole dug by a backhoe.

Tree species used were:

lacebark or true Chinese elm (*Ulmus parvifolia*) four years old, 5 1/2 to 6 feet tall with 2 1/2- to 3 1/2-inch stems near the soil line;

Japanese black pine (*Pinus thunbergiana*) four years old, 5 to 6 feet tall with 2- to 3-inch stems near the soil line. Both species had been grown during the seedling establishment period in bottomless containers which destroys the tap root and stimulates a fibrous root system.

summit green ash (*Fraxinus pennsylvanica* 'Summit') were two years old and about five feet tall when obtained from a commercial nursery and four years old and 9 to 11 feet tall with 3- to 3 1/2-inch stems near the soil line when this study began.

All trees were grown in a heavy clay loam soil and were transplanted to a site of similar soil type about one-fourth mile away. All transplanting was done during late March while all trees were dormant. Each treatment was replicated six times for each species. The tree spade used was a Vermeer T-20 mounted on the three-point hitch assembly of a 40-horsepower tractor.

All trees were planted and watered thoroughly the same day they were dug. Spring and summer rains provided good soil moisture until early August. Soils became very dry during late August and September but no supplemental watering was done.

Several assumptions were made in order to calculate transplant costs:
1) Equipment cost was based on 1/10 of 1% of the value of the machine used in each operation.
2) Labor cost was based on $5.00 per hour per man.
3) Overhead costs were calculated by multiplying the cost of labor per treatment by 30%.

Based on the assumptions made and time required, the following transplanting costs were determined:

Lifted/Hole preparation	elm	pine	ash	average
Tree spade/tree spade	$4.38	$4.65	$3.55	$4.19
Tree spade/backhoe	3.71	3.68	4.28	3.89
B&B/backhoe	9.67	9.16	7.28	8.70
Pulled/backhoe	4.85	5.52	did not work	5.18

Since all trees were transported only about one-fourth mile, transport time did not become a major factor. However, in most landscape situations transport time would become a very important consideration, especially if the tree spade was driven several miles between sites. Transport distance may also influence the performance of trees pulled from the soil with many exposed roots, unless additional measures were taken to prevent root desiccation.

On September 23, a visual grade was taken for the lacebark elm and Japanese black pine (1 = best appearance and 4 = poorest appearance) and length of current season's flush was measured on the Japanese black pine and summit green ash. Visual grade of lacebark elm and Japanese black pine was highest (indicating more stressed appearance) when the trees had been transplanted by a tree spade and planted into a tree spade-dug hole, treatment 1 (Table 18.1). Appearance of lacebark elm trees, transplanted with treatment 2 (tree spade into a backhoe hole), or treatment 3 (B & B into a backhoe hole) or treatment 4 (pull method into a hand-dug hole) were similar, and all were significantly better than treatment 1 (tree spade into tree spade hole), Figure 18.1.

Japanese black pine grew most when transplanted with treatments 2, 3, or 4, and the length of the current season's flush was significantly shorter when trees were transplanted with treatment 1 (Table 18.1). In addition to a shorter flush of growth, Japanese black pine dug with a tree spade and planted into a tree spade-dug hole (Treatment 1) also had an overall unthrifty appearance (Figure 18.2).

Summit green ash grew best when transplanted with treatment 3 (B & B) as compared to either tree spade treatments (Table 18.1). The difference in the summit green ash appearance and length of new growth when compared to other test species may be related to the manner in which the trees were grown prior to initial planting in the field. Air root-pruning during the seedling stage greatly increases the quantity of fine fibrous roots as compared to trees grown in conventional ground beds. In the limited volume of soil in the tree spade ball, more roots on the elm and pine were transferred to the new site compared to the ash. Likewise, air root-pruning probably increased the success of the pull method with the elm and pine.

Table 18.1. Effects of transplanting method on visual grade or length of new growth of trees after one growing season.

	Treatments			
	(1)	(2)	(3)	(4)
	Tree spade/	Tree spade/	B & B/	Pull method/
	Tree spade	backhoe	backhoe	backhoe
Tree species	hole	hole	hole	hole
		Visual Grade*		
Lacebark elm	3.5	2.2	1.8	2.4
Japanese black pine	3.5	2.0	1.7	2.0
		Average New Growth (inches)		
Japanese black pine	6.0	9.6	11.0	10.1
Summit green ash	2.6	2.3	6.2	--

*Visual grade based on 1 = best appearance and 4 = most stressed appearance.

It is interesting to contrast treatments 1 and 2. The success of the tree spade-dug tree in the larger planting hole, (treatment 2) suggests that glazing of the tree spade-dug ball is not a problem. When loose backfill can be placed in intimate contact with the face of the ball following transplanting, the new roots produced readily grow **out** through the glazed surface. On the other hand, when a tree spade-dug tree is placed in a tree spade-dug hole, airspaces are likely to occur in numerous positions around the ball. In addition, both the face of the ball and the face of the hole may be glazed, depending on soil type and moisture conditions. Root penetration into the face of a glazed surface is probably much more difficult than root emergence through the back of a glazed surface.

Figure 18.1. Lacebark elm foliage density and relative leaf size with tree spade-dug tree in a tree spade-dug hole (left) and typical response of other treatments, (right) in September after transplanting in March.

The fact that the conventional balled-in-burlap technique was not superior to the tree spade and backhoe hole combination suggests that digging machines can be used with a similar degree of success as with B & B, if the seedlings are root-pruned initially. The pull method deserves more attention, particularly when transplanting large trees. This may be a way to retain more roots capable of aiding re-establishment without the awesome weight encountered with very large soil balls.

Note that the pull method did not work on the green ash. As lifting force was applied, the straight-grained ash wood split. We also tried drilling the hole for the pin just below branches with no benefit. With certain species with wood that splits easily, this technique may not be practical.

446

Figure 18.2. Japanese black pine foliage density and length of current season's flush of growth with tree spade-dug tree into a tree spade-dug hole (left) and typical response of other three treatments (right) in September after transplanting in March.

Further Techniques Explored. Because it is expensive to dig large tree-planting holes by hand, improvements in tree spade-dug holes are being sought. Tree spades compact and glaze the hole walls by their pressure as the blades are inserted into the soil. It is impractical to manually roughen or disturb the face of the tree spade-dug hole. Even if the soil is roughened to break any glaze of the face of the tree spade-dug hole, new roots would still be

447

forced to grow into undisturbed soil which is relatively low in oxygen in most situations. One proposed improvement is to hand-dig a tree spade-dug hole at least two feet larger in diameter to provide well-aerated backfill (6).

A tree transplant study was conducted to determine if the planting/filling process around tree spade-planted trees could be improved (2). The study was conducted using Japanese black pine (*Pinus thunbergiana*) and 'Hopa' flowering crabapple (*Malus* X 'Hopa') and four treatments:

1) tree spade-dug tree planted into a tree spade-dug hole, with normal efforts made to water-in soil around the root ball;

2) tree spade-dug tree planted into a tree spade-dug hole with approximately one cubic foot of soil added to the bottom of the hole and made into a mud slurry. The volume of the mud slurry was enough to fill the air spaces around the root ball from the bottom of the hole to the soil surface as the root ball was lowered into place, thus preventing any air pockets (Figure 18.3);

3) tree spade-dug tree planted into a tree spade-dug hole with a ring of soil approximately eight inches deep and eight inches wide removed from around the top of the tree spade-dug hole. This soil was then used to backfill and water-in around the tree, thereby reducing or eliminating the air space in the upper eight inches of soil and any glazing in the surface eight inches of soil where the tree roots are most concentrated and active;

4) tree spade-dug tree planted into a hole approximately four feet by four feet by 30 inches deep, dug with a backhoe. The tree spade-dug tree was held in the hole by the blades as the soil was backfilled. When all backfill soil was in place, the blades were removed and the tree was watered-in (Figure 18.4).

Figure 18.3. About one cubic foot of mud slurry was made in the bottom of the hole for Treatment 2. The volume of mud was adjusted so that when the tree spade-dug tree was inserted into the hole the thick mud would just reach the soil surface.

The tree spade used was a 30-inch Vermeer. The crabapples were 12 feet tall with two-inch stem diameters; the Japanese black pine were six feet tall with two-inch stem diameters. Both tree species had been grown on a clay loam soil. The planting site was an unproductive; very heavy clay with shallow topsoil. All trees were watered well following transplanting and numerous rains occurred until mid June. No further watering was done. Trees were evaluated by measuring 10 new shoots per tree after three months. For both species, shoot growth was best for treatment 4, the tree spade-dug tree in the backhoe-dug hole (Table 18.2).

By mid August, the flowering crabapples were visually evaluated for summer heat and drought tolerance using a 1 to 10 rating where 1 = small leaves and much stress while 10 = large leaves and little, if any, stress. Again treatment 4 was best (Figure 18.5, Table 18.2).

449

Figure 18.4. The tree spade was positioned over the backhoe-dug hole, then the spade was lowered and soil back-filled around the blades before the blades were removed. The backfilling was mostly done by a second tractor with a box blade.

Little benefit was seen from treatments 2 and 3, the mud slurry and loosened top ring of soil, compared to treatment 4, backhoe-dug hole. It appears that loosening the soil surrounding the transplanting root mass is the most practical means of reducing the stress of transplanting trees. This benefit is probably due almost exclusively to improving soil aeration. The reduced soil density allows more rapid root growth from the root ball into the surrounding soil.

450

Table 18.2. Average length of 10 new shoots of Japanese black pine and Hopa flowering crabapples, for each of four transplanting treatments.

Tree Species	Tree spade dug hole (1)	Tree spade dug hole with mud slurry (2)	Tree spade dug hole with loose soil rim (3)	Backhoe dug hole (4)
Crabapple avg. shoot length	11.8 cm. (4.6 in.)	8.6 cm. (3.4 in.)	13.5 cm. (5.3 in.)	20.3* cm. (8 in.)
Crabapple visual rating^	2.6	3.5	3.7	9.4
Pine--avg. shoot length	1.5 cm. (0.6 in.)	3.1 cm. (1.2 in.)	5.4 cm. (2.1 in.)	11.7 cm. (4.6 in.)

*Averages in horizontal line followed by the same l
^Visual ratings from 1 to 10 where 1 = very poor appearance and 10 = excellent appearance.

When a tree is transplanted, new root growth occurs mostly at the cut ends (Figure 18.6). Oxygen plays a key role in this process just as it does when rooting a cutting. There appear to be many simularities between the two because a tree transplanted B & B or with a tree spade is a huge cutting, in a way. Once new roots have initiated from the cut ends, their further function and requirments are like other roots. Oxygen is still important but not as critical as in the root initiation process. In the case of a tree spade-dug tree planted into a tree spade-dug hole, the new roots are forced to develop either into the narrow space or loose soil caused by the imperfect fit of the two cone-shaped masses of soil or into the undisturbed soil on the planting site. In either case, the aeration and general conditions for the production of new roots are poor.

Figure 18.5. The tree on the left was typical of the crabapples transplanted into the large holes dug by the backhoe. Even though the trees were not given any supplemental water during the summer, foliage was dense, dark green and no internal leaves were turning yellow or beginning to drop as of late August. No measurable rain had occurred for seven weeks prior to these photos. The tree on the right was typical of plant response to the other treatments. Of the 18 trees in the three poorer treatments, only two had died. However, all appeared unthrifty and had very small leaves. These findings emphasize the importance of loosening a large volume of soil when planting to reduce transplanting stress.

452

By contrast, when a tree spade-dug tree is planted into a larger hole and the backfill soil is loosened and aerated, a much more favorable environment exists for new root development. This difference in the rapid production of new roots may not make the difference of life or death, however, it can make the difference between trees with severe stress and trees with only moderate stress. The overall landscape contribution of the two trees for the first two, three, or four years following transplanting is vastly different and well worth the extra expense.

Figure 18.6. Development of new roots following transplanting occurs almost exclusively at the cut ends. Consequently, roots of trees dug with a tree spade and planted into a tree spade-dug hole are forced to develop into undisturbed soil. This is more difficult for coarse new roots from large cut roots than for small roots growing through the soil naturally.

Literature Cited

1. Cool, R.A. 1976. Tree spade vs bare root planting. Jour. of Arboriculture 2:92-95.

2. Bridel, Robert, B.L. Appleton, and Carl E. Whitcomb. 1983. Planting techniques for tree spade-dug trees. Jour. of Arboriculture 9:282-284.

3. Flemer, W. 1982. Successful transplanting is easy. Jour. of Arboriculture 8:234-235.

4. Furuta, T. 1982. Influences on root determine transplanting success. Amer. Nurseryman 156(7):65-69.

5. Hamilton, D.F. and S.D. Verkade. 1982. The development and care of a healthy root system. Amer. Nurseryman 156(6):73-80.

6. Himelick, E.B. 1981. Mechanical tree digging and planting with a tree spade. In: Tree and shrub transplanting manual. pp. 29-32.

7. Preaus, K.B. and Carl E. Whitcomb. 1980. Transplanting landscape trees. Jour. of Arboriculture 6:221-223.

8. Vanstone, D.E. and W.G. Ronald. 1981. Comparison of bare root versus tree spade transplanting of boulevard trees. Jour. of Arboriculture 7:271-274.

9. Watson, G.W. and E.B. Himelick. 1982. Root distribution of nursery trees and its relationship to transplanting success. Jour. of Arboriculture 8:225-229.

CHAPTER 19

TRANSPLANTING LARGE TREES

TRANSPLANTING LARGE TREES

The demand for large trees following construction and grading continues to increase. In many instances, two- to three-inch diameter trees are not of acceptable size to the client. On the other hand, landscape contractors and nurserymen have consistently observed that large trees transplanted by tree spades generally perform poorly for several years before either recovery or death. This is a discussion of some of the factors involved.

Studies With Smaller Trees. Tree spade transplanting studies showed that when tree spade-dug trees were planted in a larger hole, they grew much better than when tree spade-dug trees were planted in a hole dug by the same tree spade (3). The superior growth of the trees following transplanting was due to the aerated soil around the root ball, thus providing a better environment for the rapid development of new roots. Several techniques to fill the void between a tree spade dug-tree and a tree spade-dug hole have been studied (1). It was found that tree growth in the larger planting hole was superior in all cases.

Both of these studies showed that a well aerated soil around the root ball of a tree following transplanting can assist rapid root development and subsequent growth and appearance. However, this benefit can only partially compensate for stress incurred at time of transplanting, especially the stress incurred when transplanting large trees.

Tree Size Vs. Stress. In order to better understand the stress incurred by large trees following transplanting, a study was conducted with southern magnolia (*Magnolia grandiflora*) on the University of Florida campus in Gainesville, Florida (7). The trees ranged in size from one- to five-inch stem diameter measured 4 1/2 feet above the soil. The diameter and length of each limb on each tree was measured and grouped according to size in 1/2-inch increments. By multiplying the stem diameter (rounded off to the nearest 1/2 inch) of each 1/2-inch increment times pi (3.1416) the circumference of the stem was obtained. By multiplying this value times the number of linear inches of each 1/2-inch size class, an estimate of the total stem surface area of living cells was obtained. For example, a one-inch diameter tree that had 68 linear inches of stem one inch in diameter and 236 linear inches

456

of stem 1/2 to 1 inch in diameter would have 1 x 3.1416 x 68 = 213 square inches of stem surface area on the one-inch diameter branches and 0.5 x 3.1416 x 236 = 370.5 for a total of 584 square inches of branch surface area. In this study, all branches below 1/2 inch in diameter were not considered. Ten trees in each 1/2-inch size class (based on trunk diameter) were measured for a total of 90 trees.

Most of the cells in a woody tree or shrub are dead. However, the cambium and adjacent zone of cell division constitute a layer of very active living cells surrounding all stems and roots of all dicots (most woody landscape plants except the palms). On either side of the cambium is a zone of young and active living cells: on the inside, xylem cells; and on the outside, phloem cells.

Regardless of the thickness of this layer of living cells, when the branch surface area is plotted proportionately to the size of a particular kind of tree, one begins to gain an appreciation for why the larger the tree the greater the stress following transplanting. As the stem diameter of a tree increases from one to three inches, the stem surface area of living cells increases from 580 to 5,200 square inches (Figure 19.1). This is nearly a ten-fold increase in the surface area of living cells. When the stem diameter of a tree increases from about three inches to five inches, a further five-fold increase in surface area of living cells results. Compare the mass of living cells in a tree one inch and five inches in diameter and the difference is over 40 times greater.

These findings are striking. However, consider that there is a priority of distribution of carbohydrates (energy) within a woody plant; essentially flowers, fruits, leaves, stems and roots. In other words, if flowers and developing fruits are present on a tree they will preferentially receive carbohydrates at the expense of other plant parts (2). On the other hand, if no flowers or fruits are present, the leaves utilize the carbohydrates manufactured with any excess being translocated to the stem. If there are sufficient carbohydrates manufactured by the leaves to meet the needs of all leaves and stems, some are translocated to the root system (Figure 19.2). More and Halevy (2) observed that in a rose plant in full sun, 82% of the carbohydrates produced went to young shoots, 13% went to other above-ground plant parts, and only 4.3% went to the root system.

457

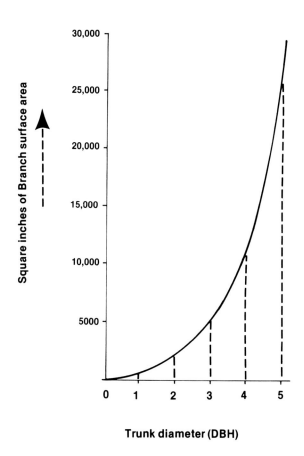

Figure 19.1. The square inches of branch surface area (an estimate of living cells) increases dramatically as trunk diameter of the tree increases. Respiration of all living cells in the top of a tree must be maintained before any appreciable energy can be translocated to the root system.

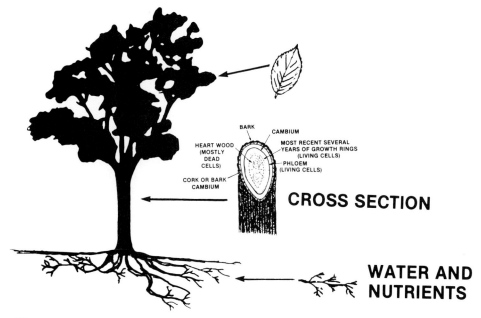

BARK

CAMBIUM

HEART WOOD
(MOSTLY
DEAD
CELLS)

MOST RECENT SEVERAL
YEARS OF GROWTH RINGS
(LIVING CELLS)

PHLOEM
(LIVING CELLS)

CORK OR BARK
CAMBIUM

CROSS SECTION

WATER AND NUTRIENTS

Figure 19.2. Movement of absorbed water and nutrients is up to the leaves via mostly living cells in the xylem and back down from the leaves via living cells in the phloem. If there is insufficient energy to meet the needs of all tissues, the plant parts most removed (stem and roots) will be the ones that suffer most.

When one considers a three- to five-inch tree recently transplanted with a substantial reduction in roots, the problem becomes more clear (Figures 19.1 and 19.2). Unless leaves and/or stored carbohydrates in the stems have the capacity to meet the needs of all leaves and all living cells in the stems, the roots receive little or none for the initiation of new roots. Thus new root growth is dependent on stored reserves and growth regulators in the roots. A good balanced nutritional program for the tree **prior** to transplanting will build the stored reserves in the stems and roots. If only a few new roots are initiated following transplanting, the leaves become stressed for water and nutrients, and thus soluble carbohydrates (energy) and growth regulating chemical production is greatly restricted. This further restricts root growth which places a greater stress on the leaves and thus the sequence of events that may ultimately lead to the death of the tree (Figure 19.3). On the other hand, the carbohydrate needs of the living leaf, stem and root tissues remain more or less constant.

This emphasizes the importance of energy (stored carbohydrate reserves) in the stems and roots prior to transplanting. The larger the tree the more critical are the stored reserves and the demand for stored reserves immediately following transplanting.

It is important to emphasize the value of well-aerated soil around the root ball following transplanting to encourage rapid root growth (1, 3). A larger planting hole at time of transplanting will probably not increase the survival of trees with low carbohydrate reserves. However, it will assist new root development of trees with adequate carbohydrate resources and reduce stress.

A theoretical analysis of the stress imposed on large trees at time of transplanting and the length of time necessary for recovery has been done (6). The model showed that when a small tree was transplanted, the length of time necessary before the root development on the new site was sufficient to support normal resumption of top growth was much less than when a large tree was transplanted, and the length of time for recovery was much greater. The model fits well with general observations of real situations over many years. The key item lacking from the model, however, is an allowance for the tremendous mass of living cells in the larger trees that must be sustained by energy from the leaves before energy can be translocated to the root system. It is this massive number of living cells, the complex array of growth-regulating compounds and the energy requirements of these cells that are primarily responsible for the poor performance of most transplanted large trees.

Because so much of this mass of living cells is present in the main stem and branches of a large tree (in excess of 60%), pruning the top of the tree has almost no effect on reducing the total energy demand. Removing all small branches in the top of a five-inch caliper tree, short of destroying the primary branch structure and thus the appearance of the tree, would only reduce the living cell mass by two to four percent. This is why top-pruning of trees provides little or no benefit in most cases. The energy-manufacturing and growth-regulating chemical production is reduced by top-pruning with little reduction in energy demand.

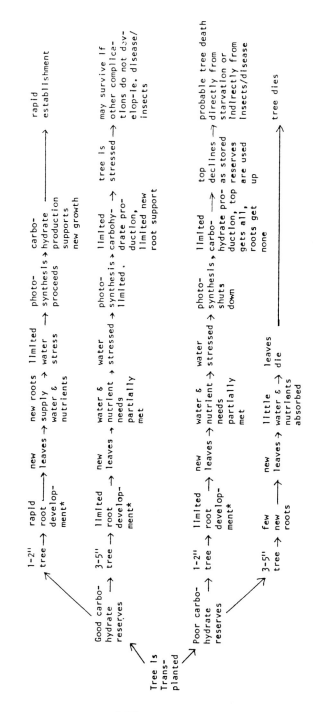

Figure 19.3. Probable sequence of events following transplanting of trees with or without good carbohydrate reserves and of small or large size.

*assuming a well aerated soil with good moisture and a reasonable supply of nutrients.

461

A Transplant Study With Large Trees. To examine this further, Whitcomb, Gray and Cavanaugh (8) designed a study to determine if top-pruning following transplanting would assist the establishment of large trees and if the methods of preparing the planting hole affect tree response to pruning. Since pruning reduced the quantity of living cells in the tree crown only slightly but substantially decreased the number of leaves available for growth regulator and energy production during the first few weeks or months following transplanting, the question was, will the benefits of a lower above-ground demand for water outweigh the loss of energy production because of fewer leaves?

Four-year-old seedlings of London planetree (*Platanus acerifolia*) with 3 1/2- to 4 1/2-inch stem diameters were grown especially for the study. The trees were grown in a clay loam soil and were transplanted into a similar but poorer soil.

The treatments were:

A. None, 20%, or 40% top pruning after transplanting.

B. Planting hole preparations:

    a. A tree spade-dug tree, planted into a tree spade-dug hole and watered in well to fill in the gap between ball and hole sidewall.

    b. A tree spade-dug tree, planted into a backhoe-dug hole approximately three times the diameter of the tree spade-dug ball but the same depth.

The tree spade used was a 30-inch Vermeer, four-blade trailer-mount type. The trees were transplanted during February. The six treatments in the study were replicated six times for a total of 36 trees. The tops of the trees were pruned prior to spring bud break but in all cases the terminal bud was **not** disturbed (Figure 19.4). Drip irrigation with two one-gallon per hour emitters per tree, was provided to prevent moisture stress the first season.

At the end of the first growing season, a substantial difference in the number of suckers at the base of the trees could be observed. Trees planted into the tree spade-dug hole with 40% top-pruning had 34 followed by 20% pruning with 30 suckers and no top-pruning had 26 suckers. Trees planted into the larger holes had substantially fewer suckers, regardless of top-pruning treatment. Those pruned 40% had 14 suckers, 20% prunind had 12 suckers and no top-pruning had 10 suckers (Table 19.1 and Figure 19.5).

462

Figure 19.4. Appearance of tree crowns following no pruning vs. 40% pruning at the beginning of the study.

Sucker growth at the base of a tree is the result of dormant shoot buds on the stem. These dormant buds create the multitude of stems which form on stumps of living trees when cut down. In the case of cutting a living tree, the entire top of the tree **and** the complex of chemical growth regulators from the terminal buds are removed. Consequently, without the continuing supply of the chemicals from the top of the tree, the dormant buds begin to grow. A similar situation occurs when a tree is pruned at transplanting and/or experiences enough stress during the transplanting process that the chemical supply of growth regulating compounds from the leaves is reduced to the point that the dormant buds in the stem begin to grow. **Suckers are the result of reduced activity and stress in the top of the tree.**

463

Table 19.1. Effects of top pruning and planting procedure on growth and quality of London planetrees.

	Tree spade-tree/ tree spade hole			Tree spade-tree/ larger planting hole		
Top-Pruned	0	20%	40%	0	20%	40%
Basal suckers, average/tree after one growing season	26	30	34	10	12	14
Length of terminal growth (inches) 1st season	4.6	3.1	3.9	9.8	6.5	6.6
2nd season	19	18.5	15.8	25.0	20.6	21.6
Total (2 years)	23.6	21.6	19.9	34.8	27.1	28.2
Overall Visual Quality	6.8*	5.2	5.6	9.0	9.0	8.0

*based on a rating scale where 1 = top dieback and poor growth, 4 = sparse foliage but no dieback, 7 = good foliage, 10 = excellent foliage and growth.

During the second growing season following transplanting, four trees died back 60% to 80%. All were trees with 20% or 40% top-pruning which had been planted into tree spade-dug holes.

Trees planted in the larger planting holes, regardless of top-pruning, had the greatest terminal growth for both the first and second growing seasons (Table 19.1). Among the three top-pruning treatments and trees in the larger planting holes, the trees with no top branches removed at time of transplanting had the greatest growth both seasons and overall for both seasons (Table 19.1). An overall visual rating at the end of the second growing season, however, showed little difference among the three top-pruning treatments as long as the larger planting hole was used. On the other hand, with the tree spade-dug hole, the trees

464

with no top pruning had higher visual quality than those with 20% or 40% top-pruning (Figure 19.6).

All of the trees planted into the larger hole regardless of top pruning were attractive, effective landscape trees the second season following transplanting.

Figure 19.5. Heavy sucker development occurred on the trunks of trees pruned 40%, especially when planted into the tree spade-dug hole.

Figure 19.6.   After two growing seasons following transplanting, the trees with no top-pruning (left) were fuller, larger and more attractive than those that had been top-pruned at planting time (two trees on the right), especially when planted into a tree spade-dug hole.

Moving Large Trees. Large trees present three major complications to the nurseryman; the large mass of living tissue in the crown that must be maintained, the volume or space requirement of the top, and the weight of the root ball.   The large mass of living cells has been covered in an earlier section of this chapter, Tree Size Vs. Stress.   It is mentioned here as a further reminder of its importance. **It must be considered.**

The volume or space requirement of the crown of a large tree sometimes prevents it from being moved.   Limbs can be tied or confined   only to some degree.   Limbs of river birch and elm can be compressed a great deal without damage.   On the other hand, honeylocust (*Gleditsia triacanthos*) limbs are quite stiff and can be flexed only slightly.   Young trees that still have the tall triangle-form are easiest to move and, in general, have the greatest likelihood of success.   Trees with multiple stems and/or strong horizontal branches often prove challenging.

466

Moist soils weigh from 100 to 140 pounds per cubic foot. Since the root ball must be kept moist, any additional watering can add more pounds to the load. For example, the London planetree (*Platanus acerifolia*) in Figure 19.7 has a stem diameter of nearly nine inches and is about 28 feet tall. The root ball is about eight feet in diameter and 30 inches deep. The Florida sand weighs about 120 pounds per cubic foot (moist), so the root ball weights about 15,000 pounds plus the weight of the tree. The ball was partially dug with a backhoe and finished by hand. The soil was wrapped in burlap and secured with four- by six-inch fencing prior to lifting.

Figure 19.7. The root ball was partially dug with a backhoe after the limbs were tied to prevent damage. The remaining ball shaping was done by hand. It was wrapped in burlap then wrapped in four-inch by six-inch mesh fencing. At intervals, the wires were twisted to draw the wire as tight as possible around the soil mass. Note the width and position of the nylon straps. The straps must be just below the center line of the root ball to prevent slippage.

In order to keep the tree in a semi-upright condition while lifting and loading, the tree was tied to the lifting straps using a broad nylon strap around the trunk (Figure 19.8) The placement of the cable and strap is very important. If the strap is placed too high in the tree, the load on the stem may be too great and breakage or damage many result. If the strap is too low, relative to the height and weight of the top of the tree compared to the soil ball, upon lifting, the entire tree and ball may become horizontal. Since it is not possible to weigh the top of the tree or the soil ball prior to lifting, experience and estimates are the only guidelines.

As for lifting the soil ball, the broader the strap(s) and webbing, the greater the distribution of the load and the less the root ball is disturbed. Since a root ball greater than eight feet in diameter requires special width and weight permits, few large root balls are dug. This means that in proportion to the root balls used on smaller trees, the root balls are quite small. Thus all possible precautions to protect the root ball must be taken. **If in doubt, use heavier equipment.** Once lifting begins, quite often it is not possible to stop and reposition or re-hook. Lifting in the nursery can be precarious since soils are soft and outriggers that provide the principal support for lifting can sink. Watch out for areas where large trees have been previously dug that may appear firm until the lift begins.

468

Figure 19.8. The tree being lifted for loading. Note the position of the nylon straps around the ball and the strap around the tree stem and padding to prevent injury. In this case, the strap around the stem was slightly too high which prevented the tree from leaning enough. The result was that getting the tree positioned on the truck was difficult. On the other hand, when lifting the tree for planting, this position would be desirable since it would help in positioning the tree upright, while still allowing for the root ball.

The tree shown in Figure 19.9 was to be moved only a few miles, with no overhead power lines, street lights, bridges or overpasses to confront the movers. Prior to digging a large tree, the route should be mapped out carefully and checked and rechecked. The size and volume of the top of a sizable tree is easy to under estimate prior to loading. An eight-foot ball placed on a truck bed four feet off the ground will clear most lines and tree limbs since any major street has a vertical clearance of at least 12 feet. When the tree is placed on a truck, the limbs against the truck bed may prevent the main stem of the tree from approaching horizontal, leaving it many feet in the air. If a tree has a multiple stem, position of the lifting cable must be positioned carefully to allow for the best hauling position in addition to the lifting position. Excess horizontal width can be worked around more easily than excess height. **Always watch for power lines and always assume they are hot. Limbs on living trees contain water and are conductors of electricity.**

In summary:

a) Digging a bigger (wider) planting hole greatly reduces plant stress.

b) Pruning back the tops of larger trees at time of transplanting does not aid survival or tree appearance, even of large trees.

c) Top-pruning in conjunction with planting trees into tree spade-dug holes was the poorest treatment.

d) Pruning tops in conjunction with a larger planting hole caused fewer suckers but provided no detectable benefit to the tree.

e) For best results, leave the top of the tree alone, except to remove structure weaknesses or broken and damaged limbs.

f) Since moisture stress of the top is a major factor that influences leaf function, one technique that can be very beneficial is to install a mist head or sprinkler in the top of the tree (Figure 19.10). This may be operated intermittently during late morning until early evening to reduce moisture stress on the new leaves. However, be careful to not over water the soil around the tree so that new root growth will be restricted due to poor soil aeration. The key is to humidify and moisten the leaves, much like the misting of cuttings. Excess water leaches chemicals from the leaves and may do more harm than good.

Figure 19.9. This tree was moved only a short distance and did not have to go under power lines or other obstacles. It is very easy to under estimate the volume and space required by a tree prior to harvest and loading.

Figure 19.10. Placing a mist or sprinkler head in the top of a large tree following transplanting can sometimes be helpful. Be careful to not over water the soil. At intervals, moisten the leaves, but do not soak the leaves and soil.

Literature Cited

1. Bridel, Robert, Carl E. Whitcomb and B.L. Appleton. 1983. Planting techniques for tree spade dug trees. Jour. of Arboriculture 9:282-284.

2. Bridel, Robert and Carl E. Whitcomb. 1981. Improving performance of trees dug and planted with a tree spade. Okla. Agri. Sta. Res. Rept. P-818:14-15.

3. More, Yoram and A.H. Halevy. 1980. Promotion of sink activity of developing rose shoots by light. Plant Physiology 66:990-995.

4. Preaus, Kenneth and Carl E. Whitcomb. 1980. Transplanting Landscape Trees. Jour. of Arboriculture 6:221-223.

5. Shoup, Steve, Rick Reavis and Carl E. Whitcomb. 1981. Effects of pruning and fertilizer on establishment of bare root deciduous trees. Jour. of Arboriculture 7:155-157.

6. Watson, Gary. 1985. Tree size affects root regeneration and top growth after transplanting. Jour. of Arboriculture 11:37-40.

7. Whitcomb, Carl E. 1983. Why large trees are difficult to transplant. Jour. of Arboriculture 9:57-59.

8. Whitcomb, Carl E., Charlie Gray and Billy Cavanaugh. 1985. Methods of transplanting large trees. Okla. Agri. Exp. Sta. Res. Rept. P-872:17-21.

CHAPTER 20

HARVESTING TREES FROM THE WILD

HARVESTING TREES FROM THE WILD

When nursery-grown trees are not available or are perceived to be over-priced, trees are sometimes harvested from the wild. This is a mixed situation at best. In some cases the land owner and/or persons digging the trees feel "trees are trees" and nature-planted trees should be just as good as nursery-grown trees and in some cases the price/cost can be attractive. This is unfortunate for all parties concerned. In most cases, unless the person(s) harvesting the wild trees have clear intentions of deceiving their customers and making only one sale, everyone loses (Figure 20.1).

Wild trees generally have strong, intact taproots that suppress lateral root development until the trees reach considerable size and even then play a role in branch root development. If in doubt, try to dig a young tree only one or two years old with taproot intact, or simpler yet, pull one up by hand.

When a seed germinates in the wild, the taproot plays a key role during the infancy stage and for the first three to ten years. The tap, or primary, root will extend downward until physical restriction (rocks, very compacted soil), or the lack of oxygen restricts growth. This may be from a few inches to many feet. Once the tap root extension slows, secondary (and more horizontal) roots begin. Root branching is much like branch development above ground. As long as the terminal or primary shoot (or root) is growing rapidly, secondary branch growth is being restricted by growth regulating chemicals produced in the tip.

In the wild, competition is fierce, soil fertility is low, moisture availability may reach the critical stage several times during the year and, because of these factors and shading by larger plants, energy levels in the young plant are very low, further predisposing it to insects, diseases and predators.

475

Figure 20.1. Wild trees generally have a strong tap root and/or roots such that few roots are present in the soil ball at harvest (above). Energy levels in the plant are very low and new roots cannot be produced without energy. Few trees dug in the wild with no prior care or conditioning survive in the landscape (below).

On the other hand, nursery-grown trees should have been grown with good fertility, limited competition, supplemental moisture either directly by irrigation or indirectly by control of competition and soil management practices and the taproot has been destroyed or highly modified by root pruning using an assortment of techniques and/or transplanting. Because of these cultural factors and root modifications the rate of growth of a nursery-grown tree is much faster than a wild tree and energy levels are much higher. Three points stand out here: 1) a transplanted tree cannot produce new roots at the cut ends of remaining roots without energy, 2) the energy must be present in the root and stem tissue of the plant at the time of harvest. The plant will die before energy manufactured after transplanting can reach a level to support new root growth and 3) once a plant is stunted, it never regains the health and vigor of a plant that has not been stunted. In studies with seedlings of several species, those stunted because of low fertility during the first three months following germination in three years never caught up with the seedlings that had not been stunted, even though both plants received identical favorable conditions after the first three-month period. This author has grown many "slow-growing" oaks seven feet tall or more in a single season (plant the acorn in April and look up to see the tip of the tree in October) by taking advantage of all the factors to minimize stress and maximize growing conditions. The two oaks in Figure 20.2 dramatize the extent of the stunting most wild trees experience.

Persons wanting to harvest wild trees sometimes argue that they can/will root prune to improve the root system before digging. The chapter on root pruning covers this point and there is no need to repeat it here except to note that root-pruning with low fertility, high competition and low energy levels in the plant can be counter-productive.

Even when wild trees survive the transplant trauma, they are weak, stressed and much more vulnerable to pests and environmental stress than nursery-grown trees. One of the key factors customers ask at retail nurseries and garden centers regarding trees is, "How fast does it grow?" Unfortunately, the emphasis on fast growth means junk trees such as silver maple get sold and planted when a properly grown oak or other desirable species would be a far better investment, and would grow nearly as fast with proper care.

Figure 20.2. One of these two oak trees is 2.5 years old while the other is only six months old. The fascinating point is that the small shumard oak on the right is the largest of 50 nursery bed-grown seedlings (two years in a bed, then one growing season in the container) while the six-month-old seedling on the left is typical of a large block of seedlings grown with minimum stress.

There is also the consideration of removal of wild trees from areas where they should remain for aesthetic purposes or to aid in erosion control or other uses. Wild trees along stream banks and ravines are both attractive and functional. On the other hand, in some areas, oaks and other species are unwanted in pastures and certain crop lands and in some cases are sprayed or pushed out and burned to make way for other crops.

If a reputable individual chooses to harvest wild trees, there are several steps that will aid the operation but by no means guarantee success:

a) Fertilize the trees according to a soil test at least one year prior to harvest and two years would be much better. Do not go overboard with excess nitrogen, about 200 pounds per acre per

478

year should be about right in most cases. If the soil test shows low phosphorus, **do** apply it even though it does not move in the soil. There will be an adequate number of fine roots in the duff, leaf litter and debris at the soil surface that it will benefit the tree.

b) Prune out any dead branches and dense internal growth at least one year before harvest. Many young wild trees have dense branches, poorly positioned throughout the crown.

c) Reduce the competition. This may mean removal of adjacent trees which deprive the crown of sunlight and/or spraying perennial weeds with Roundup at the appropriate time and in some cases applying a pre-emergent herbicide to reduce the population of annual grasses.

The combination of a, b and c will greatly increase the vigor of the following season's growth; energy levels within the plant will increase and most of the pruning wounds will be calloused over prior to harvest one or two years later.

d) Following harvest, wild trees should be placed in a holding area to determine viability for one growing season before planting into the landscape. Place the trees in RootBuilder panels (see Chapter 3 and 4) or on several layers of weed barrier fabric, surround with 1 x 2 inch mesh wire, creating a container sufficiently large so that four to six inches of soil or soil mix can be added around the parameter but no deeper than the original root ball. Line the inside of the wire frame with 40-pound roofing felt. The weed barrier fabric will provide some root pruning to any roots that grow downward, but because of the constriction, their loss will be of minor consequence to the tree at transplanting and lifting the tree will be relatively easy.

The roots that grow into the soil below will anchor the tree sufficiently to prevent blowing over. In addition, if the weed barrier fabric is used as the bottom of the "container", good field soil may be used around the root ball and drainage/aeration will be satisfactory. On the other hand, if plastic or any other material impenetrable to water is beneath the root ball, a soil mix of the type used in container production must be used to insure proper drainage. The reason for the vast differences in drainage is due to the continuous downward flow of water with the fabric vs. the perched water table caused by the impenetrable bottom. This is covered in detail in Chapter 1, "Methods of Plant Production". The greatest advantage of using soil is the buffer and nutrient holding capacity vs the soil mix. On the other hand, the soil adds more weight to the root ball. Do not use weed barrier fabric on the vertical sizes of the wire frame. The porous fabric will allow rapid water loss and growth will be restricted. In addition, if two containers are touching, roots will grow from one container into the other and make moving difficult.

e)   Fertilize the trees at a moderate rate, according to a soil test. If field soil is added, incorporate any nutrient other than nitrogen into the soil before placing around the root ball. If a container mix is used, add phosphorus, micronutrients and sulfur, if needed, before placing around the root ball, then topdress with a slow-release fertilizer or apply liquid nitrogen and potassium.

After one growing season above ground the trees that are thrifty are ready for the landscape. Fall planting is advantageous since a container or semi-container system has been established.

The economics of this scheme is marginal at best. When the cost of preparation, digging, hauling, placing in wire frames, fertilizer, pesticides and maintenance for one growing season are considered, what at first may have looked like a very profitable venture quickly loses its luster. When the further costs of all trees that die or never recover to make salable trees are added to the production costs of the few that do reach the market, little, if any, profit remains and there are certainly better ways to keep trim and fit.

Harvesting wild trees is mostly a lesson in futility, frustration and false prosperity, while giving the nursery business a black eye. Mother Nature knows how to grow trees in the wild, but a good nurseryman can do better at growing trees to transplant.

CHAPTER 21

GYPSUM AND CHANGES IN SOIL STRUCTURE

GYPSUM AND CHANGES IN SOIL STRUCTURE

In many areas there is a misconception that adding gypsum (calcium sulfate) to heavy clay soils will improve the tilth, structure and permeability. This may or may not be true, depending on the soil problem.

Gypsum and High Sodium Soils. Gypsum will improve soil tilth, structure and permeability **only** when the soil has a high level of sodium present. When gypsum is added to a soil containing substantial sodium, the calcium and sulfate separate. Calcium is a stronger element than sodium and will replace the sodium on the clay particles of the soil. The sodium is then free to react with the sulfate to form sodium sulfate which is very water soluble. The sodium sulfate then leaches downward in the soil and out of the root zone. Since the sodium has only one electrical charge and the calcium that replaced it has two, the calcium has the capacity to attach several clay particles together, thereby creating soil aggregates. These soil aggregates make the soil more friable and granular with an increased water infiltration and percolation rate.

The amount of gypsum necessary to improve the structure of high sodium soils depends on the purity of the gypsum, exchange capacity of the soil and the amount of sodium present. Application rates vary from about 1 to 10 tons per acre or more (Table 21.1). Apply no more than about four tons per acre at one application. Finely ground gypsum (#100 sieve) will react more quickly with the soil than more coarse-textured gypsum (#8 sieve). Since gypsum is only slowly soluble in water, the finer the particles, the more rapid the reaction with the soil. Gypsum incorporated into the soil two to four inches deep will have the greatest effect. Incorporating gypsum deeper simply dilutes the chemical and since the sodium accumulates primarily near the soil surface, there is generally no need for deep incorporation.

Gypsum may also be beneficial to plant growth on some acid soils where sulfur and/or calcium are deficient. This situation is much less common but may occur. In general, this may occur under conditions of acid soils, moderate to high rainfall, and the long-term use of acid-forming nitrogen fertilizers such as urea (46-0-0), ammonium nitrate (33-0-0), or sulfur-coated urea. If a soil test reveals both low sulfur and low calcium, then applying calcium sulfate (gypsum) will aid plant health. The rate would depend on the severity of the need and soil texture. A higher rate would be required on a heavy clay soil than on a sandy loam, for example.

Table 21.1. Approximate gypsum requirements of soils high in sodium (tons of gypsum per acre).

Texture	Exchangeable sodium (%)			
	15	20	30	40
Coarse	2	3	5	7
Medium	3	5	8	11
Fine	4	6	10	14

Gypsum and Low Sodium Soils. Gypsum **will not** improve soil tilth, structure and permeability unless excess sodium is present. In most areas of heavy clay soils, sodium is not the problem. Consequently adding gypsum simply adds additional calcium and sulfur to the soil. In most cases, the soils contain more than enough calcium so adding the gypsum makes the overall nutrient availability less favorable. Calcium levels in most soils, above a minimum level, create restrictions to the growth of woody plants by tying up micronutrients. Soil pH should be considered in the overall soil management, however, soil pH in the range from 4.5 to 6.5 is very favorable and should not be raised unless calcium levels are extremely low. For example, if a soil test shows a pH of 4.3 and a low calcium level (below 600 pounds of available calcium per acre) then calcium carbonate (lime) should be added to raise the soil pH to about 5.5 and raise the level of calcium up to 600 to 1000 pounds per acre. On the other hand, if magnesium is also low, dolomite (calcium and magnesium carbonate with about 20% calcium and 10% magnesium) should be used to raise the pH and increase levels of both elements. However, if the level of calcium in the soil is low and the soil pH is already 5.5 to 6.0, then **do not** add calcium carbonate or dolomite as the availability of the micronutrients, especially iron, manganese and copper will be decreased. In this case, add gypsum to supply calcium. Gypsum will have little or no change on soil pH.

483

Since gypsum is a neutral salt, that is, for every acid-forming fraction (sulfate) there is a basic-forming fraction (calcium), no change in soil pH occurs. Magnesium sulfate is another example of a useful neutral salt that has little, if any, effect on soil pH while increasing the level of a useful element.

Alternatives. If heavy clay soils are the problem, and they do not contain excess sodium, the only practical solution is the addition of some structural material to improve soil tilth and structure. Adding organic matter will improve soil tilth, texture and permeability, but only for relatively short periods of time. For example, adding peat moss will aid the structure of a heavy clay in Oklahoma for little more than one year before the organic matter is decomposed by microorganisms. Growing a soil building crop such as sudex does a good job (see Chapter 7, "Rebuilding Nursery Soils"). Adding sand, calcined clay, pea gravel or other non-organic structurably stable material, will help **only** if enough is added to reach the threshold point. The threshold point is that amount of sand required to hold all of the clay particles apart. If 10% sand is added to a heavy clay, the tilth, texture and porosity of the clay soil **is not** changed sufficiently to influence porosity. This is because as long as there are enough clay particles to completely surround the sand granules, you have simply made concrete. However, at some point, perhaps 25% to 30% sand, when there is no longer enough clay particles to surround each sand granule, the soil tilth, texture and permeability will be decidedly and **permanently** changed. (See the chapter on plants in containers in *Establishment and Maintenance of Landscape Plants* by Carl E. Whitcomb, for further information and procedures for determining the threshold point for improving soils) No two soils are the same, therefore, there are no broad general recommendations for the amount of sand required to reach the threshold level and permanently change the soil.

Another factor to consider is the depth of the soil to be changed. If only the top three to four inches need to be changed, the quantity of sand required will be one-half the quantity needed to change the soil to a depth of six to eight inches. Also keep in mind that if the top three to four inches of soil are made more permeable by adding sand, what will happen to the water after it percolates to the bottom of the amended soil. If the water simply accumulates at this point, little, if anything, has been accomplished. Consider the entire soil drainage profile before adding soil amendments. There are few worthwhile, short-term and inexpensive solutions to soil drainage problems. Adding organic matter generally provides no permanent benefit. Adding enough sand can provide permanent changes in soil texture and permeability.

APPENDIX

Comparative costs (1985) and approximate rates of various herbicides or combinations of herbicides.

Pre-emergent herbicides	Appropriate cost/unit	Cost/lb. of chemical	Rec. rate of appl. per acre	Rec. rate of actual product	Cost per appl.
Goal (liquid only)	$54.00/gal.	$34.00	1.5 to 2.5	1 to 2.5 gal.	$51 to $85
Ronstar (2% granules only)	$80.00/100 lbs.	$40.00	1.5 to 2.5	75 to 125 lbs.	$60 to $100
Surflan (wettable 75% powder)	$58.50/5 lbs.	$ 6.00	1.5 to 2.5	2 to 3.3 lbs.	$24 to $40
(liquid)	$59.00/gal.	$15.00	1.5 to 2.5	1.5 to 2.5 qts.	$22.50 to $37.50
Treflan (liquid)	$28.00/gal.	$ 7.00	2.0 to 3.0	2 to 3 qts.	$14 to $21
(5% granules)	$70.00/100 lbs.	$14.00	2.0 to 3.0	40 to 60 lbs.	$28 to $42

Post-emergent herbicides					
Roundup	$84.00/gal	$21.00	2 to 4 lbs.	2 to 4 qts.	$42 to $84
Cacodylic acid (Dilic Phytar 560, etc.)	$20.40/gal.	$ 8.20	2.5 to 4 lbs.	1 to 1.5 gal.	$20.40 to $30.60

Cost of combinations of herbicides (tank mixes)

Product	4 quarts Roundup	+	2.5 quarts Surflan	
Cost	$84.00		$37.50	= $121.50
	2 quarts Roundup	+	2.5 quarts Surflan	
	$42.00		$37.50	= $ 79.50
	1 gallon Phytar 560	+	2.5 quarts Surflan	
	$20.40		$37.50	= $ 57.90
	1 gallon Phytar 560	+	3 quarts Treflan	
	$20.40		$21.00	= $ 41.40

	4 quarts Roundup	+	1.5 gallons Goal	
	$84.00		$85.00	= $169.00
	2 quarts Roundup	+	1.5 gallons Goal	
	$42.00		$85.00	= $127.00
	1 gallon Phytar	+	1.5 gallons Goal	
	$20.40		$85.00	= $105.40

Calculating Solutions PPM

Percent	Dilution	PPM	Grams/liter	Oz./gal.
1.0	1:100	10,000	10.0	0.35
0.1	1:1000	1,000	1.0	0.03
0.01	1:10,000	100	0.1	0.003
0.001	1:100,000	10	0.01	
0.0001	1:1,000,000	1	0.001	

One part per million (ppm):
   by weight = 1 milligram (mg) per kilogram (kg)
   by volume = 1 microliter (ul) per liter (l)

Example: You desire an 800 ppm solution **or** 800 ul per 1000 ml (one liter). The stock solution is 4.5% or 45,000 ppm.

Equation: $C_1 V_1 = C_2 V_2$

In this case: C_1 = 45,000 ppm (the stock solution)
   V_1 = volume of C_1
   C_2 = 800 ppm (final concentration desired)
   V_2 = 1000 ml or 1 liter

45,000 ppm (C_1) X ___?___ (V_1) = 800 ppm (C_2) X 1000 ml (V_2)

800 X 1000 = 800,000   and   45,000/800,000 = 17.87 ml

Thus, 17.78 ml in 1000 ml (1 liter) = 800 ppm

MEASURES AND EQUIVALENTS

1 inch is 2.54 centimeters. 1 centimeter is 0.394 inch

1 yard is 0.914 meter.   1 meter is 1.09 yards

1 kilogram (kg) is 1000 grams or 2.2 pounds.

1 gram (g) is 1000 milligrams or 0.035 ounce (U.S).

1 milligram (mg) is 1000 micrograms.

1 mg/liter is 1 part per million (ppm).

1 ppm is 1 mg/liter, 1 mg/kilogram, 0.0001%, 0.013 ounces by weight in 100 gallons (water).

1 liter (1) is 1000 milliliters (ml) or cubic centimeters (cc), 1.058 fluid quarts, and weighs 1 kilogram (water).

1 milliliter or cubic centimeter of water is 0.035 fluid ounces and weighs 1 gram.

1 pound is 16 oz., 453.6 grams, 0.12 gallons (water), 0.0155 cu.ft. (water), 2 1/4 cups of sugar, 4 1/2 cups of flour.

1 ounce is 28.35 grams.

1 gallon is 3.785 liters, 8.34 pounds (water), or 0.133 cubic feet.

1 cubic foot is 7.5 gallons, 62.4 pounds of water, 0.80357 bushels (U.S.)

1 gallon is 4 quarts, 8 pints, 16 cups or 128 fluid ounces.

1 quart is 2 pints, 4 cups, 32 fluid ounces, 64 tablespoons, or 0.946 liters.

1 pint is 2 cups, 16 fluid ounces, 32 tablespoons, 454 grams, 0.473 liters, or 1 pound (water).

1 ounce per 1 gallon is 7490 ppm.

Useful measurements (continued)

1 cup is 8 fluid ounces, 227 grams, 1/2 pint, 16 tablespoons, 48 teaspoons.

1 fluid ounce is 2 tablespoons, 6 teaspoons, 29.6 milliliter or cubic centimeter or 28.4 grams.

1 tablespoon (U.S.) is 3 teaspoons, 1/2 fluid ounce, 1/16 cup or approximately 16 grams.

1 percent is 10,000 ppm, 10 g/liter, 10 g/kilogram, 1.33 ounces by weight per gallon (water), 38 grams per gallon (water), 8.34 pounds per 100 gallons (water).

To convert Fahrenheit (F) into Centigrade (C), subtract 32 and multiply by 5/9; thus 68 degrees F equals 20 degrees C.

To convert Centigrade to Fahrenheit, multiply by 9/5 and add 32; thus 55 degrees C equals 131 degrees F.

Conversion Factors for the Nurseryman: English and Metric

To convert lbs./acre to kg/hectare, multiply lbs./acre by 1.121.

lbs./acre	kg/hectare	lbs./acre	kg/hectare
1/2	0.560	4	4.484
3/4	0.840	5	5.605,
1	1.121	6	6.726
1.5	1.680	8	8.968
2	2.242	10	11.210
2.5	2.803	12	13.452
3	3.363		

To convert lbs./cu.yd. to kg/cu.m, multiply lbs./cu.yd. by 0.595.

lbs./cu.yd.	kg/cu.m	lbs./cu.yd.	kg/cu.m
1/2	0.2975	5	2.974
3/4	0.445	6	3.570
1	0.595	7	4.165
1.5	0.892	8	4.760
2	1.189	10	5.948
2.5	1.487	12	7.140
3	1.784	14	8.328
4	2.380	16	9.520

Conversion Factors (continued)

To convert gallons to liters, multiply gallons by 3.785

1 gal. = 3.785 l or 231 cu.in.	1 lb. = 454 grams
2 gal. = 7.6 l	1 kilogram = 1,000 grams
3 gal. = 11.4 l	or 2.2046 pounds
5 gal. = 18.9 l	1 cu. yd. = 0.765 cu.m
7.5 gal. = 28.4 l	1 meter = 39.37 inches
10 gal. = 37.9 l	1 decimeter = 3.939 in.
15 gal. = 56.8 l	or 0.328 ft.
20 gal. = 75.7 l	1 centimeter = 0.3937 in.
1 inch = 2.54 centimeters	1 yard = 0.9144 meter

1 foot = 3.048 decimeter or 30.48 centimeters

Approximate metric equivalents:
 1 hectare = about 2 1/2 acres (2.47 acres)
 1 kilogram = 2 1/5 pounds (2.2046 pounds)
 1 meter = 1.1 yards or 3.3 feet.
 1 liter = 1.06 quarts, 61 cubic inches
 1 cubic meter = 61,026 cubic inches or 1.31 times greater than a cubic yard, 264 gallons.
 1 cubic foot = 7.48 gallons or 28.316 liters.
 1 gallon water = 8.326 pounds.
 1 cubic foot water = 62.43 pounds.

TO CHANGE:	TO:	MULTIPLY BY:
inches	centimeters	2.54
feet	meters	.305
miles	kilometer	1.609
meters	inches	39.37
kilometers	miles	.621
square inches	square centimeters	6.452
square yards	square meters	.836
cubic yards	cubic meters	.765
cubic meters	cubic yards	1.308
quarts	liters	.946
liters	quarts	1.057
ounces	grams	28.35
pounds	kilograms	.454
kilograms	pounds	2.205

Toxicities of Various Chemicals Used in Nurseries*

Toxicity Rating	Class	LD 50 (mg/kg)	Probable lethal dose for 150 lb. man
1	extremely toxic	less than 5	less than 7 drops
2	very toxic	5-49	7 drops to 1 teaspoon
3	moderately toxic	50-499	1 teaspoon to 1 ounce
4	slightly toxic	500-4999	1 ounce to 1 pint
5	almost non-toxic	5000-14,999	1 pint to 1 quart
6	non-toxic	15,000 and above	more than 1 quart

Common Name	Trade Name	LD 50 (mg/kg)
Herbicides:		
1. sodium arsenite	Atlas A, Triox	10
2. Paraquat	Paraquat	150
3. 2,4,5-T	various brands	300
4. copper sulfate	various brands	300
5. 2,4-D, 2,4-DB	various brands	600
6. cacodylic acid	Phytar 560	830
7. monosodium methylarsenate	MSMA	700
8. dicamba	Banvel D	1,040
9. vernolate, EPTC	Vernam, Eptam	1,800
10. DSMA	Ansar, Sodar	1,800
11. DCPA	Dacthal	3,000
12. dichlobenil	Casoron	3,160
13. atrazine	Atrazine	3,180
14. diuron	Karmex	3,400
15. trifluralin	Treflan	3,700
16. glyphosate	Roundup	4,900
17. simazine	Princep	5,000
18. ansulam	Ansulox 4.0	8,000
19. dalapon	Dowpon	9,300
20. alachlor	Lasso	9,300
21. benefin	Balan	10,000
Fungicides:		
1. Benlate	Benlate	9,590
2. Captan	Captan	10,000

Toxicities of Various Chemicals (continued)

Insecticides:
1. Temik	Temik	1
2. Parathion	Parathion	8
3. Toxaphene	Toxaphene	69
4. lead arsenate	(0.1 gram lethal to man)	100
5. Diazinon	Diazinon	175
6. pyrethrin	various aerosols	200
7. Chlorodane	Chlorodane	475-500
8. carbaryl	Sevin (dermal)	450
9. Malathion	Malathion	1,500
10. Methoxychlor	Methoxychlor	5,000

Fumigants:
1. B-9	2,000 ppm gas may be fatal to man)	1 mg/l

Growth Retardants:
1. B-9	Alar	8.4 gm/kg
2. Cycocel	Cycocel	670 mg/kg

Other Common Items: (for comparison)
1. gasoline		150
2. caffein	coffee	200
3. aspirin		750
4. sodium chloride	table salt	3,320

- -

*based on white rates, materials given orally

Toxicity Rating	Class	LD 50 (mg/kg)	Probable lethal dose for 150 lbs. man
1	extremely toxic	less than 5	less than 7 drops
2	very toxic	5-49	7 drops to 1 teaspoon
3	moderately toxic	50-499	1 teaspoon to 1 ounce
4	slightly toxic	500-4999	1 ounce to 1 pint
5	almost non-toxic	5000-14,999	1 pint to 1 quart
6	non-toxic	15,000 and above	more than 1 quart

GLOSSARY

Abscission layer. The partial or complete arrest of a tissue at the base of the leaf that causes the leaf to drop.

Annual. A plant which lives for only one growing season, completing its life cycle from seed to seed.

Apical. The point or tip as of a stem or root.

Apical dominance. The suppression of side-shoot development by the terminal bud (shoot tip).

Artificial mix. Soilless mix.

Asexual propagation. Production of new plants from shoot, stem, leaf, or root pieces (by cuttings, division, layering).

Auxins. A group of hormones (plant growth regulators) that induce growth through cell elongation.

Axillary. In the angle formed by a leaf an stem.

B & B. Balled and Burlapped.

Bacterium (plural: bacteria). A one-celled microscopic plant that lacks chlorophyll and multiplies by fission. A few cause diseases but most are helpful.

Balled and Burlapped. Plants dug with roots inside soil roughly in the shape of a ball. This root-ball is then tightly wrapped in burlap to keep it from breaking apart when handled.

Bare-root stock. Nursery stock with little or no soil on the roots.

Bed. An area for growing plants, either outdoors or in greenhouses, or an area of level ground area (bed) in a greenhouse for propagation and/or growth of plants.

Bedding plants. A wide range of plants that are propagated and cultured through the initial stages of growth by commercial growers and are then sold for use in flower and vegetable gardens.

Blindness. The condition when a plant bud stops developing. It is a frequent problem of roses, during low light periods, and of the terminal buds of some tree species following transplanting.

Broad-leaved evergreens. Broad-leaved plants which retain green leaves year round.

Bud break. When resting buds resume growth.

Budding. Joining a small piece of bark (and sometimes wood) having a single bud onto the trunk, branch, or twig of a rooted plant so the single bud grows a new preferred plant.

Calcined clay. Montmorillonite clay, baked at a high temperature, which makes it rigid (it no longer shrinks or swells when wetted or dried). This material can be added to a growth medium to improve the air/water relationship.

Caliper. Diameter of plant's main stem (trunk) measured six inches above ground where the trunk is four inches or less in diameter and 12 inches above ground for larger sizes; the determining measurement in nursery stock grading, usually applied to trees and commonly expressed in inches.

Callus. Mass of cells that develops from and around wounded plant tissues, such as the base of cuttings and at the junction of a graft union.

Cambium or more correctly, cambial zone. The cylindrical zone of meristematic tissue between the heartwood and the bark of a dicot tree or shrub.

Capillarity. The movement of water through a porous material caused by the attraction of water for the particle surfaces. The smaller the particles, the stronger the attraction.

Carbohydrates. The basic food substances manufactured by the leaves generally referred to as "energy" by the author.

Chloroplast. The structure in the cells of the leaves where the chlorophyll is located. The site where carbohydrates and starches are manufactured.

Chlorosis. Leaves become yellow from the loss of chlorophyll. Can be due to nutrient disorder, virus, chemical spray injury, excessive light intensity or disease.

Compensation point. That light level where the amount of food (carbohydrates) manufactured by the leaves just equals the amount of food used by the cells of the leaf in respiration.

Conifers. Needle-leaved plants that produce seeds in cones; most conifers are evergreens; includes pine, spruce, fir, cedar, cypress, false cypress, yew, hemlock, redwood, and ginkgo.

Constant fertilization. Application of dilute fertilizer with each watering.

Container capacity. That level of moisture in a container with a specific growth medium where no further water will drain out because of the perched water table in the bottom of the container and adhesive and cohesive forces.

Culls. Undesirable or inferior plants; a relative term with many interpretations.

Cultivar. A cultivated variety; originating and persisting under cultivation; plants that are true to type from vegetative propagation; synonymous with variety.

Cutting. A portion of a stem, leaf, or root placed in a medium to grow roots and thus into a new individual plant.

Damping-off. A disease caused by a number of fungi, mainly *Pythium, Rhizoctonia*, and *Phytophthora*. The symptoms include decay of seeds prior to germination, rot of seedlings before emergence from the root medium, and development of stem rot at the soil line after emergence, causing seedlings to collapse.

Deciduous. Refers to perennial plants which lose leaves in fall or whose tops die down over winter.

Defoliation. Dropping or shedding of leaves of plants.

Desiccation. The process of drying. Desiccation of plants results from a lack of water or excessive salts.

Dibble hole. A cavity formed in a container growth medium by an object, generally the size and shape of the liner pot or tube.

Disease. A plant is said to be diseased when it develops a different appearance or when it changes physiologically from the normally accepted state. These differences are called symptoms. Disease can be caused by such unfavorable environmental conditions as temperature extremes, insects, or pathogenic organisms such as nematodes, fungi, bacteria, or viruses.

Division. Process of cutting a clump type of plant into sections.

Dolomite or dolomitic limestone. Material applied to a growth medium to supply both calcium and magnesium carbonates. It also raises the pH of the medium.

Dormant. A term applied to plants or seed which are in a state of dormancy; plants that are alive but not growing.

Emulsifiable concentrate. Formulation of pesticide or herbicide in which the pesticide or herbicide is dissolved in a petroleum solvent and emulsifier mixture, which holds the pesticide in suspension when agitated with water.

Energy. The carbohydrates and starches manufactured in the leaves of green plants.

Fertilizer injector. A machine that accurately combines a certain amount of concentrated soluble fertilizer with a known volume of water in a water line. The injector can be powered electrically or from water pressure.

Field-growing. Method of growing nursery stock directly in soil in the field as opposed to growing in containers.

Foot-candle (fc). A unit of light intensity equal to the direct illumination on a surface everywhere one foot from a uniform point source of one international candle. It is equivalent to 10.76 lux. Light intensity may vary from a maximum in summer from 10,000 fc or more to 2,000 or less in winter.

Fritted trace elements. Micronutrient elements infused in soft glass that slowly dissolve when added to a growth medium.

Fumigants. Chemicals used to fumigate soils, media, or plants; fumigants come in a liquefied or solid form, becoming a gas, vapor, or smoke when released or ignited.

Fumigation. Killing of insects, diseases, weeds, nematodes, or other organisms with a gas, smoke, or vapor.

Fungicide. Chemical that kills or suppresses fungus.

Fungus. An undifferentiated plant lacking chlorophyll and conductive tissues.

Fungus gnats. Small flies in the family *Sciaridae*; maggots feed on fungi and decaying organic matter and on plant roots and stems.

Gallon can. A metal or plastic container of 1/2- to one-gallon capacity. A very loose term referring to container volume.

Grading. Classifying plants according to quality or size.

Grafting. A method of propagation where a stem portion, with two or more buds, of one plant is joined with another plant, having roots, to form one new plant; joining a scion with the trunk, branch, or twig of a rooted plant.

Granular. Formulation in which the herbicide is mixed with a coarsely ground carrier such as coal, corn cobs, or calcined clay, to be applied dry to the soil surface and incorporated or watered-in.

Growing season. From spring into fall, as commonly used.

Growth medium. A soilless, artificial mix or a pure material (such as peat moss or pine bark) used for growing plants; media is the plural of medium and refers to more than one growth medium.

Harden off. Exposing plants gradually to low or varying temperatures, less humid or drier conditions, or higher light or other unaccustomed growing conditions to acclimate them to more difficult growing conditions, such as outdoors, or to being away from mist; to toughen plants to withstand handling and/or less desirable conditions.

Hardy plants. A relative term to describe plants which can withstand the cold and other weather conditions in the area where they are to be grown.

Herbicide. A chemical to control weeds.

Hormone. An organic substance produced in one part of the plant and translocated to another part where, in small concentrations, it regulates growth and development.

Host plant. A plant that is invaded by a pest or disease organism.

Humus. The relatively stable fraction of the soil organic matter remaining after the major portion of added plant and animal residues has decomposed.

Hydroponics. A system of growing plants in which water constitutes the growth medium.

IAA (indole-3-acetic acid). A naturally occurring auxin produced in apical meristems of both roots and shoots.

IBA (indole-3-butyric acid). A synthetically produced auxin.

Inoculum. The pathogen or its parts that can cause disease; that portion of individual pathogens which is brought into contact with the host.

Internode. The portion of a plant stem between two nodes. The node is the portion of the stem where one or more leaves are attached.

Interveinal. Pertaining to the space among the vascular tissues (veins) on a leaf.

Larva. The immature, wingless, and often wormlike form in which some insects hatch from the egg, and in which they remain through an increase in size and other minor changes until they assume the pupa stage.

Leaching. The most effective method of reducing high levels of soluble salts. Water the growth medium: the first application dissolves the salts, and the second watering flushes excess salts from the soil.

Leader. The dominant, central branch of a tree or shrub.

Leggy. Refers to a plant which is unattractive because it has not leafed out at the base, leaving bare and exposed trunks or branches.

Light saturation. The maximum amount of light energy that a leaf or other tissue can utilize under a given set of condition.

Liner. A young plant of suitable size for planting in rows (lines) in the field or in containers for growing on into larger plants; a nursery term.

Lining out stock. Plants large enough to be planted or lined-out in a row; a nursery term.

Liquid feed. Applications of dilute fertilizer through the irrigation system.

Media. Growth media, the mix, or substrates in which plants are grown. Sand, peat moss, pine bark, and vermiculite are examples of ingredients in container growth media.

Meristem. A tissue composed of embryonic, unspecialized cells actively or potentially involved in cell division. An apical meristem is a meristem located at the tip of a shoot or root.

Methyl bromide. Chemical soil sterilant, usually sold in cans as a liquid under pressure. A dangerous gas that must be handled with care.

MHOS. Unit used to denote amount of soluble salts in a soil, determined by a Solu-bridge instrument.

Micronutrients. The trace elements required in small quantities for plant growth; specifically, iron, manganese, zinc, copper, boron, and molybdenum.

Microorganism (microbe). A small living organism that requires the aid of a microscope to be seen.

Mist propagation. System used to supply intermittent mist water sprays over the cuttings. Electrical control devices are used to turn the mist on and off.

Mycelium. The hypha or hyphae that make up the body of a fungus. Mycelium are the microscopic threadlike strands that make up the body of a fungus.

NAA (naphthalene acetic acid). A synthetically produced auxin.

Necrosis. The state of being dead and discolored.

Node. The position on a stem where leaves and buds are located.

Osmocote. A resin-coated slow-release fertilizer that can be added to a potting medium prior to planting or as a top-dressing after planting. It can be used to provide nutrition throughout the duration of a crop, or it can be used at rates that will require supplemental liquid fertilization.

Parts per million (ppm). Measurement used to denote concentration of growth regulators, fertilizer solutions, and gases. A ratio of materials; one gallon in one million gallons equals one ppm.

Pasteurization. Process whereby harmful organisms are killed; differs from sterilization, which eliminates all organisms.

Pathogen. Infectious agent that causes plant disease.

Peat moss. Partially decayed plant material, often used as an ingredient in a growth medium. Generally very acidic.

Perched water table. See page 243.

Perlite. Volcanic rock heated to about 98 degrees C (1,800 F), causing it to expand and become porous. The horticultural grade is a coarse aggregate and is best suited for mixing with other components for making very light-weight mixes for growing plants.

pH. A measure of the degree of acidity or alkalinity. The values range from 0, which is the most acid, to 14, which is the most alkaline, with 7 being neutral.

Phloem. A tissue in plants that trahsports energy downward from leaves to other plant parts, including stems and roots; the tissues outside of the cambial zone.

Photosynthesis. The manufacture of carbohydrates from carbon dioxide and water in the presence of chlorophyll, using light energy and releasing oxygen.

Phytophthora. Latin name for a genus of fungus that causes plant disease, generally a root- and crown-rot pathogen.

Phytotoxicity. Injury to a plant or plant part, caused by a chemical or environmental condition.

Post-emergent. An herbicide to kill existing weeds.

Pot-bound. Condition when the roots of a plant begin to wrap around or entwine the root ball inside of a container.

Pre-emergent. An herbicide that must be applied before the weed seed germinates

Propagation. Producing new plants from parts (cuttings, layers, division, grafts, buds, tissue, bulbs, tubers, rhizomes, corms) of whole plants, or from seeds.

Pruning. Removal of plant parts to improve the health, size, or shape of a plant.

Pythium. A fungal pathogen, water mold, soil inhabitant, and common cause of root rot and damping off of seedlings.
Recontamination. Contamination with pathogens that occurs after pasteurization or sterilization.

Respiration. Those biochemical processes which result in the consumption of oxygen and carbohydrates, the evolution of carbon dioxide, and the release of energy. Respiration has the reverse effect of photosynthesis.

Rhizome. A horizontal underground stem which forms both roots and shoots at its nodes.

Root ball. With container plants, the root system plus growth medium in which roots are growing.

Root pruning. Cutting of roots of plants to induce a more compact root system.

Rooted cutting. A cutting which has grown new roots.

Rooting compound. A chemical which promotes or hastens the rooting of cuttings.

Rooting hormone. Same as a rooting compound.

Sand. A mineral particle measuring 0.05 to 2.0 millimeters in diameter.

Scarification. A mechanical or acid treatment applied to certain seed to reduce the hard, impervious seed coat and to permit seed germination.

Seedling. A small plant grown from seed.

Semi-hardwood cuttings. Stem cuttings taken from the partially matured wood of new shoots.

Senescence. The process of growing old; aging.

Shifting. Usually means "shifting up": shifting from a smaller container to a larger one, such as from a one-gallon one to a three-gallon one.

Softwood cuttings. Stem cuttings from the soft, succulent, new spring growth.

Soil. The upper, heavily weathered layer of the earth's crust which supports plant life. It is a mixture of mineral and organic materials.

Soil mix. A mixture of bark, sand, peat, or other inorganic and/or organic materials used for growing plants. Generally no field soil is used.

Soil sterilization. Applying a chemical (soil sterilant) to a soil to prevent plant growth (especially of weeds) for one or more years.

Solenoid valve. An electrically activated valve which controls the flow of gases or liquids. Such valves can be activated by a time clock to control the rate of flow.

Solu-bridge. Apparatus that measures the electrical conductivity of a soil solution and is used to determine the soluble salt concentration.

Spider mites. Various species of mites in the family Tetranychidae that are plant parasites.

Spores. The reproductive unit of fungi; analogous to seeds of higher plants.

Steam pasteurization. A heat treatment, usually with 160 degrees F (56 C) aerated steam, for selective control of insects, diseases, nematodes, and most weeds.

Steam sterilization. A heat treatment using 212 degrees F (100 C) steam on the growth medium before planting to kill all weed seeds, insects, diseases, nematodes, and other organisms.

Sticking. Placing of cuttings into the propagation medium; "stuck" cuttings are those which have been placed into propagation medium.

Stock. Nursery plants for sale.

Stock plant. A plant from which cuttings may be taken.

Stomates. Pores or openings, generally on the underneath side of a leaf where carbon dioxide enters and water vapor is lost to cool the leaf tissues.

Strap-leaves. Leaves whose margins are partially or completely missing so that the leaf is narrower than normal, often resembling a strap.

Stratification. A seed treatment of low temperatures that is often needed to break dormancy and stimulate seed germination.

Superphosphate. (0-20-0), a granular material that can be added to a soil mixture to supply phosphorus. Contains about 9% actual phosphorus.

Surfactant or wetting agent. A chemical used to alter the surface properties of liquids. Surfactants are added to pesticide sprays to reduce the surface tension of the spray liquid, thereby enabling it to spread out more readily over the plant leaf surface. Surfactants are also used to improve the initial wetting of growth media.

Systemic. Spreading internally throughout the plant. Some pesticides are systemic, as are some pathogens.

Texture. The relative proportion of various sizes of mineral particles in a given soil or growth medium.

Tiller. Twigs or shoots that arise from the base of a plant.

Tilth. The nature of a soil following cultivation. A soil in tood tilth has a granular texture as opposed to large clods.

Transpiration. The loss of water from the leaves of plants.

Tropism. A growth response or bending toward or away from a stimulus. Geotropism is in response to gravity: roots grow toward, and shoots away from, the center of earth's gravity. Phototropism is in response to light: shoots tend to grow toward light.

Vascular tissue. Tissue in the root, stem, leaf, or flower stem, including phloem for conducting organic substances throughout the plant, xylem for conducting water and nutrients primarily from the roots to the shoot, and supporting fiber cells. Vascular tissue in leaves is often called veins.

Vermiculite. Mica compound heated to about 738 degrees C (1,400 F). Plate-like structure that retains both water and fertilizer. Used for mixing with other materials for growing plants.

Verticillium. Name of a genus of fungus that causes plant disease; a root and vascular pathogen.

Wettable powder. Formulation of pesticide in which the pesticide is mixed with a finely ground clay, which holds the pesticide in suspension when agitated with water.

Wetting agent. See surfactant.

Wholesaler. One who sells to retailers; one who does not sell directly to consumers.

Xylem. A tissue in the plant that transports water and nutrients upward from the roots to the foliage. Cells connected end-to-end form xylem tubes. Vessels are the predominant xylem cells in flowering plants and have open ends. Tracheids predominate in the conifer (pines, etc.) xylem; rather than having open ends, they have pits along their sides connecting to adjacent tracheid cells. Vessel and tracheid cells are non-living at the time they carry out the function of water and nutrient transport.

INDEX

A

Abscission, 206, 294

Absorbed, 135, 160, 165, 171, 178, 191, 195-196, 199, 208, 379, 392, 394, 398, 402-403, 406, 459

Accelerate, 62, 69, 167, 186, 209, 280, 368, 399

Accumulation, 98, 106, 135, 137, 210, 220, 289, 294, 342, 353

Adsorb, 176, 184, 196, 345

Aeration, 21, 44, 49-50, 164, 222, 248, 253, 342, 353, 421-422, 442, 450-451, 470, 479

Air-pruned, 27-28, 30-31, 45, 68, 72, 73-75, 79, 83, 87, 93, 115, 126, 133, 422

Alfalfa, 229-230, 419

Algae, 63, 352

Alkaline, 155, 211, 344, 354

Aluminum, 156, 386, 389, 391, 394, 431

Aluminum sulfate, 156

Amendments, 130, 154, 227, 233-234, 239, 241, 246-247, 274, 485

Ammonium, 155, 159, 168-169, 171, 173-175, 177-178, 195-197, 208, 226, 353, 482

Anchor, 53, 86, 93, 247, 479

Anchorage, 38, 118, 141, 143, 144

Ansar, 393

Anti-backflush, 351

Aphids, 322, 358-359, 405

Apical, 61, 133, 314, 422

Apical dominance, 25

Arsenic, 393-394

Asexually, 262

Atrazine, 386, 407

Auxins, 261

B

Backfill, 130, 445, 448, 453

Bacterial, 196

Bags, 58-60, 62, 64-65, 93, 145, 147, 255

Balled-in-burlap, 1, 5, 9-10, 13, 22, 93, 261, 268, 272, 392, 424-425, 441, 443, 446

Bareroot, 421-422

Bark, 8, 13, 23, 65, 123, 227, 233, 250, 253, 277, 284, 298, 304, 307-308, 310, 368, 370, 379
Bark-peat-sand, 99
Benzine, 361
Bermudagrass, 226, 378, 395, 397-398, 408
Bicarbonates, 155, 211, 342, 344, 353-354
Birch, 28, 53-55, 93-96, 98, 100, 104, 120, 141-142, 236-238, 466
Bittercress, 356, 358-359, 384-385, 405, 409
Blackgum, 7
Boron, 154, 157, 160, 162-163, 171, 187, 189, 195, 208, 217-220, 342, 345
Branching, 7, 25-29, 41, 45-46, 53-54, 58, 64-66, 68, 70, 72, 74, 79, 85, 88, 93, 98, 115-116, 118, 133-134, 140-141, 179, 271, 284, 286, 299-300, 302, 306, 307, 422, 475
Bromacil, 386, 392, 406
Buds, 8, 99, 120-122, 133, 135-136, 206, 210, 212, 214, 216-217, 239, 271-272, 274-275, 301, 304, 316, 318, 322-323, 328, 379, 381, 421, 432, 436, 463
Buffer, 21, 82, 191, 346, 425, 479
Burlap, 5-6, 10, 11, 14-15, 103, 126, 467

C
Cable, 143, 144, 468, 470
Cacodylic, 378, 380, 393-394
Calcined, 362, 484
Calcium, 154-157, 160, 164, 168-171, 174-179, 181-184, 188-189, 195-196, 198, 208-212, 219, 342, 344-345, 353-354, 482-484
Calcium sulfate, 169
Calibrating, 363-365
Caliper, 16, 56-57, 72, 99, 117, 130-133, 141, 234-237, 239, 261, 263, 266, 289, 299, 397, 460
Callous, 295, 305, 308, 322, 479
Callus, 118, 279, 308-310, 328
Capillarity, 128, 243
Carbohydrates, 21, 164-166, 177-178, 186, 196, 206, 274, 394, 457, 459
Carbonates, 170, 344
Casoron, 360
Cation, 181, 210
Chloride, 159, 169, 173, 175, 177, 180, 200, 226, 342, 345
Chlorophyll, 202, 212

509

Groundcover, 331, 392
Growth-regulating, 460
Grow-bags, 150
Gro-Safe, 392
Gypsum, 170, 174-175, 177, 179, 181, 482, 483,

H

Hardiness, 23, 180, 232, 277, 428, 439
Harvesting, 92-93, 103, 105, 108, 120, 122, 131, 144, 146, 150, 327, 442, 475, 480
Health, 17, 21, 25, 29, 106, 140-141, 143, 177, 197, 253, 272, 423, 477, 483
Heat-tolerant, 239
Heeled-in, 8
Herbicides, 228-229, 356, 359-362, 364-365, 368, 370-373, 375-377, 381, 384, 386, 391-395, 399, 402, 404-410, 412, 416-417, 419
HoleStar, 113-114
Hollofil, 107, 109
Hormone, 266, 286
Hyvar, 386-387, 392, 402, 406

I

IBA, 261-262, 264-266
IBDU, 169, 192, 196
Incorporation, 170, 188, 228, 375, 381, 383, 482
Indolebutyric, 261, 266
Injury, 14, 121, 124, 166, 198, 217, 235, 239, 265, 282-283, 343, 345, 361, 365, 367-368, 371-372, 381, 386-387, 389, 391-395, 397-398, 407, 419, 425-426, 428, 431, 435-436, 438-439, 441, 469
Intercrop, 229-230, 413, 415-416, 419
Iodine, 138
Iron, 49, 154, 157, 162-163, 171, 187-189, 195, 198, 202, 206-208, 211-213, 217, 353, 399, 483
Irrigation, 19, 34, 107, 116, 123, 150, 159, 170, 174, 181, 184, 192, 196-197, 200, 210, 217, 235-236, 238, 244, 248, 250, 262, 329, 331, 335, 338, 340, 343-346, 349-354, 356, 362, 365-366, 377, 396-397, 402, 405, 410, 415-419, 462, 477

J-K
Johnsongrass, 378, 395
Karmex, 371-372, 386, 391-393, 402-403
K-mag, 169, 171

L
Lasso, 371-372, 409-410
Leaching, 159, 169, 173, 196-197, 353, 370
Lead, 19, 304, 339, 459
Leader, 116, 273, 275, 289, 306, 313-319, 321-322, 324-325
Legumes, 229
Lespedeza, 230, 419
Lime, 156, 170, 177, 211, 226, 483
Liners, 60, 82, 114, 145, 243

M
Macro-nutrients, 195
Magamp, 169
Magnesium, 154-157, 160, 162-164, 167, 169-171, 175-177, 181-184, 188-189, 195, 202-209, 219, 290, 344-345, 483-484
Magnesium-deficient, 204, 206
Manganese, 154, 156-157, 161-163, 171, 187-189, 195, 202, 206-208, 211-214, 217, 353, 483
Manure, 224-227
Media, 21, 50, 89, 184, 368, 408-409, 428-430
Microfoam, 86, 427, 431-432, 435-436, 439
Micromax, 188, 206, 208, 253
Micronutrients, 50, 158, 160, 171, 176, 178, 182, 184-186, 188-189, 195, 198, 206, 208, 216-217, 342, 353, 480, 483
Microorganisms, 371, 484
Micro-environment, 173
Molybdenum, 154, 163, 171, 189, 195, 208, 218, 219
Monocots, 206, 284
Mulch, 8, 11, 87-88, 123-124, 415-416, 421
Muriate-of-potash, 226

N
NAA, 261
Napropamide, 360
Necrosis, 217, 391
Nitralin, 410

Phosphorus, 107, 116, 154, 157-160, 167-169, 175-176, 178-181, 184-185, 189, 192, 195, 197-200, 202, 208, 211-212, 219, 226-227, 285, 290, 479, 480
Photosynthesis, 193, 277, 286
Phytar, 378, 393
Phytophthora, 19, 329
Phytotoxicity, 361, 408
Plant health, 14
Plant nutrition, 161
Poast, 395
Polyethylene, 42, 58-62, 64-65, 68, 92-93, 147, 255, 333, 358, 386, 427, 431-432, 436
Post-emergent, 359-360, 362, 375, 378-380, 393-395, 412
Potash, 154, 169-171, 175, 177
Potassium, 154, 157-160, 167-171, 173-177, 180-181, 184-185, 189, 191-192, 195, 199-202, 208, 226-227, 250, 285, 290, 353, 480
Pramitol, 386-387, 389-392, 402, 407
Pre-emergent, 359-362, 367-370, 373-374, 377-380, 382, 383, 393, 395-396, 399, 402, 416, 479
Princep, 360, 370, 386, 391-392
Probe, 154
Prometon, 386-387, 390-392, 407
Propagation, 29-31, 45-47, 73, 89, 262, 265
Prowl, 372
Pruning, 26, 31, 45-46, 68, 72-73, 89, 114-117, 133, 145, 150, 207, 259, 268-272, 274-277, 279, 281-287, 289, 294, 295, 299-301, 303-305, 307-310, 312, 314, 318, 320-325, 328, 373, 419, 460, 462-465, 470, 473, 477, 479

R
Ratios, 161, 171, 189, 345
Regeneration, 23, 89, 266, 286, 473
Regulators, 459, 463
Replanting, 8, 442
Residue, 224, 227, 371, 394
Re-established, 25, 145, 255
Rhizobium, 416
Rhizome, 385, 393, 398
Ronstar, 359-360, 362, 367-368, 370-372, 379-381, 408-410
Root growth, 9
Root pruning, 44

Root quality, 26
Root stimulators, 261
RootBag, 88, 105, 108, 113, 115, 128, 147, 149, 417
RootBuilder, 78-79, 81-82, 84-88, 125, 128, 423, 479
RootMaker, 45-46, 73-77, 86, 88
Root-absorbed, 396
Root-bound, 33-34, 36-41, 88, 136, 145, 243, 252-255
Root-branching, 88, 127
Root-modifying, 44
Root-pruning, 68-69, 72, 79, 90, 114, 147, 280, 282-285, 382, 444-445, 477
Root-trapping, 67, 79-80
Roundup, 378-381, 394-401, 408, 417, 419, 479
Rout, 367

S
Salt index, 168
Sanitation, 356, 359
Saturated, 14, 85, 124, 127, 243
Scorching, 426
Seedlings, 25-26, 28-31, 34, 45, 47, 55-56, 58, 60, 73, 75, 77, 88-89, 93, 115, 133, 142, 254, 262, 266, 269, 285-287, 299, 333, 379, 417-418, 446, 462, 477-478
Seeds, 226, 356, 358, 367-368, 375, 385, 395, 405-406, 417
Shrinkage, 85, 124, 423
Simazine, 372, 386, 391-392, 402-403, 405
Slow-release, 159, 160, 168-169, 173-174, 179-180, 188, 190-192, 196, 227, 239, 250, 285, 370, 480
Solubility, 156, 168, 170, 177, 189, 213, 217, 370-372
Spiraling, 30, 68, 75
Sprays, 206, 212, 261, 266, 371, 375, 399
Spray-stake, 330
Spring vs. fall planting, 258
Sprinkler-irrigated, 159
Staking, 72-73, 81, 292, 294, 308, 311, 322, 334
Sterilant, 386, 402, 405-407
Sterilization, 402, 406
Stolons, 230, 331, 398, 416-417
Stomates, 165, 279
Stress, 5, 8, 11-12, 34, 37, 52, 74, 82, 85-86, 92, 99, 120, 123, 125, 130, 145, 166-168, 172, 177, 197, 237-238, 243, 248-250,